In Radical Pursuit

Critical Essays and Lectures

In Radical Pursuit

W. D. SNODGRASS

HARPER & ROW
Publishers 1817

New York · Evanston · San Francisco · London

THE FOLLOWING ESSAYS originally appeared in the publications noted and are reprinted by permission of the appropriate editors: "Finding a Poem," *The Partisan Review;* "Master's in the Verse Patch," *New World Writing;* "A Rocking Horse," *The Hudson Review;* "Crime for Punishment," *The Hudson Review;* "Glorying in Failure," *The Malahat Review.* Related earlier versions of "That Anguish of Concreteness" appeared in *The New York Review of Books* and *The Hudson Review.* The present version first appeared in *Essays on the Poetry—Theodore Roethke,* ed. Arnold Stein, University of Washington Press, and is reprinted here by permission.

"Glorying in Failure" was delivered as the first annual Leo Hendrick Memorial Lecture at Oliver College, 1974.

"Moonshine and Sunny Beams" was delivered as the annual Hopwood Lecture at the University of Michigan, 1974.

"Analysis of Depths" was delivered in the Spaulding Distinguished Lecture Series, 1969, at the University of New Hampshire and published for limited circulation in their monograph series.

FIRST EDITION

Designed by Gwendolyn O. England

Library of Congress Cataloging in Publication Data

Snodgrass, William DeWitt, 1926–
    In radical pursuit.
    1. Literature—Addresses, essays, lectures. I. Title.
PN37.S57   809.1   73–14290
ISBN 0–06–013917–X

For Camille

Contents

Four Studies in the Classics

Preface

I hope I do not belabor the obvious in noting that I did not conceive this book as a unit. These pieces were written over a very long period, at various times and for various purposes. Whatever unity the book achieves must come from the fact that all its parts are products of one mind; I have long pursued the same problems. Indeed, the essay which I first began *(A Midsummer Night's Dream)* is also the one I finished last. On the other hand, several of these pieces were completed many years ago, while others were both begun and finished quite recently. It has been a considerable delight to me to find that the most recent essays seem not only easier in style, but far more radical in their perception of their subjects.

In general, writing prose is so difficult for me that I never attempt it until I feel fairly sure I have something new to say about a subject. Most often this has led me into areas beneath the consciousness of the author himself. That is partly because other more conscious areas of the work have already been fully covered by other critics; partly because I feel that the unconscious areas of thought and emotion are of far greater importance than conscious belief or intention. Nonetheless, I do not intend any of my interpretations to be definitive or to exclude any of the more conscious interpretations. Coming to literature as an amateur, not as a specialist, my aim is to broaden the reader's experience of the work of art, not to limit or control it.

My teachers were the New Critics and I have always felt grateful to them. I do not think I write like them, though I may still have a tendency toward argumentative overkill. The New Critics taught us to read, so they had to prove that understanding was possible; that is no longer necessary. I hope my own essays lean toward a broader humanism—one less concerned with being right, and more concerned with enrichment. I believe my models to be such pieces as Santayana's essay on Lucretius, Simone Weil on *The Iliad,* and W. H. Auden on "Balaam and his Ass."

Of my Four Personal Lectures the earliest, "Tact and the Poet's Force," was first delivered at a writers' conference. This is the only piece here which deals with literary theory—tries to relate its problems to the nature of literature. It only seems to be less personal than the three following lectures which begin in analyses of my own poems and worksheets. Coming after the followers of Eliot and Pound, many poets of my generation took it as a special challenge to bring direct statements of feeling and idea back into poetry. Having struggled at this for ten or fifteen years, I tried in this essay to tell a group of younger poets what I had learned about how this might be possible.

"Finding a Poem" and "Poems about Paintings" deal more obviously with my own work. One relates my poetic practice to my personal life; the other works toward a direct personal involvement with five paintings. My study of these paintings was intimately involved with my psychoanalysis in Detroit; I may well have claimed insights here which would be more properly credited to Dr. Sanford Izner. The fourth lecture, "A Poem's Becoming" is my only attempt to relate my creative work to the overall tendencies of our culture.

Only one of these lectures, "Finding a Poem," has previously appeared in print.

Of my Four Studies in the Moderns, that on Roethke is a redaction of two earlier pieces; that on John Crowe Ransom was originally part of a symposium arranged and edited by Anthony Ostroff. The essay on D. H. Lawrence is the earliest of the pieces in this volume. The study of Dostoievsky was also finished long ago, although I have tried now to loosen its prose and fill some of its gaps.

The Four Studies in the Classics were all completed in recent years. Neither the essay on *A Midsummer Night's Dream* nor that on *The Iliad* has appeared previously.

Some of my friends are openly alarmed by my political and social views. I believe that I am neither a "utopian Fascist" as one friend calls me, nor an "old-line Stalinist" as I sometimes call myself. Auden, I think, once called Chekhov a liberal who aspired to the a-political. If I must be pigeonholed, I would like to hear something like that said of me. True, most of my remarks are skeptical of liberalism and democracy. That is partly because nearly all American intellectuals are liberal democrats and there is little point in saying what we all know—or have all, at least, said. I see almost as little value in proclaiming our virtues as in denouncing the faults of others. But this is also partly because we live in a time when it is too clear that our old cheerful dogmas have failed. We should no longer be too proud to learn, even from Fascists and Stalinists. That does not mean that I think Fascism or Stalinism—or any other such form—necessarily superior. My suspicion is that such matters are not the real problem. But even if they were, why assume the problem has an answer? Anything that has an answer is no problem.

This whole question is complicated because I write sometimes as artist, sometimes as private citizen. Most of my liberal friends think that what is good for the artist is good for society, and vice versa. I wish I could share this pleasant view. On the other hand, I do not think the artist and citizen unalterably opposed or that one can be sacrificed to the other's benefit. The real point—and this is where I most disagree with my friends—is that we simply do not know, either as citizens or artists, where we are going or what we want, what would be good for us and how to get it if we *did* know. The world, and we ourselves, are far too complex to be accounted for in any political doctrine, philosophical doctrine, conscious ideation.

Perhaps (and only perhaps) it would be nice if such abstractions controlled our lives. In that case, ideas might become interesting. To me, however, it seems that every important act in our lives is both propelled and guided by the darker, less visible areas of emotion and personality. Those, I think, are the resources I am seeking, the roots I have tried to pursue.

W.D.S.

Acknowledgments

Over a period of years I have received fellowships from the Guggenheim Foundation, the Academy of American Poets and the National Endowment in the Arts which have helped me work on several of these pieces. I am also grateful for periods in residence at both the MacDowell Colony and Yaddo.

I must express gratitude to those friends on whose intelligence, affectionate concern and discretion I have so often depended. I have elsewhere mentioned Dr. Sanford Izner and (indirectly) William Wasserstrom and Richard Gollin. I have drawn constantly upon Donald Hall, George P. Elliott and Donald Dike. Once again I would thank that lady to whom this volume, like many things, is dedicated.

Four Personal Lectures

Tact and the Poet's Force

I want to begin by reading, for my text, a poem from a children's record called "The Carrot Seed":

> Carrots grow from carrot seeds;
> I planted one to grow it.
> I'll water it; I'll pull the weeds.
> Carrots grow from carrot seeds.

On the record, this is the song of the hero, a little boy who plants one single carrot seed, believing it will come up. Every day he cultivates around the seed, waters it, pulls up weeds; every day he watches for his carrot. Meantime, his older brother stands around singing:

> Nyaa, nyaa, it won't come up;
> Nyaa, nyaa, it won't come up;
> Won't come up; won't come up;
> Nothing's coming up!

Even worse than that, this little boy has parents. They say, "Well, your carrot *might* come up, but you mustn't feel too badly, *if.* . . ." and they have a little song:

> Grownups know a lot of things
> That little boys can't know,
> So don't be disappointed, if
> Your carrot doesn't grow.

Faced by this multitude of skeptics, our hero can only reply by singing, once again, his credo:

> Carrots grow from carrot seeds;
> I planted one to grow it.
> I'll water it; I'll pull the weeds.
> Carrots grow from carrot seeds.

This is a story, then, about faith. This little boy has a theory about life and growth in the universe, about his relation to natural processes; it is his answer to all questions, all doubts. One must admit that he has better luck with *his* theories than most of us have with ours: one day, in a mighty fanfare, a regular sunburst of trumpets and kettle-drums, the biggest carrot in the whole world springs up. When his astonished family asks him what in the world's going on out there, he replies in the most matter-of-fact tone:

The carrot. Came up.

He shows neither surprise nor triumph: this is exactly what *had* to happen; he had always *known* this.

After I had heard this record several times, I sat down to read the record jacket. I got a severe shock. I could recall that little boy's voice saying, with plangent certainty, "I know it." But those words weren't on the jacket. They weren't on the record either—he had never said them. I heard them, yet he had not said them. What happened, apparently, was this: when he sang

4

> Carrots grow from carrot seeds;
> I planted one to grow it.

I must have thought ahead, half-consciously, and tried to guess the rest of that old familiar stanza-form:

> I'll water it; I'll pull the weeds
> And it will grow, I know it.

Instead, when he got to that last line, he fooled me—he simply repeated the first line, his cherished principle:

> Carrots grow from carrot seeds.

Now the problem I want to raise is this: Why, when the story is already about a little boy's feeling that "he knows it," and when the poem so openly prepared a place for him to say that, why didn't he say it?

Let me leave that question hanging for a moment, to establish a second text—a slightly more conventional one. Early in the "Elegy Written in a Country Churchyard" is a passage where Gray describes the "solemn stillness" of the twilit landscape around the church. He can hear a few beetles droning, a few sheepbells tinkling; everything else is silent

> Save that from yonder ivy-mantled tow'r
> The moping owl does to the moon complain
> Of such as, wand'ring near her secret bow'r
> Molest her ancient solitary reign.

That passage admittedly does not share many qualities with "The Carrot Seed." Yet these two poems are alike, I think, in showing a very high degree of tact—a tact so highly refined that both passages are colored (perhaps even controlled) by crucial words or phrases which are never even spoken.

If you go back through the many different versions of this poem which Gray published during his lifetime, you discover something

5

surprising. The earliest version and the deathbed version give that stanza exactly as I read it. All the many intervening versions, however, have instead of a "secret bower" a "sacred bower." And I submit that the purpose of the word "secret" is not to convey that the owl's bower is hidden—that's of no importance one way or the other—but rather to suggest that some "sacred" power, to which this owl is related, looks down over the scene.

Several factors contribute to this sense of sacredness. First, the physical presence of the church and graveyard; second, the similarity in sound between "secret" and "sacred"; third, both "secret" and "bower" already have holy connotations because of their use in the Bible and other earlier literature; finally, the interplay between "secret" and the phrase "ancient solitary reign." It's a mighty unusual owl that has an "ancient solitary reign"—you won't find him in Roger Tory Peterson. Thus, all resources have been used to suggest that crucial word "sacred." All resources, that is, *except* assertion.

The most interesting thing here, though, is that Gray had had that word "sacred" consciously in his mind, even published it. But he finally repressed it. For his final version, he must have decided that his first impulse—"secret"—was right; that the passage was better and the bower perhaps more sacred, if that sacredness was created by suggestion and atmosphere, not by assertion.

I must ask you to believe that poetic examples of this sort might be multiplied almost endlessly. The problem I want to address, then, is that old question asked so often by exasperated businessmen—my father among them—"Why don't you guys, you poets, say what you mean?"

I believe—and I hope this sounds either dangerously revolutionary, or else hopelessly old-fashioned—that it is a poet's business to say something interesting. Something so interesting and so valuable that people should stop whatever it is they are doing and listen . . . should stop thumbing through their order books, turning the dials on the TV, chasing the secretary around the desk. Truly, none of those things is trivial. The pursuit of a living, of some opinion to shape your life, of love—you must offer people something more valuable so they can dare to stop.

Of course, I am not saying that people *will* listen if you do say something interesting; quite the reverse is true. Unfortunately, people prefer writing that is dull, so most writing is intentionally dulled for its reader. Its real aim is the domination of that reader's spirit by the writer, or by those who pay him. That is best accomplished by being dull and so stultifying the reader's intelligence, his ability to discriminate, to make his own choice. This is true, of course, not only of such written material as newspapers, novels, and magazines, but of all forms of communication—radio, television, movies, nine-tenths of the talking done by merchants, teachers, parents. Their aim is to control —to get us to choose this whisky or that political group, this tobacco or that god, this brand of coffin or that system of values. In order to control our choice, they limit our area of vision, our awareness of the choices; the best way to do that is simply to say over and over again the things we have already heard and given at least nominal acceptance.

To such purposes, the artist—the man who wants to be interesting —stands constantly opposed. He always says something we have not heard before; he always suggests possibilities. This, however, makes him suspect if not actually hated, for we resist anything new with terrible ferocity.

That is understandable. We have done much magnificent theorizing about the world; the world remains a mystery. Man may become extinct, tyranny may prevail, your business fail, your wife leave you, tomorrow. There is a strong possibility that no idea works *all* the time. All the ideas carry guarantees, of course; the only trouble is that nobody knows where you go to get your money, or your life, back. This terrifying possibility that no idea always works is suggested every time someone offers us a new fact or a new idea. The more ignorant we are, the more sluggishly we think, then the more desperately we cling to the hope that our ideas are adequate. They clearly are not. The only way we can reassure ourselves is simply to deny the existence of anything which does not fit our preconceptions. So, all tyrants pander to our prejudices. We, in relief and gratitude, will give over control of our lives to anyone or anything that will just repeat to us those dangerously comforting half-truths we have invented about our world.

If, however, we fear any new fact or idea because it implies freedom of vision, we fear far more any new person, because he implies freedom of choice. We hate the man we can't disarm by slipping him into a stereotype, the man who won't fit our preconceptions about Man. Feeling as inadequate as we do, we automatically assume that anyone different must be better. And *that* we do not permit. So, we enforce our weaknesses upon each other. We hate the man who reminds us of the value of our differences.

We hate him even more because he reminds us that we are ourselves, not by force of circumstance, but largely by our own choice. If we do not approve of ourselves, we could have chosen differently; we can still choose differently tomorrow.

Unfortunately for the writer, he will always have to frighten people, and in just these ways. He can say nothing worth hearing, nothing worth stopping for, unless he says something new and different. He can only do that in one of three obvious ways:

First, he might have a new idea.

Second, he may have a new set of details and facts structured within old ideas.

Third, he may have a new style; that is, he may have a way of talking which symbolizes a new and different person.

If there are other ways to be interesting in a poem I have not seen them.

I want to devote the rest of my paper, then, to an analysis of the problems presented by this classification. First, and though many modern critics would disagree, I do believe a poem may have value simply for the idea it expresses. This is true, however, only if the idea is a new one—and there is nothing about which people more willingly fool themselves. It rather seldom happens; still it is possible: a writer *could* have a new idea. Let me give an example by the British poet Philip Larkin: a poem addressed to Sally Amis, the newborn daughter of his friend Kingsley Amis.

BORN YESTERDAY
for Sally Amis

Tightly-folded bud,
I have wished you something
None of the others would:
Not the usual stuff
About being beautiful,
Or running off a spring
Of innocence and love—
They will all wish you that,
And should it prove possible,
Well, you're a lucky girl.

But if it shouldn't, then
May you be ordinary;
Have, like other women,
An average of talents:
Not ugly, not good-looking,
Nothing uncustomary
To pull you off your balance,
That, unworkable itself,
Stops all the rest from working.
In fact, may you be dull—
If that is what a skilled,
Vigilant, flexible,
Unemphasised, enthralled
Catching of happiness is called.

This idea—that Sally may be luckier to grow up neither specially gifted nor good-looking—is only new in some relative sense. We have all suspected it at some time—perhaps about our own children—but it so quietly overthrows our ordinary values about success and happiness that we usually repress it. So, in some vital sense, a new idea. And it is worth our time to listen to a man who believes this so earnestly that he can look at the newborn daughter of his friend and can honestly wish her to be ordinary so that she can be happy.

In this poem the idea has interest *as* an idea. Larkin gives almost no concrete details—he doesn't need them. Again, there is almost nothing of interest in the style, the voice; the man who could honestly speak this new idea was, automatically, a new and interesting man. Unfortunately for any of us who write, though, the bloom is already rubbed off that subject—in that poem, by that poet. From now on, a writer cannot merely by its use say anything new or valuable; that's been done.

So, one of the things I am doing here is to rebel against an old commandment of my schooldays: Thou shalt not use abstract words or ideas in thy poem. Although the abstract words—truth, justice, happiness, democracy, love, kindness, etc.—are usually dull, that is because they are normally used to narrow the field of vision, to keep people from seeing. There is no reason they cannot be used to widen vision, if the writer is either more honest or more capable of abstract thought than most of his culture is. It is not impossible to be interesting when talking about ideas or when using ideational language; it is merely improbable. The poet's chosen vocation is to try something improbable.

There are, however, two hints. First, most people who are very anxious to tell you their ideas have none. That's why they're anxious to tell them. Second, if you *are* looking for a new idea, you are more likely to find it close to home. Any truth worth mentioning is probably something we all know far too well already but which we are laboring to obscure. Freud once remarked that he was considered one of the

10

geniuses of his age because he had made three discoveries—no one of which was unknown to any nursemaid on the whole continent! When Larkin says, "May you be dull" or, in another poem, "We all hate home/And having to be there" he has widened our vision to include something we always knew. This releases the energy we have wasted trying to hold it out of sight; at the same time, it suggests whole new areas of possible choice. It does not control which of the choices we shall make; it only makes us freer to choose, more responsible to the thing we *do* choose, and stronger to support it.

Now I certainly am not suggesting that a poem can never state any idea unless that is a new idea. In any poem, there may very well be a statement of idea, which poem we, however, will value for other qualities. This can come about in a great number of ways. It happens perhaps most commonly, certainly most significantly, when an idea is discovered by the poem itself to be already underlying one of its own patterns of words and facts. The *discovery* of any such idea (or emotion—I am using the terms quite interchangeably) is one of the most exciting events in our world; it has a value quite distinct from any value inhering to the idea *as* an idea. Consequently, just such a discovery is very often the climactic action of a poem. Let me give a single example, a poem by Rilke, which I give in a rough prose translation:

AN ARCHAIC TORSO OF APOLLO

We will not ever know his legendary head
Wherein the eyes, like apples, ripened. Yet,
His torso glows like a candelabra
In which his vision, merely turned down low,

Still holds and gleams. If this were not so, the curve
Of the breast could not so blind you, nor this smile
Pass lightly through the soft turn of the loins
Into that center where procreation flared.

If this were not so, this stone would stand defaced, maimed,
Under the transparent cascade of the shoulder,
Not glimmering that way, like a wild beast's pelt,

Nor breaking out of all its contours
Like a star; for there is no place here
That does not see you. You must change your life.

You must change your life. You wouldn't walk across the street to hear *that*. How many people tell you that each week? And with what a multitude of ulterior motives! Enjoy life; eat at Fred's! Give wings to your heart; Northwest Orient Airlines! The poet's motive is only that you become someone discovering that; someone looking at the statue and having the impression that its lost eyes have somehow spread through the whole trunk. Now the whole body seems to watch *you;* you came to the museum to look at the statue; it is looking at you. Suddenly, the discovery of this idea—You must change your life —transforms the whole poem. You see that this body, maimed as it is, does not show you *its* inadequacy, but *yours*. This experience, and the emergence of the idea from it, is worth crawling miles for. What you do with that experience is your business.

So much for the handling of ideas. Let me turn now to the problems of tact in handling details. I want to take an extreme example: "Protocols" by Randall Jarrell. In this poem, several German children tell of their trip to the concentration camp at Birkenau in Odessa, and of how they were put to death in gas chambers which were disguised as shower rooms. You may not know that the poison gas, phosgene, smells like clover or hay—hence, the smell of hay mentioned at the end of the poem. Again, as the children are entering the camp, they see a smokestack; they think it's a factory.

PROTOCOLS

We went there on the train. *They had big barges*
that they towed,

We stood up, there were so many I was squashed.
There was a smoke-stack, then they made me wash.
It was a factory, I think. *My mother held me up*
And I could see the ship that made the smoke.

When I was tired my mother carried me.
She said, "Don't be afraid." But I was only tired.
Where we went there is no more Odessa.
They had water in a pipe—like rain, but hot;
The water there is deeper than the world

And I was tired and fell in in my sleep
And the water drank me. That is what I think.
And I said to my mother, "Now I'm washed and dried,"
My mother hugged me, and it smelled like hay
And that is how you die. And that is how you die.

How many poets tried to write this poem and failed! How many could not resist saying that this is evil—that it is wrong to kill children. That is not worth saying. If the reader doesn't know that by now, there is no use *your* telling him. Everyone agrees that other people should not kill children; we only disagree as to when it may be necessary, what might be more important, and whether or not children *are* being killed. Jarrell's business, here, is to show that this reality exists, children *are* being killed. He has had the tact to see that any statement of idea would have weakened his poem.

But beyond this, he has seen the need for an extreme tact in choice of details. How many poets could have resisted the brutal guard who would beat the children and curse them for Jewish swine?—the weeping and hysterical sobbing?—the final horror when the Jews discovered the phosgene in the shower, the rush for the door, the strangling and trampling? They are all true—all happened at some time. Why are they kept out of the poem?

First, the strategy of argument suggests that when the facts are so strong you make a better case by showing your opponent's argument

13

at its best. If at its best it is horrifying, you needn't argue the rest. This is Jarrell's strategy. The children rather enjoy the trip; everything is exciting, like a trip to a big city department store. The guards appear only as "they" who give orders to wash. Thus, we are not distracted into questions of manner; the real problem here is not *how* people should kill children, it is the reality that people *do* kill children.

But there is another reason why restraint is so crucial here. This subject lies in an area where we give habitual consent without real belief. For years, all the communication media told us about the German extermination camps; as a result, many of us were surprised to find that they really *did* exist. Not that we had ever said, even to ourselves, that the news reports were false. Rather we accepted them in their own spirit: as self-comforting rationalizations proving our own moral superiority and justifying our policies. Yet, we knew that the existence of such camps did not really account for our foreign policy; knew that we would have been told roughly the same things even if they had not been true; knew that even if the facts were true, they could be selected in accordance with any desired effect. We accepted the stories about concentration camps much as we accepted the advertisements that appeared beside them: we don't believe the tobacco really *is* better, we just buy it. Most of us already desired or accepted our government's policies, so we accepted the stories about concentration camps without really *believing* them.

We had so often used these truths *as if* they were lies, we could no longer believe in them. Such subjects become almost impossible to write about—during the war, in fact, Auden said they *were* impossible. Yet, if you cannot write about these, almost the key subjects to our civilization, why would anyone go to the terribly hard work that writing is? Jarrell shows what is required—a complete removal from any ulterior motive, an absolute dedication to the object and the experience.

Oddly enough, we find that Jarrell's understated version is nearer the literal fact than is the propagandist's version. In such camps there was little public brutality; that would cause hysteria or resistance and hinder the efficient operation of extermination procedures. Besides, the guards, however much trained in brutality, remained pretty much ordinary people. They reacted much as you or I might have. Unloading bodies from gas chambers drove most of them mad in about three months. That job had to be given over to trustees *(sonderkommando)* who could themselves be gassed when *they* went mad. Of course, some of the guards were brutal—many of us, when we think we're doing something wrong, do it with greater emphasis, hoping this proves it right. But most of us react differently. Most of us who operate gas chambers, hang nooses, or electric chairs prefer to do so with every demonstration of kindly concern, since we too want to believe ourselves kindly and gentle people.

Yet this question of nearness to literal truth can be very misleading. What the writer seeks is imaginative truth; and *that* Jarrell's poem has. You know at once that this is no news editor trying to arouse your feelings (or his own) to the support of some particular line of action; these are merely several children who died there, who tell you exactly, simply and directly, what it was like, how it felt. They would not *dream* of enlisting you. Hence they are more real than propaganda's children ever become; too real for anyone's comfort. They might be of any nationality; so might their guards. And this makes the poem terribly threatening, indeed. It does not say "He did it," or even "You did it"—it merely says "This is." It leaves open the horrifying possibility: "I did it. We *all* did it. We all *could* do it."

To write this poem, you must first be willing to imagine yourself as a child in the situation—a *real* child, who might even enjoy parts of the trip. Then, you must be willing to imagine yourself a guard—this is the real test—and see how you would act. You must admit that moral weakness *could* lead you into such a position, could at least strongly tempt you. Until you are willing to admit that you share some part of humanity's baseness and degradation, you cannot write about humanity's dignity and gentleness. Of all the ulterior motives, none is more common, none more debilitating, none more damning, than the pretense to moral superiority.

To show what happens in the absence of this kind of tact, let me take a passage from a man who, in his earlier works, had been a very fine poet indeed, Kenneth Rexroth. *The Dragon and the Unicorn* tells about a journey through Europe shortly after World War II. After describing the miseries of the poor in Capri, Naples, and Sorrento, Rexroth turns to address an imaginary reader:

> Sitting there, reading this in your
> Psychoanalyst's waiting room,
> Thirty-five years old, faintly
> Perfumed, expensively dressed,
> Sheer nylons strapped to freezing thighs,
> Brain removed at Bennington
> Or Sarah Lawrence, . . .
> . . . you
> Think this is all just Art—contrast—
> Naples—New York. It is not. Every time
> You open your frigidaire
> A dead Neapolitan baby
> Drops out.

This is probably one of the most significant of ideas for us—that our prosperity is based on the poverty, even the starvation, of others. Yet no man in his right mind could think that a new idea; any man capable of hearing that has heard it. What does Rexroth offer in voice and detail, what of himself does he contribute, to bring his idea to life again? Only the most blatant hyperbole, whose purpose clearly is not to introduce people to a reality they want to ignore, but rather to impress upon them his moral superiority. This amounts to an act of spiritual violence intended to dominate the reader and force his acceptance.

Such spiritual colonialism is as inimical to art as its techniques are inimical to peace when employed by nations. Such a failure of tact could come about, I think, only because of a deep insecurity in the writer. If he really thought his idea were adequate, would he quite so desperately need my agreement? Yet this kind of insecurity tends to dog the heels of any older idea, since the longer an idea is around, the more we will be aware of that idea's failures to cover the complexities of the world and of our minds. As John Jay Chapman remarked, anything you've believed more than three weeks is a lie. Yet it's true, too—as true as the first day you found it. But if your mind is at all active, so many qualifications will soon arise in your consciousness (not to mention the subconscious) that even that idea's complementary opposite must also be represented if we are to do justice to our minds.

Carrots *do* grow from carrot seeds. However, after planting a garden several years ago, I can report to you that carrots also do *not* grow from carrot seeds. This may have something to do with the fact that farmers plant them broadcast.

Our prosperity *is* based on the poverty of others. I would furnish you no excuse for ignoring that. Yet we must also see that it is based on the prosperity of others; many other people's prosperity is based on *ours*. Many valuable things and many revolting things exist because of that prosperity; you will not sum up your knowledge of it or your feelings about it in any simple statement.

The problem is that most people, once committed to any line of thought, cannot endure the unavoidable weaknesses and complexities of their position. They shout their idea louder and louder, hoping to quiet everyone else's doubts and especially their own. Soon, every claim to certainty is a proof of doubt. The man who really *does* know something will show it in his actions and his tone of voice—like the little boy in "The Carrot Seed." And it does seem that somewhere we must mention that however much we admire his confidence, his faith, he *was* wrong.

Too many people, however, outgrow Rexroth's kind of naïveté only to adopt its complementary opposite—a spurious superiority. They

17

mature enough to see that no idea will permit them to be right all the time, so they reject *all* ideas. They become intellectuals. They live only to demonstrate their detachment from all positions, their utter superiority to any belief or any feeling. To them, the greatest sin is passion or energy. *Our* problem, I think, is to discriminate, yet not lose the ability to believe and act; to belong energetically to the world without being an idiot. We can do this only if we have the strength to live inside human limitations, to know that it *is* better to have lived, even though this means being wrong a good part of the time.

In contrast to Rexroth's poem, I want to quote another poem on the same subject, "The Golf Links" by Sarah Cleghorn. I think that these four lines demonstrate, as little else can, the strength that comes into the poet's voice when he has the inner security to let the facts speak in their own ungarnished strength.

THE GOLF LINKS

The golf links lie so near the mill
That almost every day
The laboring children can look out
And see the men at play.

This brings me to the problems of tact in style—and in a certain sense I have been talking about this problem all along, since the way we use ideas or facts is a part of our style. The particular point of my argument has been to prevent some misuse of facts or ideas from destroying the poet's voice in his poem.

If that is not to happen, a very great deal must be left to the tone of voice, the choice of language, the suggestiveness of words. As an example, let me take one of the most familiar poems in the language:

STOPPING BY WOODS ON A SNOWY EVENING
—*Robert Frost*

Whose woods these are I think I know.
His house is in the village though;

He will not see me stopping here
To watch his woods fill up with snow.

My little horse must think it queer
To stop without a farmhouse near
Between the woods and frozen lake
The darkest evening of the year.

He gives his harness bells a shake
To ask if there is some mistake.
The only other sound's the sweep
Of easy wind and downy flake.

The woods are lovely, dark and deep,
But I have promises to keep,
And miles to go before I sleep,
And miles to go before I sleep.

Why *does* so much have to depend on the furtive tone of "He will not see me"? On the despair implied by "The darkest evening of the year"? (Some readers apparently thought they could find that on their light meter!) On the sleep and death associations of "easy" and "downy"?

Simply because Frost must remain faithful to the truth of the experience; must resist the temptation to a spurious superiority. When the woods speak to you, they don't say, "Commit suicide"—or if they do, you'd better have someone look to your woods; they're getting thinned out. If you hate yourself, they say (as they say in a poem of Robert Lowell's), "Cut your own throat. Cut your own throat. Now. Now." If you hate your world, they say—in the softest, gentlest voice, "You are *so* tired; surely you deserve a *little* sleep. We are lovely, dark and deep." To weaken the seduction of that voice would be to destroy the poem.

Just as the writer must give up all pretense to intellectual superiority, he must give up also all pretense to moral superiority. No man detached enough to use the word "suicide" would be standing there to "watch [those] woods fill up with snow." "Suicide" is committee language. It is always easy to say "I am a terrible sinner" or "I have suicidal urges" or "I have an Oedipus complex." You *say* you have troubles; you sound so superior to them that you belie your own statement in making it. The hard thing, the strong thing, is to say in simple, personal language, how that problem affects the pattern of your life.

Frost unquestionably knew he was writing about a suicidal urge; he may have known that this was probably related to a desire for the womb. To have said so would have been a gross failure in humility. Again, however, this humility is terribly threatening to those who do not happen to share it. We all would like to think ourselves far above such feelings. But just as Larkin's poem cannot choose in favor of home (as it does) until it has faced the fact that "we all hate home," so Frost's poem cannot honestly choose life (as it does) until it has humbly admitted how good death sometimes looks.

Studying the worksheets of this poem, it appears that "downy" was one of the last words added to the poem—it appears that Frost felt once he had found this word he had guaranteed the poem's experience, the seductive call of the woods to just step in and fall asleep, to have it downier and easier than this life ever gives it to you. No doubt, Frost could easily have picked a more "deathy" word and so have made his meaning unmistakable—even to those with a vested interest in misunderstanding. At the same time, this would demonstrate his command of the situation, his detachment from it. Not only would this distract his attention from the experience; it would strongly suggest that his real aim was our admiration for him, not our participation with him.

Why, finally, is all this tact required? Why must ideas and emotions be repressed from conscious statement into details and facts; repressed again from facts into the texture of language, the choice of words, connotations; repressed finally into technical factors like rhyme and echoes of other words. Why must we even depend on words like

20

"sacred" or "I know it" which aren't in the printed poem at all? For two reasons which are really one: we aim at truth to experience and we aim at powerful expression. We are concerned here with problems of inmost belief and of strong emotion—and these again are areas of habitual disbelief. We simply do not credit people's conscious statements in these areas. And for very good reasons—most people simply do not use their conscious minds for the discernment or the revelation of the truth. They use their conscious minds to disguise themselves from others and from themselves, to make themselves look better than they are.

We simply do not believe anyone who talks very easily about matters of great feeling or ultimate belief. We are more impressed by the man who implies, almost by accident, that a bower is sacred to him or that "He knows it." We are not impressed with this kind of talk unless we see that the feeling is strong enough to force its way out past some sort of reticence.

Auden once wrote:

> The mouse we banished yesterday
> Is an enraged rhinoceros today

He was referring to the way we often repress some idea or feeling, which then collects great strength and spreads through the whole pattern of our lives. Often enough this process is terribly destructive; sometimes it is very useful. The poet's chief business is the revelation of the pattern of our lives, regardless of whether he approves of that or not. Thus, he has more use for an enraged rhinoceros in his poem than for a mouse. Too much consciousness, misapplied, leads directly to mousy poems.

So the poet imitates life, often, by carrying on in his poem a process similar to that of our life. He takes some idea, ordinary enough in itself, and represses it from conscious assertion, so that it can spread into the details, the style, the formal technique. Like the lost eyes of Rilke's statue, this lost consciousness spreads throughout the whole trunk; it soon stares out from every pore. Since it is out of the reach of conscious assertion, we know it is less liable to manipulation toward any false motive; its genuineness is more nearly guaranteed.

Thus, in his work, the poet faces that same problem faced daily by the individual conscience. We know that we must restrain some part of our energies or we destroy ourselves. Yet, as we turn our energies back against ourselves, they too may destroy us. In the case of mental and emotional energies, they can make us short-sighted, cramped in mind, dull, dispirited. We must learn to restrain and refocus our powers in such a way that we will not be right at the expense of being dead and worthless; must learn to be, though necessarily both right and wrong, yet stronger, livelier, fitter to survive, and more worth the effort of preserving.

Finding a Poem

In the Introduction to his *Collected Poems,* Robert Frost writes:

It is but a trick poem and no poem at all if the best
of it was thought of first and saved for the last. . . .
No surprise for the writer, no surprise for the reader.

If this is true, revision may be one of the most important creative acts; it is certainly the creative act most easily studied.

I find that my own revisions fall into two categories. First, many appear to be purely stylistic. I was raised, poetically, in a highly intellectual atmosphere; William Empson was my first love. When one of my poems goes bad, I almost always have to go back and write it longer—develop, openly and extensively, ideas which I have been trying to imply intensively. This does not involve changing the poem's denotational sense, only its way of speaking. That does not mean that such changes are unimportant; it is at least possible to argue that a poem's style—that quality of voice which suggests qualities of mind —that this *is* its basic meaning.

Second, however, and more immediately significant, are those revisions which I will call conceptual. Sometimes a poem *does* surprise you by taking itself out of your well-meaning hands and deciding for itself what it will say. Sometimes you find that your poem has taken you into an area where words have resonance, where the words and images echo through many areas of your thinking. You have approached something basic to that pattern of ideas and emotions and feelings which *is* your mind; you find out something of what *your* meaning is. Nine chances out of ten, this is something far different from the well-intended pseudo-beliefs which you offer yourself and your world everyday.

In this paper, I want to record one of the few lucky times this has happened to me. To do this, I shall have to become, for the moment, a sort of earnest graduate student of my own poem. I shall have to present a first and a last version of it and try to unfold the changes or recognitions inside my mind which caused the differences between these versions. And since the mind never lives divorced from its objects, since no perception endures apart from the thing perceived, I shall have to investigate the objects and events of my personal life which then concerned me, and which led me to define what I then believed.

Several years ago, I wanted to write a poem for my daughter, Cynthia, from whom I was separated by divorce from my first wife. I had already written four or five poems for my daughter, one for each season over a period of about a year and a half. This new poem, I thought, would be for the spring of 1954. I had collected a set of reminiscences and images about Easter, rebirth and repetition, eggs, birds, and flight. I had not analyzed these images; I only felt that they "belonged together" in one poem. What such a poem might mean, I had no inkling. When no further ideas came to me, I decided to set about trying to write the poem anyway, to see if a pattern would emerge in the actual writing.

For some time I had been fascinated by the purely syllabic metric I had seen in remarkable poems by Marianne Moore, W. H. Auden, Kenneth Rexroth, and by my friend Donald Justice. I chose this metric for my poem, hoping it might open some new rhythmic possibilities to me, but hoping also that it would let me drop into occasional stretches of flat prose which might balance the rather "poetical" quality of the images I had collected. The stanza I hit on had a syllable count which ran 5, 7, 4, 7, 6, 8, 12, 9 and rhymes which ran a, b, a, b, c, c, d, d. (You may notice that stanza 4 is metrically faulty in several places.) This, then, is the first version which I produced when I tried to versify my cluster of images:

HEART'S NEEDLE, vi.

> Easter comes around
> again; the river rising,
> the rigid ground
> melting. When you come you bring
> an egg dyed lavender.
> We shout along these banks to hear
> our voices returning from the hills to meet us.
> We need the landscape to repeat us.
>
> Here where you were born
> we watched the sundown swallow
> dive, drive and turn,
> we skimmed stones or might follow
> the killdeer from her nest;
> we walked where, in their day of rest
> lovers lay always on the riverbanks. You still
> live nearby, on the opposite hill.
>
> After the windstorm
> of July Fourth, all summer

through the light, warm
haze we heard great chain saws chirr
like iron locusts, watched crews
of squirrelmen climbing to hack loose
limbs twisted, torn in the shattering wind, cut free
the wrenched branches that could sap the tree.

By the park's birdrun
we once found, loose, outside,
a buff pigeon,
proud, brown-spatted. When I tried
to take her, she flapped so
fiercely in my grip, I let her go.
The keeper came and we helped snarl her in a net.
You bring things I'd as leave forget.

I mind how the red-
winged blackbird flapped her wild wings,
dived at my head,
scolding how her frail nest swings
there, where the tall reeds sway.
I recollect here your first May—
rain and the river rising, the killdeers flying
all night over the mudflats crying.

I showed this poem, for criticism, to a number of my friends at the
University of Iowa. Most of them liked it in a lukewarmish way; one
said that it sounded a little like an imitation of my earlier poems about
my daughter. And, when I came back to it, I had to admit that I still
didn't know what it was about. I could see that the image of hacking
the limbs off the trees was related to my separation from my daughter
(I had previously described this as an animal gnawing off one of its
limbs to get out of a trap); the pigeon fluttering out of my hands was
related both to my letting her go in the separation and also to the way
she sometimes ran away to make me chase her. The blackbird in the

last stanza seemed to be my first wife "protecting" her nest; the killdeers crying over their flooded nests implied some sense of grief over the breaking up of the home. These things all made sense and were all memories which the child's return might cause to be reborn in me. But this did not seem enough. No adequate pattern had emerged. I wasn't sorry to have written the poem, but I couldn't say that I thought much had happened.

Besides, what was the Fourth of July (stanza 3) doing in my Easter poem? Of course there *had* been a terrible windstorm that night in Iowa City. Many wires and trees came down, the power failed, and all the people watching fireworks in the park barely escaped when the storm passed ten feet over their heads. I knew that my daughter had been in the park with her mother that night, though I was not. At that time I was separated from the family; that particular evening I was at a birthday party for the girl who later became my second wife. Thus, that night had held a good deal of significance for me. Yet none of it was *in* the poem, nor did it seem to me that it *should* be. While I was writing this stanza, most of these problems had already occurred to me, yet something had wanted to keep that phrase about the Fourth of July. I had a moment of wild panic at the thought that perhaps I was becoming patriotic in my old age. Happily, I was soon able to quell *that* chimera. Yet, I still had my dilemma: if the Fourth of July didn't mean patriotism, what *did* it mean?

At this point, I put the poem aside, hoping that something might happen if I looked the other way. One Sunday morning several weeks later, I was sitting in a Quaker meeting when one of the members said something that annoyed me. In rough paraphrase, it went, "The measure of man's freedom is that he alone is given the power to reject God." I am always bothered by people, especially Quakers, who talk about God—I started going to meeting to escape people who talk about things they don't know about. My own habit is to paraphrase such statements, substituting for the term "God" either "Nature" or "Life," since those are at least terms about which I think a person might know something. When I tried paraphrasing the Quaker's statement, I found myself confronting one of my own central problems. Shortly, I heard myself saying that, in Nature, man alone has the choice to withdraw from the reality in which he lives, and so has the power to die, either metaphorically or literally. I was specially concerned about this then, because I had recently returned from my sister's funeral. A shy, quiet girl, subject to asthma attacks, she was closely involved with her family, lived at home even after graduation, and was employed by her father. One year after the storm I mentioned earlier, she got up out of bed and fell dead—on the morning of the Fourth of July. It would be hard to say *why* she died. Neither her asthma nor any of its complications appeared severe enough to end her life—not if she had really wanted to go on.

But I was now once again disturbed about this, for my daughter had just had an asthma attack. I felt that this was *her* way of refusing her life. (It happens that I was wrong about this, but that has no essential bearing on the poem; what matters is that I *did* believe this and was profoundly disturbed by it.) I felt that I must find some way to tell her that she must choose what reality was possible—that she was, of course, full of rage and regret for what she could not have, but that she was hardly alone in that. She still must choose what was unavoidable. This was the particular rebirth I wanted that year.

It was not until after the meeting that I realized I had been talking about my poem. It must have been this whole complex of problems about freedom, breathing, and asthma which had smuggled the Fourth of July into the poem. This, too, must link with the ironic rhyme-word "free" in the passage about cutting limbs off the trees, and again with the lines about snarling the pigeon in a net, for I apparently felt that I had helped snarl my daughter in a tangle of smother-love. It seemed to me—and I have often found this to be so —that my poem could develop a structure adequate to my experience only if, like the old sonata form, it carried two separate thematic areas at the same time. Plainly, the whole problem of freedom and guilt, which had at first been so very subordinate, must now be developed into a major thematic area, perhaps into the dominant theme.

I went about this in two ways. First, I added new material. After my original first stanza, I added a new one about the time when the child took her first breath and, with it, accepted her life. At the end of the poem, I added two stanzas: first, one stanza about her present refusal of breath (presented, however, as a memory of an earlier attack); finally, a stanza to sum up what I wanted to say to her, and what could only be said more or less doctrinally, but which I hoped was new enough, or personal enough, to be worth an abstract statement.

Since this new material brought with it a progression from the time of the child's birth to her present illness, it seemed that the material already in the poem should be rearranged to fit this chronological order. This involved numerous small changes which will be obvious; the largest change involved taking the original last stanza (about the blackbird and the killdeers), which dealt with the breakup of the marriage, and moving this material back before the original third stanza (about hacking the wrenched limbs off the trees), which dealt with the divorce and separation.

I found, also, that to make these additions and changes, I had to change my stanza pattern by adding one more syllable in each of the first three lines of every stanza, and two more syllables in the fourth line. Finally, I had to give up my lines about stone-skipping and the Sunday lovers on the riverbank. This nearly broke my heart, but I promised myself to work them into a later poem. Like almost every other promise I have ever made myself, this one remains unfulfilled.

As I now describe this process, it may sound very purposive and tidy—simply deciding what the poem needed, then writing it. Actually, the process was more a sort of interminable bumbling, trying one thing after another until something felt right. The final version now stands as the sixth poem of a cycle entitled "Heart's Needle."

Easter has come around
again; the river is rising
 over the thawed ground
and the banksides. When you come you bring
 an egg dyed lavender.
We shout along our bank to hear
our voices returning from the hills to meet us.
We need the landscape to repeat us.

 You lived on this bank first.
While nine months filled your term, we knew
 how your lungs, immersed
in the womb, miraculously grew
 their useless folds till
the fierce, cold air rushed in to fill
them out like bushes thick with leaves. You took your hour,
 caught breath, and cried with your full lung power.

 Over the stagnant bight
we see the hungry bank swallow
 flaunting his free flight
still; we sink in mud to follow
 the killdeer from the grass
that hides her nest. That March there was
rain; the rivers rose; you could hear killdeers flying
 all night over the mudflats crying.

 You bring back how the red-
winged blackbird shrieked, slapping frail wings,
 diving at my head—
I saw where her tough nest, cradled, swings
 in tall reeds that must sway
with the winds blowing every way.
If you recall much, you recall this place. You still
 live nearby—on the opposite hill.

After the sharp windstorm
of July Fourth, all that summer
through the gentle, warm
afternoons, we heard great chain saws chirr
like iron locusts. Crews
of roughneck boys swarmed to cut loose
branches wrenched in the shattering wind, to hack free
all the torn limbs that could sap the tree.

In the debris lay
starlings, dead. Near the park's birdrun
we surprised one day
a proud, tan-spatted, buff-brown pigeon.
In my hands she flapped so
fearfully that I let her go.
Her keeper came, And we helped snarl her in a net.
You bring things I'd as soon forget.

You raise into my head
a Fall night that I came once more
to sit on your bed;
sweat beads stood out on your arms and fore-
head and you wheezed for breath,
for help, like some child caught beneath
its comfortable woolly blankets, drowning there.
Your lungs caught and would not take the air.

Of all things, only we
have power to choose that we should die;
nothing else is free
in this world to refuse it. Yet I,
who say this, could not raise
myself from bed how many days
to the thieving world. Child, I have another wife,
another child. We try to choose our life.

This was, I thought, a better poem, more personal and so more universal. But that, in all seriousness, seemed a minor matter. It seemed more important that I had discovered what I needed to say. Looking back at the earlier poem, I can now see that it was sentimental and insincere. For, in the structure which it built (or jerrybuilt), it pretended that my feelings of grief were very important; they were not. Of course I had such feelings, but I had put them at the climactic point of my poem, not because they were actually important climactic feelings in my mind, but rather because I had carried those killdeers around with me for so many years waiting for a poem to put them in, and because the grief which they connoted seemed an obvious (because stereotyped) climax for a poem.

I am left, then, with a very old-fashioned measure of a poem's worth —the depth of its sincerity. And it seems to me that the poets of our generation—those of us who have gone so far in criticism and analysis that we cannot ever turn back and be innocent again, who have such extensive resources for disguising ourselves from ourselves—that our only hope as artists is to continually ask ourselves, "Am I writing what I *really* think? Not what is acceptable; not what my favorite intellectual would think in this situation; not what I wish I felt. Only what I cannot help thinking." For I believe that the only reality which a man can ever surely know is that self he cannot help being, though he will only know that self through its interactions with the world around it. If he pretties it up, if he changes its meaning, if he gives it the voice of any borrowed authority, if in short he rejects this reality, his mind will be less than alive. So will his words.

A Poem's Becoming

Since they depend so heavily upon unconscious energies, the intellectual and creative vanguard must usually work upon problems of which they can only later, if even then, become fully conscious. Yet, insofar as we are critics, it is our business to ask, "Where have we been going? Where are we now? Where are we going next?" And insofar as we are creative artists, we may well listen to our own answers, since (dangerous as that information is) it may be useful to have some conscious notion of what's in the air, of what could now be discovered, of "Where's the action?" In this paper I want to investigate some of these problems, exploring what I take to be the great artistic and intellectual revolution of the sixty years from about 1870 through about 1930, the smaller counterrevolution through 1960 or so, and finally to make some guesses about where we may now be going.

I want to begin in what may seem a strange way—by looking at two versions of my poem "A Cardinal" and considering the differences between these versions and what is implied by such changes. I once wrote that when one of my poems goes bad, I always need to rewrite it, longer. That sounded naïve to me, even when I wrote it, yet it certainly was true and I now* see that it has rather extensive implications. Looking back over my worksheets, I find that the revisions I have made during most of my career are of a sort no one would have made, nor would I have done so, in an earlier part of this century. I think this change is symptomatic of far-reaching changes, not only in myself, but in the general atmosphere because of that counterrevolution which first began about 1930 but which only reached me some time later. By now, of course, it is obvious in the work of a great many artists, and already the more advanced of these have abandoned it and gone on in other directions.

Let me begin, then, with an example—a poem I started many years ago—a poem about my own inabilities to write a poem. The first version had no title:

> I wake late and leave
> the refurbished quonset
> where they let me live.
> I feel like their leftovers;
> they save me for the onset
> of some new war or other.
>
> There rises from the campus
> its pined and hemlocked park;
> inside this narrow compass
> I prowl toward my horizons
> of thrush and meadowlarks,
> but each step brings a silence
> near by me to some small

*Throughout this lecture, "now" refers to 1960 or so, when it was delivered. It was then titled "An Overview: 1870–1970."

still voice: a scared hush lurks
around me, like a smell.

Sitting to try my meters,
I hear under the prose
of factories and motors
an old, unselfish cadence:
a life they cannot praise
rehearsed by air cadets;
from the municipal airport
where golf balls veer like tracers,
grave engines rumble their part.

But who has pitched this wriggling
leg of grasshopper
onto my proper scribblings?
The sleek, satanic cardinal
above me sings for supper
his appetite's vain ordinal.
Absurd! Birdsong's the vital
claim to their comeuppance;
he outspeaks his squatter's title.

All bugs and these pert birds
witness once more their voices
though I, still, in their weeds
still stalk my specimen words,
replenishing the verses
of nobody else's world.

That version of my poem has five stanzas of varying lengths. The final version came about eight years later, has thirty stanzas, and is handled very differently, indeed. Yet you may notice that the first and the last stanza are almost completely unchanged. The middle three stanzas, however, have been expanded into twenty-seven stanzas! The poem is now called

A Cardinal

I wake late and leave
the refurbished quonset
where they let me live.
I feel like their leftovers:
they keep me for the onset
of some new war or other.

With half a ream of paper
and fountain pens, equipped
with ink and ink eraser,
a book to hunt up words,
and the same old manuscripts,
I tromp off to the woods,

the little stand of birches
between golf course and campus
where birds flirt through the branches
and the city will be hushed.
Inside this narrow compass
I crash through underbrush,

beer cans and lovers' trash
in search of my horizons
of meadowlark and thrush.
Yet near me, here, it's still.
I carry a scared silence
with me like my smell.

At each of my footsteps
one of the insect noises
in the tall grass, stops.
The weeds sing where I leave.
All the living voices
evade me like beliefs.

Well, let them look *me* up

and take their own sweet time;
I've come to set up shop
under this blue spruce
and tinker at my rhymes.
God knows it's little use;

God knows I have spent ages
peering like a stuffed owl
at these same blank pages
and, though I strained to listen
the world lay wrapped with wool
far as the ends of distance.

And what do I hear today?
Little that sounds mine—
in town, across the way,
mill whistles squeal;
now, closer by, the whine
of a freight car's wheels;

out on the superturnpike
the cattle trucks and trailers
lumbering toward next week;
beyond, from the county airport,
where golf balls veer like tracers,
great engines thunder their part

in this devil's Mass
of marketable praise.
Oh, they've all found *their* voices.
And now I catch a meter
under this heavy prose
of factories and motors:

the college air cadets
are on their grinder, marching,
counting out their cadence,

one two three four, creating
for the school and market
the ground bass of our credo—

faith in free enterprise
and our unselfish forces
who chant to advertise
the ancient pulse of violence.
Meantime, I fuss with phrases
or clamp my jaws in silence.

Watch out; what's this red
bird, fluttering up to perch
ten feet from my head!
See the green insect wings,
pinched in his beak, twitch.
He swallows it. And sings.

Speak of the bloody devil!
Old sleek satanic cardinal—
you get your bellyful,
maintain the ancient Law,
and celebrate this ordinal
of the red beak and claw.

You natural Jesuit,
sing, in your fine feathers,
Hosannah to Appetite;
announce to the woods and hills
the one god of our fathers
is living in us still;

sing for the flyboys, birdy,
in praise of their profession;
sing for the choirs of pretty
slogans and catch-phrases
that rule us by obsession;
praise what it pays to praise:

praise soap and garbage cans,
join with the majority
in praising man-eat-man,
or praise the young who sell
their minds to retire at forty.
With honor.
                Go to hell!

Good God! This is absurd!
A veritable scarecrow!
I curse out a poor bird
for daring feed his belly;
now my bird has flown
and left me in this gully.

It is absurd, absurd
Darwinian self-pity!
As if a self-made bird
would sign his days to sergeants,
his soul to a committee,
or call himself a bargain!

As if I'd never heard
what the birds' song means;
as if I'd ask a bird
to mortify his body.
Wait; from the next ravine,
he's singing again, already.

And he outspeaks a vital
claim to know his needs;
his song's a squatter's title
on his tree and the half acre
in which he hunts and breeds
and feeds the best he's able.

To enemies and rivals,
to mates and quick beetles,

39

he sings out for survival:
"I want my meals and loving;
I fight nobody's battles;
don't pardon me for living.

The world's not done to me;
it is what I do;
whom I speak shall be;
I music out my name
and what I tell is who
in all the world I am."

We whistle in the dark
of a region in doubt
where unknown powers work,
as watchmen in the night
ring bells to say, Watch out,
I am here; I have the right.

It should be recognized
I have not come sneaking
And look for no surprises.
Lives are saved this way.
Each trade has its way of speaking,
each bird its name to say.

We whistle in the dark
to drive the devils off.
Each dog creates his bark.
Even I, in Navy blues,
I whistled *Wachet Auf*
to tell the sailors who.

He's back; obliquely flying
under a trail of vapor,
our sky's white center-line.
A robin goes by, wrestling
a streamer of toiletpaper

his mate might want for nesting.

Selfish, unorthodox,
they live upon our leavings.
Boys or cats or hawks
can scare them out of song.
Still, long as they are living,
they are not still for long.

Each year the city leaves
less of trees or meadows;
they nest in our very eaves
and say what they have to say.
Assertion is their credo;
style tells their policy.

All bugs, now, and the birds
witness once more their voices
though I'm still in their weeds
tracking my specimen words,
replenishing the verses
of nobody else's world.

Few will deny that that is longer. But there are other differences, too—very significant ones. First, as the poem becomes longer and more extensive, much less compressed and intensive, the speaker's voice has been explored much further, tends to become much more of a human voice, much less of a poetical or stylized voice. Second, with this, the speaker tends to become more human—even somewhat absurd—may curse at a bird, get so pumped up with his own rhetoric that he will act ridiculously and so become recognizable, even to himself. Third, although both poems involve a conflict of feeling, in the first version the opposed emotions tend to be locally present so that the poem seems always to be fighting within itself, line by line, or word against word within the line. In the later version, the opposed emotions tend to be sorted out into separate parts of the poem: in the

41

early part, the speaker is blaming on the society his inability to write
—saying "How could anybody write a poem in a crass, materialistic
culture like this?" Later, he decides that has rather little to do with
it—he's only trying to blame on someone else what is really a problem
of his own internal economy of energy. Fourth, in the final version
there is a marked turning point of emotion within the poem, a *peri-
peteia* if you like, which precedes and leads to the climax; and that
is the moment when the speaker decides that he has been being
absurd. Within the poem, then, he's had a chance to be absurd, to
change his mind and go another direction, and that leads him on
directly to a climax and to action.

It seems to me *now* that in revising this poem, I was trying to write
out of it the influence of my education—an education based very
heavily on that great revolution of the last century; in poetry, particularly that of the great French Symbolists. Thus, in school, we had been
taught to write a very difficult and very intellectual poem. We tried
to achieve the obscure and dense texture of the French Symbolists
(very intuitive and often deranged poets), but by using methods similar to those of the very intellectual and conscious poets of the English
Renaissance, especially the Metaphysical poets. I need hardly say that
this was a very strange combination.

My first published poem started like this:

> June, and the Tigerlily swam our hedge
> Like gold fish in the inmost sea's most green
>
> Awakenings. Fondly, we gathered the bloom.
> Thus: Dis. In our inquisitive, close room
> The Lily parched and clenched to a fist
> Which could then neither fierce nor pure subsist.

Of course you recognize that this is a poem about the loss of religious
faith? The Tigerlily is meant to stand for Christ, who, like Persephone,
was gathered away into the underworld by a dark god, Dis or Pluto
—our own inquisitive spirit—but who might be reborn later in the

poem. I got seriously upset when one critic said this poem had no intellectual content; he said he wouldn't demand a metaphysical conceit (which, of course, the poem *was*), but he would like to have it talk about something besides plain old flowers. I had so packed my poem with intellection that he thought it had none! I was much more distressed, though, when another critic praised my poem as a piece of description by someone who had really gone out and looked at the world. (The one thing I certainly had *not* done and wouldn't have thought of doing.)

If, at that time, I wanted to write a poem about my marriage and the troubles it had gotten into, I costumed myself as "Orpheus" and wrote:

> Stone lips to the unspoken cave;
> Fingering the nervous strings, alone,
> I crossed that gray sill, raised my head
> To lift my song into the grave
> Meanders of unfolding stone,
> Following where the echo led
> Down blind alleys of our dead.

Or I took another disguise. We had been taught that we mustn't talk directly about our feelings or use the first person singular, we must turn our feelings into a landscape, make what's called an objective correlative. I wrote:

> Our fields were a crust of pure form.
> We crossed on katatonic brooks
> To our four walls and shut the doors. . . .

But, of course, that's so hair-raisingly bad as to be somewhat misleading.

Much symbolist poetry, and poetry written under its influence, was very good indeed. Neither should I be construed as arguing that clear poetry is better than obscure poetry. That is not true; it was merely true *for me* at that particular time. However, a shift of this sort has gone on in poetry generally, and in recent years much of the best poetry tended to share the qualities of my second version, while much of the worst tended to resemble my earlier version.

In the late 1940s, the finest voice in British poetry was probably either William Empson or Dylan Thomas. Surely no one has forgotten what Dylan Thomas sounds like:

> It was my thirtieth year to heaven
> Woke to my hearing from harbour and neighbour wood
> And the mussel pooled and the heron
>   Priested shore
> The morning beckon
> With water praying and call of seagull and rook
> And the knock of sailing boats on the net webbed wall
>   Myself to set foot
>   That second
> In the still sleeping town and set forth.

Or again:

> Altarwise by owl-light in the half-way house
> The gentleman lay graveward with his furies;
> Abaddon in the hangnail cracked from Adam,
> And, from his fork, a dog among the fairies,
> The atlas-eater with a jaw for news,
> Bit out the mandrake with to-morrow's scream.

William Empson, the prophet of ambiguity, sounded like this:

BACCHUS

> The god arkitect whose coping with the Flood
> Groyned the white stallion arches of the main
>   (And miner deeps that in the dome of the brain
>   Take Iris' arches' pupillage and Word)
> Walked on the bucking water like a bird

> And, guard, went round its rampart and its ball
>   (Columbus' egg sat on earth's garden wall
>   And held the equitation of his bar;

a passage which, for all its differences of approach, for all its hyper-conscious multiple puns, ends up sounding surprisingly like the Thomas poem before it.

The finest voice in British poetry by the early 1960s was Philip Larkin, who sounded like this:

CHURCH GOING

> Once I am sure there's nothing going on
> I step inside, letting the door thud shut.
> Another church: matting, seats, and stone,
> And little books; sprawlings of flowers, cut
> For Sunday, brownish now; some brass and stuff
> Up at the holy end; the small neat organ;
> And a tense, musty, unignorable silence,
> Brewed God knows how long. Hatless, I take off
> My cycle-clips in awkward reverence.

It is an astonishing difference. But the same thing happened in American poetry—which during that period, and until the appearance of Ted Hughes, was much more lively and creative than was British poetry.

In the late 1940s our most powerful younger voices were those of Hart Crane and Robert Lowell. In "The Bridge" Hart Crane sounded like this:

> . . . .O Thou steeled Cognizance whose leap commits
> The agile precincts of the lark's return;
> Within whose lariat sweep encinctured sing
> In single chrysalis the many twain,—
> Of stars Thou art the stitch and stallion glow
> And like an organ, Thou, with sound of doom—

> Sight, sound and flesh Thou leadest from time's realm
> As love strikes clear direction for the helm.

A few years later, Robert Lowell sounded like this in "The Crucifix":

> How dry time screaks in its fat axle-grease
> As spare November strikes us through the ice
> And the Leviathan breaks water in the rice
> Fields, at the poles, at the hot gates to Greece;
> It's time: the old unmastered lion roars
> And ramps like a mad dog outside the doors
> Snapping at gobbets in my thumbless hand.
> The seaways lurch through Sodom's knees of sand
> Tomorrow. We are sinking. "Run, rat, run,"
> The prophets thunder, and I run upon
> My father, Adam.

By the early 1960s, the dominant voice in American poetry was probably still that of Robert Lowell, but a Lowell so changed as to be scarcely recognizable. In the ending of "Terminal Days at Beverly Farms," he speaks again of a father, his actual, literal father:

> Father's death was abrupt and unprotesting.
> His vision was still twenty-twenty.
> After a morning of anxious, repetitive smiling,
> his last words to Mother were:
> "I feel awful."

Again, in "Memories of West Street and Lepke" he writes of time:

> Only teaching on Tuesdays, bookworming
> in pajamas fresh from the washer each morning,
> I hog a whole house on Boston's
> "hardly passionate Marlborough Street,"
> where even the man
> scavenging filth in the back alley trash cans,
> has two children, a beach wagon, a helpmate,

and is a "young Republican."
I have a nine months' daughter,
young enough to be my granddaughter.
Like the sun she rises in her flame-flamingo infants' wear.

You will probably have to grant me, then, that a change rather of the order I've described did go on in a good deal of the poetry of that period. Thus the earlier drafts of my own poem reflected the poetry written before this shift, the later version reflected the changes which went on in so much poetry during the 1950s (though we can now trace hints of this change much earlier). Or, more accurately, these revisions probably did not "reflect" this shift; most artists found it for themselves, only to discover later that a similar shift was going on independently in the work of others.

In order to discuss, however, what's gone on in these last twenty or thirty years, I must go back first and define how I see that great artistic and intellectual revolution which began around 1870 in the work of the French Impressionists and Symbolists and came to us in the work of Pound and Eliot, but against which, since the 1930s, a steady countercurrent was developing which by the middle 1950s came into full flower. For to artists of my generation, that originally revolutionary movement had become something fixed, domineering and oppressive. We had come to have a tradition of academic experiment, experiments using thoroughly predictable materials and reaching thoroughly predictable answers.

I must make it clear, however, that we certainly did not feel that the leading figures of that revolution were negligible or trifling. Rather we felt them to be so great as to be definitive. By taking the direction of Rimbaud or that of Freud, one could only go on dwindling as the traditions founded on their insights became more and more academic and binding. If there was one thing we didn't need, it was any more little Freuds, any more little Rimbauds.

Now that we have been able to throw off this overbearing influence,

I have had some opportunity to go back and see more of what it was we were rebelling against—rather like a son going back to study his father once he's thrown off his dominance. My chance to make this study came recently when I started writing a series of poems based on paintings by the great Impressionist and post-Impressionist masters. The Impressionists, of course, hold the same position in painting as that held in poetry by my old masters, the Symbolists.

Looking back over the work of the Impressionists and especially of Claude Monet, I began to suspect that they had initiated and carried out an astonishing attack against form, had led a direct attempt to destroy matter and release energy.* They wished their paintings not to represent any object, but rather that light which emanated or radiated from the object. As a result, very quickly the object simply disappeared, was translated into light, a form of energy. At first you had the energized surface of the canvas, recording the impression of light upon the eye and devoid of any moral or ideational interpretation. But very quickly painting passed beyond this; in later works the primary reality is not that of the represented light, but rather the reality of the paint which represents it. The real subject of the painting was that energy suggested in the style and technique of creating the paint surface, the human qualities represented by *this* choice of paint, *that* balance of mass and color, *that* kind of brush stroke—a tendency already well advanced in the work of Manet and carried to its fullest extreme in our own Action Painters.

These same drives quickly became apparent and even dominant in the other arts as well. Composers began to break down the solid forms of musical form, the sonata, rondo, etc., the forms of harmony, of rhythmical regularity. The Symbolist poets, so directly the counterpart of the Impressionist painters, began tearing down the old prosodic forms, syntactical forms, subject matter. Just as the painting lost

*In "Poems About Painting" I have commented at length on Monet and his crucial part in this process, so I shall confine my remarks here to broader outlines.

its desire to tell any story or even to represent objects, so the Symbolist poem usually has no narrative, no plot, no actors, no action; the language surface takes on a life and drama of its own. The "actors" of such a poem are certain key words and phrases which establish timeless conflicts, relationships, tensions among themselves. Even the objects in such a poem will be broken down and lose reality. Rimbaud, for instance, in his great poem "Memoire" writes:

> The green and faded dresses of the girls
> Are willow trees where dart out the unbridled birds.

What do you see here?—willow trees or little girls in green dresses? Both and neither. For those objects do not have primary reality. What is really real is that charge of symbolic energy released by the collision of the two objects. Once again, we have an energized surface where objects are not real in themselves but are broken down to release symbolic energies.

At the same time this was happening in artistic circles, similar processes were taking place in all the areas of our life. You had the breakdown of the family, of religious belief, social structure, imperial and governmental forms, political beliefs—all of these forms being broken down so as to release energies frozen into these forms. In general, all intellectual predispositions were breaking down around us —which in a way demands that we all become artists—something for which we are profoundly ill-equipped. The great climax of the process is found, I think, in Freud, who broke down what we had always taken for the solid forms of personality and so released those frozen energies. In the physical sciences, we have something entirely comparable (something intellectual, however, rather than emotional) in the relativity theories of Einstein; and the whole process has its grand anticlimax, of course, in the actual smashing of the atom, the taking of the whole process literally—simply breaking down physical matter and releasing part of its energies. But this *is* an anticlimax—it is carried out by those who are affected too literally and directly by such a drive to be very creative, and its effect is severely limited. It may end your life; it cannot deeply affect its quality as can Freud or Monet.

How could a whole culture come to be so obsessed, so possessed by this compulsion to break down form—an aim no other culture would have thought desirable, or even possible? We do know that certain artists and thinkers can experience their bodies at an almost chemical, almost molecular level. Rilke, not conscious that he was dying of leukemia, wrote to a friend, "I feel a new constellation rising in my blood." Shall we imagine that a few artists, aware of the basic insubstantiality of their substance, began to conceive the possibility that all matter could be dissolved, all forms decomposed? Scarcely; most of these artists were acting under just as much compulsion as were those in the grip of social revolutions, and were as little conscious of what they were really doing.

But they *were* under the influence of a closely related drive: the old Faustian hatred of human form as such, man's rage against man's limits. As this drive is expressed by the common man in politics, social revolution and mental illness, it is clear that the two root forms of this hatred are the child's fear and hatred of his sexual form and his hatred of the facts of inequality—hatred of his parents for being large and powerful, for feeding him and showing him how helpless he is. In later life, of course, this may grow into a hatred of injustice, of harmful social inequalities; it may also grow into a hatred of all that is truly superior.

In the hands of the ordinary man, such compulsions more often have taken a destructive turn, though the slogans have always been noble and promising. Lacking inventiveness, the ability to channel these forces into positive or creative areas, the common man must act them out directly and literally: copulate with all and any, dress like the opposite sex, try to become the opposite sex, obliterate all sex differences. (Can it be that Christine Jorgensen really stands at the apex of Western civilization?) In the name of self-expression, the average man will create a world of total sameness and conformity so that he may be a neuter and none may judge against him. Yet in rejecting difference, he has already committed himself to the mediocre and must attack all that is stronger, more gifted, more realized.

Similarly, he is fixed in an ambivalent struggle with those he sees as powerful, must attack each authority in turn, his father, his country, his civilization. Again, this may take place under noble doctrines and may locally have beneficial results when turned against actual tyrannies. Yet we can be reasonably sure that most people will replace one tyranny with another either stronger or more subtle. We see an apparently endless round of self-defeating social revolutions, each carried on in the name of freedom because its real aim is always tyranny, the loss of freedoms most people can neither use nor bear. If Monet and Beethoven could not bear their creative freedom without turning to damage themselves, how much less could the common man? Thus, while the culture itself has failed so abysmally that it is now on the verge of collapse, during this same period its artists and thinkers (driven by the same forces) have been unbelievably inventive, have done work of such audacity and brilliance that future times will find it almost beyond possibility.

Daring as this intellectual and artistic revolution was, it reached artists of my generation in a seriously debased and decayed form. It has always had a number of regressive and backward tendencies which, as the movement passed to second-rate minds and became institutionalized, became dominant and oppressive. To see these regressive tendencies more clearly we may consider the treatment of time in Symbolist poems—though we could trace the same tendencies in other areas.

Despite all its relation to the skeptical and scientific revolution, the Symbolist revolution was basically psychological and religious; in some ways it was more a revulsion than a revolution. You may recall the very exalted tone of my post-Symbolist examples. Symbolist poetry tended to keep the tenor and the language of religion, without its substance. Symbolist poetry, in its attempt to concretize a mood and

51

hold it suspended, in its rejection of matter and external reality in favor of the internal reality, the symbol, the "image" of Rilke, this poetry becomes in effect a search for a state of Being, a rejection of that world of Becoming in which we are born, grow, and die. The work of art comes to symbolize a changeless realm, a realm where things do not move (and so, perish). You will notice, if you study the Symbolists, nearly all their poetry is obsessed with stasis of some sort —no matter whether it seeks it and celebrates it, as in Yeats's "Byzantium" and "Sailing to Byzantium" and in the example of Hart Crane I read, or whether it finds that stasis and laments it—as a psychological rather than religious state. The stasis of my own poem, with its katatonic brooks or my other poem and its inability to write a poem. Or you can find it in the great poems of the period: Rimbaud's "Memoire" ends with a picture of himself as a man dredging from a little boat, chained in the slime of the river bottom, and unable to reach to either the yellow flower—woman—or the blue—man. Again, one of Mallarmé's most famous poems shows him as a swan frozen into the ice of a lake. Or, later, Rilke's famous panther pacing in the cage,

> For him, there are a thousand bars;
> Behind a thousand bars, no world.

Now because of this obsession with stasis, one of the first kinds of matter to disappear from the Symbolist poem is the dramatic character. It is essential that there be no actors and no real action or the poem will start moving; it will change its mind and decide to do something, thus defeating its own purpose. The poem is usually a monologue, but it must never be a dramatic one, must never change its mind, must never reach a decision and start off into action. Because of that, we have our emphasis on irony in modern criticism—the demand that any attitude stated must be immediately countered and balanced and frozen by its opposite; constant balance must be maintained.

Thus, the Symbolist poem tends to exist outside of time. In the poem, time very seldom passes. Even more remarkable, the reader does not experience the poem in its own reading time; instead, he can take infinite time to experience all the symbolic amplifications of the words, balancing the richnesses of the poem back and forth until he can hold them all in his mind at once, together with all the necessary biographical data, footnotes, critical commentaries. He must become like the mind of God, holding past, present, and future—and footnotes—and critical interpretations—all in timeless suspension. This accounts also for that elevation of tone so common in the later Symbolists; this, like the style of Milton, is meant to suggest to you a meaning, an elevation of spirit, an existence beyond description. This also accounts for the importance of ambiguities, puns, myths, symbolic linkages in this poetry. The ideal Symbolist poem would probably be only two words long, but those two words would carry the symbolic meaning of all human experience. For this is only one more form of literary hedge-hoggism, to use Isaiah Berlin's term. It stems from a pseudo-religious or pseudo-metaphysical attempt to sum up the all in some one idea-statement or belief or symbol. For a while, the symbol took the place of any religious or metaphysical equation of all our disparate experience. Perhaps things could all be related because they might have symbolical relations. Hence the great emphasis recently on what is called anagogical meaning in poets like Dante. It is an attempt to cut down on the terrible disparity and incongruity of our world.

This, then, is the poetical pattern I see as dominant from about 1870 till about 1930, and it is largely by opposition to this pattern that the poets since 1930 have operated, poets roughly from Auden to the present generation. The general process has been a further secularization, a return to *this* world; our poems exist here—they are poems of Becoming, not poems of Being. They tend to be deliberately place-centered: Hugh Staples in his study of Robert Lowell remarks that the very titles of his poems tend to reflect the growing importance of places in Lowell's thought and work—such titles as "91 Revere St.," "Dunbarton," "Terminal Days at Beverly Farms." James Wright's earlier poems take place in Martin's Ferry, Ohio; my own in Beaver Falls, Pennsylvania, or Iowa City, Iowa. Anne Sexton's in Newton Lower Falls, Massachusetts. Philip Booth's in Castine, Maine.

Poets tended to be much more interested in the problems of this world—problems of politics, marriage, business. We are almost all of us delighted if we can squeeze into a poem some new physical detail, something no one ever put in a poem before—not only for its symbolical sense, either, but for its literal value as a *thing.* For me, personally, this change was all part of a psychotherapy I was involved in in Iowa City—where I noticed as I talked to my doctor that one of the persons in that room sounded like a psychiatry textbook—and it wasn't him. I noticed that where I was always talking about the Oedipus complex, he kept asking me how I was going to pay my rent—I was astonished to find that he was interested in the problems of this world and only became interested in symbology when some tangle of symbols was preventing me from operating practically in this world. But, at the same time, other poets were coming to much the same sort of decision in other ways. We have come to value matter and the physical world —perhaps because we are in much more real danger of losing them than people ever were before.

Along with this go very significant changes in the use of time in a poem. Time *does* pass in the poems we write now—people change and things happen there. And the poem itself is meant to be experienced in its own reading time. You're meant to read through it from beginning to end, as a piece of dramatic dialogue spoken by someone to someone and for some personal reason. The poem may have to be read over and over again to reveal its richnesses—if it has any—but it is a dramatic process taking place in time and involving change. Not a stasis produced outside of time.

Our models in the past ten years are much less likely Donne and Rimbaud and Eliot than Chaucer and Hardy and Frost. Our poems are much more likely to include dramatic actors and speakers. Insofar as we are able, we try to value human personality, as such, and regardless of whether we approve of it—for we are in great danger of losing *that,* too.

This has brought with it a comparable lowering of tone—at best, a humanity of tone. The earlier examples that I read you tended always to be very hierarchical, celebrant, enchanted, magical. The better poems being produced right now tend to be common-sensical, stylistically almost ordinary—such a voice as you might hear in this world, not a voice meant to lift you out of this world. In short, we have not only dropped the subject matter of religion, as had our predecessors the Symbolists; we have tended to drop also its tenor and language—its energy if you like. Speaking only for myself, that religious ecstasy so dear to the later Symbolists (as it is to some of the "beat" poets of the present time) seems to me very much like their other ecstasies—drunkenness, dope, sexual perversions. Sometimes great fun, no doubt, but an ecstasy—literally, a "standing outside," a removal from the world which we feel both a duty and a practical necessity to revere. In the words of Rimbaud, these things are a derangement of the senses; most of us tend to value our senses and to try in all possible ways to preserve them. We seek to regain our senses—we go to colleges, to psychiatrists, to conferences—we try to keep both our reason and our reasonability as alive as possible. Perhaps because we feel in more imminent danger of losing them.

We tend to be foxes, not hedgehogs; pluralists, not monists. We tend to live by our physical senses and our wits—not by some one rule we hope we can apply to every situation we may encounter. We seek Becoming, and we find it in all ranges of experience. In its decline, the Symbolist poem was often a terrible temptation to conspicuous admirability. "Look how symbologically brilliant, how morally alert I am!" For the first part of this world we want to escape is ourselves. Now I find that I want my poems not to be so admirable; I want them to have more of my own absurdity, pomposity, monstrousness, silliness. That, of course, is one of the chief reasons my poems have gotten longer. If you write down only your brilliant or your moral thoughts, you are going to write very short poems, indeed! This change, of course, leads to something more dramatic: instead of the poem's attitudes being always balanced, now each part of the poem can have its own opinions, some good, some bad, some silly, some brilliant—and you can get from part to part only by changing your mind, by changing your heart. Somebody decides something, and this is usually either the effect or the cause of action. That, I think, is where we are now.* The counterrevolution has been of some value, I believe, especially in overcoming an influence that had become academic and warped. Yet to some extent that very rebellion of ours has been limiting; so long as we define ourselves by rebellion against Rimbaud, we are still limited by him.

I would like to suggest that what we are now going to do is probably to extend our interest in Place, and externality, into an investigation of Space. Not only because we live in a Space Age, but also because this carries with it certain broader problems of metaphysical space—problems of moral limits (or moral space), problems of psychological space, of what the psychologists call propreoception, the awareness of the self as positioned in space relative to other objects and other selves. And these problems are precisely the problems obsessing the best thinkers of our period. We are like the Greeks in this. Being great explorers of physical space, having pushed back their own limits as far as they dared, they were obsessed with the problems of limit—moral and practical limit. How far can you go? Can you get away with it?

But I believe that the reinvestigation of moral, practical, imaginative, and emotional limit has already been begun by our younger poets. Two of the poets usually associated with the so-called beat group, Robert Duncan and Denise Levertov, have both been attacking this problem. My only fear about their work is that they will attack it in so overconscious and doctrinaire a manner that they may distract

*I would remind the reader that the present time of this lecture is roughly 1960. These remarks do not apply to most American poets in the period since.

the problem into the shallower areas of the mind—such areas as artistic dogma and literary politics—and away from those deeper and less conscious areas from which all real creativity and discovery must come. After all, if it has become something we can talk about in our everyday lives, can even use in our literary dogfights, that proves that it isn't really a deep or rich enough discovery to last long.

I first began to think consciously about this problem when I was on the stage at an arts festival in Vancouver, B.C., together with Robert Duncan. There Anne Halprin, the dancer, began to talk about her feeling that the coming art form was the dance because it was best equipped to investigate the nature of space and to create an art form of objects or intelligences positioned in space and relative only to each other; and this, she felt, was our world and our awareness of it. Though I felt that her own dancing handled this problem poorly, I was terribly impressed with her statement, felt that I'd heard something which might be really archtypical.

I was very happy to see, then, that the very next book by Robert Duncan was called *The Opening of the Field,* and that one of the poems in it was called "The Dance." I was also very disappointed, indeed, not to like the book nearly so well as some of Duncan's other work; feeling that he hadn't investigated the problems very richly. Here, however, is a sample:

THE DANCE

    from its dancers circulates among the other
        dancers. This
    would-have-been feverish cool excess of
        movement makes
    each man hit the pitch co-
        ordinate.

    Lovely their feet pound the green solid meadow.
        The dancers
    mimic flowers—root stem stamen and petal
        our words are,

our articulations, our
measures.
It is the joy that exceeds pleasure.

Perhaps I am wrong about the book—many of my friends think it very
good—among them, Denise Levertov, whose poem on this subject
impresses me rather more.

Miss Levertov's poem strikes me almost as an abstract poem dealing with this subject, or more probably an allegory of the subject—
man existing between freely created tensions, with no reality but the
call of his own appetites and the gravity of those objects around him.
Her poem is called "The Rainwalkers" and I will quote it entire.

THE RAINWALKERS

An old man whose black face
shines golden-brown as wet pebbles
under the streetlamp, is walking
two mongrel dogs of dis-
proportionate size, in the rain,
in the relaxed early-evening avenue.

The small sleek one wants to stop,
docile to the imploring soul of the trashbasket,
but the young tall curly one
wants to walk on; the glistening sidewalk
entices him to arcane happenings.

Increasing rain. The old bareheaded man
smiles and grumbles to himself.
The lights change: the avenue's
endless nave echoes notes of
liturgical red. He drifts

between his dogs' desires.
The three of them are enveloped—
turning now to go crosstown—in their
sense of each other, of pleasure,

of weather, of corners,
of leisurely tensions between them
and private silence.

   That seems to me a good example of an allegorical treatment of this
subject—for I see Miss Levertov as chiefly an allegorical poet—and
yet it seems to me limited to the depths that so abstract or idea-bound
a treatment can hope for. A poem that seems to me a really large poem
in this direction, a poem that seems really profound, is *Fever and
Chills* by George P. Elliott. A book-length poem, it is a story about
a man who starts an affair with his best friend's wife (who is also his
wife's best friend) in order, deliberately, though not consciously, to
find out if the world does have a limit, if you can get away with
anything. What he finds out is a thing of terrible bleakness and terror
—yes, you can get away with it. Yes, you can do it; nobody will stop
you. It is probable that in time you will make a mess of your life that
way and will come even to hate the girl—though not even that is sure
—yet it's probable, since you never really loved her in the first place
but were only using her for a sort of experiment. The poem contains
this sort of meditations:

                    This man who loved his countryside
                    Whose country's ways were part of him
                    Loathed the State he had been reared in.
                    With each vote, he had pronounced
                    Of his own will: Let the State be.
                    And the State (already) was.
                    It had used his will like a wrench.
                    Proudly to bring forth two new things
                    Which it had swaddled from cradling
                    Parachutes and eased through summer air
                    Annihilating two cities
                    He did not hate as much as that.
                    He ceased to vote, so withholding
                    His will, but did not rise against.

Half-declining and half-holding
The citizenship his birthright.
The State, indifferent to him,
Had wills enough to wrench together
All the sleek offspring it wanted
And to do with them as it pleased.
Not only in the State did this
Man's will not rule as he would like
But in his own home and in himself.
His will's perfection lay with her
Consummate perfection in acts
Done secretly, in such darkness
He could not see what they meant or
What it meant that he had done them.
Half-dreaming, outspread, he performed
A safe phantasy of danger:
Himself was the person of the sky;
Stars were his atoms; his form was
An incarnation of vacancy
Made visible by casual stars;
Through this so-imagined void, sped
Cold no-things of macrocosm
Which had such energy, that if one
Should hit one planet of one star,
The person should no longer be,
For re-explosion of the stars.
So, half-awake on his friend's bed,
He imagined his pleased body—
Which micro-physics conceived as
Matterless and nearly empty—
Streaked vagrantly by cosmic rays
So potent: if one bombed into
One least moon of his least hangnail

Solar system . . . but it would not,
10 to the nth . . . but it could . . .
His hand stirred onto her, his eyes turned.
She lay facing the wall, sleeping.
He saw no stars in her moist skin.
She had the smooth abrupt shoulders
Of a medieval statue queen
And a mole in the small of her back.

Although an excerpt can suggest neither the eccentricity nor the musicality of the poem's language, it is still wonderfully impressive to encompass a subject range running from politics and atoms bombs, to domestic relations, to modern physics' conception of the cosmos, then suddenly back to the most immediate reality—the girl lying naked on the bed. The poem ends shockingly. The affair ultimately grows stale, both finally reveal it to their spouses, the families are broken up, he grows ill and is sent to the hospital:

Before he had quite recovered,
Susan was to join her husband.
The night before she left, they met.
He desired her because he thought
He ought to. For the first time, his
I want you failed to generate
Hers. She lay with face averted
And helped him make what had been love;
She thought he wanted to. Even
Then, their bodies could not quite fail.

His wife, who did not reprove him,
Also did not forgive him, but
She wanted him back, and he went.

An astonishing poem, I think. Deeply dedicated to this world. Exploring deeply those very problems of moral limit, of relativism, of meaninglessness that I've been considering.

In suggesting that this may be the next direction that we are going, I realize that I am making a wild guess.* (I realize also that if I were to make the problem too convincingly explicit I might be doing no one a favor.) But I cannot help feeling that this vision of ourselves as dancers in an endless space, finite dancers in a space not infinite but undefined, puts us in line with the greatest and most courageous thinkers of our past—for instance with that relativism proposed so long ago by Renaissance men like Giordano Bruno, but which so very few have dared to follow up and explore. If we do not take the opportunities offered us, we shall be left far behind by the physical sciences and we shall develop no spiritual power comparable to our physical power. (Not that I suggest that even if we profoundly explored this problem we would be able to control our physical force and so guarantee our survival. The only salvation which art offers is the salvation of having done a great work.) If we fail in this, succeeding generations (supposing there are any) can quite justly think of us as moral, intellectual, and imaginative cowards and will perhaps find in our obliteration—which is in all events imminent—no great loss.

*On the whole, I think that the most vital poems of the last ten or fifteen years have borne out this prediction. I did not at all suspect, however, that the method they would use to investigate an ethical and psychological space would be the polyvoiced poem. I refer particularly to *The War of the Secret Agents* by Henri Coulette, *Gunsight* by Theodore Weiss, and John Berryman's incredible *77 Dream Songs.*

Vincent Van Gogh. THE STARRY NIGHT (1889).
Collection, The Museum of Modern Art, New York.
Acquired through the Lillie P. Bliss Bequest.

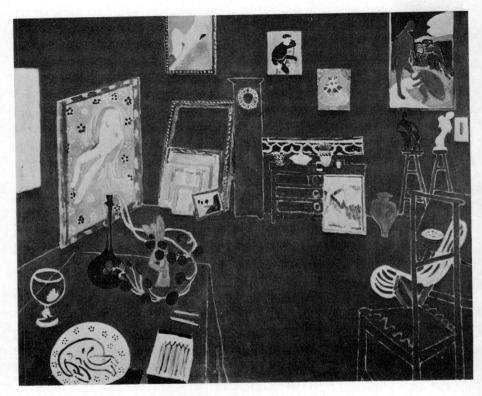

Henri Matisse. THE RED STUDIO (1911).
Collection, The Museum of Modern Art, New York.
Mrs. Simon Guggenheim Fund.

Edouard Vuillard. MOTHER AND SISTER OF THE ARTIST (c. 1893).
Collection, The Museum of Modern Art, New York.
Gift of Mrs. Saidie A. May.

Claude Monet. WATER LILIES (c. 1920).
Collection, The Museum of Modern Art, New York.
Mrs. Simon Guggenheim Fund.

Edouard Manet.   EXECUTION OF THE EMPEROR MAXIMILIAN (1867).
Städtische Kunsthalle Mannheim, West Germany.

Poems About Paintings

Some years ago, a prominent art magazine suggested that I should write a poem based on a painting or sculpture; they promised in return to pay me well, print my poem handsomely, and offer it to a large, distinguished audience. Noble aims those seemed to me. Being very young and innocent, I scarcely imagined all three promises could be false. And by the time I had wakened to the bloody facts, I could only thank the editors for taking advantage of me; I had never been seduced to better purpose.

The only trouble was that I knew nothing about painting or sculpture. Still, I was determined not to let ignorance stand in my way; I only needed a brain to pick. Once, for a single evening, I had taught a course in modern art. I had warned my employers beforehand that I knew nothing about art. "But," they said, "this is Adult Education; you don't need to know anything!" Since the class was to meet in a small lovely mansion and would include excellent dinners, warm sherry, and high pay for me, I overcame my scruples. Alas, corruption would not have me; only two students appeared. Yet, giving up those two was the worst loss of all. They were what every male teacher dreams of: exquisitely beautiful young women, willing to say just what they thought, intelligent, lively, and totally ignorant. We had held the first meeting, anyway.

They were housewives; their friends thought modern art was neat and groovy; were they crazy? "For instance, *that,*" they said, pulling a slide out of our prefabricated teaching kit. We dropped it into the projector and there appeared "The Starry Night" by Vincent van Gogh. What about it, we wondered? "What about it?" clamored the dark, flashing one. "It's terrible!" What's terrible, we wondered? "What's terrible? Just look at it—everything there is heaving, bulging, swirling all over the place. It won't even stand still. What kind of world is that? There's not one thing in that whole painting that will stand still except that little church, there, at the center!"

Then, of course, followed a long, stunned silence while the lady listened to what she'd said—and while we listened, too. In ten sentences she had produced the main key to the painting's iconography and structure. When we started talking again, we all had plenty to say. For nearly an hour we were filling in implications: the balance between the little town, square-cut, solid, firm, and the vast sky, swirling and bursting in some enormous spasm of energy; the twelve tiny lights of the town and the twelve huge lights of the sky; the small angular shapes of the town and the vast, curved, strangely sexual shapes of the clouds or the Milky Way overhead; the mountains like an ocean ready to break over the square roofs; the huge flamelike cypress in the foreground and the tiny blue formal spire in the mid-distance. Finally, the way the town, for all its squared solidity, seems almost to be floating away from the watcher; certainly, it has now receded beyond his reach.

Oddly enough, I don't think any of us knew then that this was really the little church where Van Gogh's father had preached at Zundert, which he painted again and again throughout his life, and which he in one way and another was always trying to go back to.

Trying now to write my poem, I was again fascinated by the painting and by the lady's responses to it. Could I use this as a basis for a poem? No; not inside my deadline. For one thing, the style was too drastic—the paint laid on in great flat dabs and slashes, apparently with a palette knife, bare chunks of canvas showing through, painted surely at white heat. I had spent years unlearning such stylistic violence. My teachers had been mostly post-Symbolists, a school directly parallel to the post-Impressionist painters like Van Gogh, especially in their stylistic extremity. Rebelling against my teachers, I had tried to build a very simple, unobtrusive style, one which would direct attention toward the thing talked about, away from me or my way of talking. I could hardly turn back now to showier styles I had forsaken as a student. On the other hand, I could hardly investigate so violent a painting in any very calm or reasoned style of writing. Eventually, I might try it; not now.

During that same evening's "teaching," though, we had talked about another painting, one that seemed more immediately accessible. The second slide we looked at was an almost equally famous canvas, "The Red Studio" by Henri Matisse. Here the lady and I had a crucial disagreement; this led us, again, into the center of the painting.

Probably the most conspicuous feature of this canvas is its use of the same brick-red color for the floor, walls, ceiling, even the major pieces of furniture. There is no gradation of color—the lines marking the floor, the corners of the walls, the ceiling, the outlines of the furniture, all are merely scratched into the red paint—perhaps with the wrong end of the brush. This color, and the room so saturated with it, seemed to me quite gay, lively, energetic. The lady, on the other hand, found it absolutely terrifying.

To her, it made the room insubstantial and dangerous; if you set your foot down there, you would surely crash through. The only solid things there, showing the colors of real objects in the real world, were the art objects—paintings, ceramics, etc. It was as if all the rest— walls, floors, furnitures—had somehow been energized. Just as she

65

had found the chaos and energy of Van Gogh's picture frightening, she found this insubstantial energy frightening. I never decided that I was wrong; I certainly decided she was right. Now, I hoped that if I could discover how we were *both* right, I might have my poem.

I began by just sitting for long periods with the slide, free-associating to it—picking my own brain for a change. The first thing that came to mind was a very dangerous and energetic rug in my psychiatrist's office several years before. Talking to him, I often sat on the couch with my legs folded up under me. Meantime his rug would glow a ferocious and threatening red. If I had put my foot down, it would surely have crashed through, might have been devoured or burned to a crisp. Actually, in its natural state, at rest, that rug had been green. Yet I never discovered that, never saw the rug in its normal state, until the therapy was nearly finished. Apparently, my mere entry into that room was all it took to induce a raging, bloody red in the fibers of that green and inoffensive rug.

That called to mind my childhood nightmare—one I had only three or four times, but which reduced me to utter panic. The walls of my room would turn vague and fuzzy; buzzing softly, they would start to close in on me, very, very slowly. What they wanted to do to me I never found out—my parents had always arrived in time.

The next thing that the fiery, containing walls of Matisse's studio recalled was one of the older theories of the universe. The ancients had thought the world was contained by a series of concentric spheres, each composed of a different material. The outermost was the Empirean, a sphere of fire containing all the universe. One of the late Roman magi—I had to look him up: Protesilaus—had even believed he could *see* that wall of fire with his naked eye. He apparently affected the whole universe much as I had affected my psychiatrist's rug.

This ancient theory led me to newer ones: first, Dante's idea of the planets and the universe all contained within God's love, yet energized and turned by that same love; second, the more recent theory of ether, that all-pervasive substance (or nonsubstance) from which all matter and energy are formed and within which they turn.

I should not let you think that all my associations were learned or sublime. My next recollections were of a record by Mort Sahl. On it, he had recalled his early days in a boys' reformatory surrounded by an electrical fence. You would wake up at night and find the boy in the next bunk gone, then you'd hear him outside: "Bzzzzzzzt!" And he'd come back in: "Fssst! Wow! Hotttt!!!" It was, he said, a deterrent to initiative.

My own childhood had had two such devices, one delightful and exciting, one grotesque and fearful. The first had been a Dodgem—everyone's favorite ride at the carnival. It, too, was contained in a highly charged cage, an electrical fence. Strange now to think of the little cars as planets circling inside their own closed system, all contained (like Dante's friendly little universe) in a grid of benign energy—a close and spark-filled heaven to which they must reach for the power they needed. They might almost be praying.

When I was a boy, except for those buzzing walls of my nightmare, we'd had only one device that made a sound like Mort Sahl's fence. It hung outside the drugstore. On warm Sunday evenings, we would hang around drinking Cokes, watching the girls go past, and hearing the sounds of the more courageous insects: "Bzzzzzzt!" Could that have discouraged *our* initiative?

Matisse's painting, incidentally, also seemed concerned with women. Two kinds of women (or two attitudes toward them) seemed to be represented by the paintings on those red walls. During our Adult Education evening, we had talked about this, too, without fully realizing that each of those paintings within the painting represents a specific earlier canvas by Matisse. On the left is a huge canvas of an ethereal blond nude, stylized and idealized, scattered about with flowers or stars; opposite to this, on the far right, is a group of dark-skinned bathers, perhaps natives, whose bodies show that same earthy, energetic color as the artist's walls. The rest of their world is full of natural color—all the colors missing from the world of the artist's studio.

If there is a central figure in the room, it seemed to be the man in the painting high on the central wall between two other canvases. To me, he looked like a sailor. He seemed drawn between these two feminine images, though the green curve of his legs and lower body suggested a strong list toward the earthier women on the right. This motif is repeated in the objects on the long table in the foreground. At the left is another idealized nude, painted on a white bowl; on the right appears what might be a statuette of an earth-colored woman, or perhaps only a cypress knee. The green curve of the "sailor's" legs is echoed here by a green plant, one of whose bines circles the darker girl caressingly.

Surely this must be off the subject. So far, I had been dealing with images either of a terrible destructiveness or of a rather womblike containment. My Protestant upbringing said I should not now let myself be distracted by women, ethereal or earthy. Still, this was no ordinary room; it was an artist's studio, a kind of womb, a place of creation. And it didn't seem entirely improbable that one's feelings about women might have something to do with his feelings about creativity and creation—creation in the world or creation of the world. Perhaps the point was that the artist had somehow managed to surcharge with energy all the ordinary surfaces of his room, of his life, so that the room had been able to conceive and bear these objects, at the same time becoming dangerous and insubstantial.

And that led to a stranger notion, one of the most recent theories of creation and the nature of the universe. Was it possible that the artist, perhaps before the scientist, had found a way to untie molecular structure, to dissolve matter and so release a part of its energy? Could this account for the strange destructive potential of the room? Did not most modern artists make a related transformation, breaking down the solid substance of the world and of their own work, so as to release energy? Was this only a figure of speech? Or did the figure of speech itself point to a basic similarity between the obsessions of the modern artist and those of the modern scientific theorist?

I was beginning to be interested, to feel that if I could get relativistic theory and Dodgems, Mort Sahl and Protesilaus into the same poem, I might have something. One thing I did *not* have was a dramatic occasion. I found that in the painting's strange, almost inhuman hollow quality. Where, for instance, is the artist himself? We see his qualities portrayed everywhere, perhaps even see his portrait in the painting of the "sailor." Where was the man who painted himself? Or painted his studio in place of himself? Why should we have that empty space at the center of the canvas, the very place where the artist *should* stand? I found myself imagining that perhaps he *had* put his foot down there, had been burned or swallowed up by his room. Perhaps he had devised this way to give his surroundings such energy, to fertilize them so they might give birth. So, he has become his paintings. But at the very center of his world is an empty space, an absence. Perhaps the matter he has dissolved and destroyed in order to create new forms, new orders, is himself.

This, then, is the poem I came up with.

MATISSE: "THE RED STUDIO"

There is no one here.
But the objects: they are real. It is not
As if he had stepped out or moved away;
There is no other room and no
Returning. Your foot or finger would pass
Through, as into unreflecting water
Red with clay, or into fire.
Still, the objects: they are real. It is
As if he had stood
Still in the bare center of this floor,
His mind turned in in concentrated fury,
Till he sank

Like a great beast sinking into sands
Slowly, and did not look up.
His own room drank him.
What else could generate this
Terra cotta raging through the floor and walls,
Through chests, chairs, the table and the clock,
Till all environments of living are
Transformed to energy—
Crude, definitive and gay.
And so gave birth to objects that are real.
How slowly they took shape, his children, here,
Grew solid and remain:
The crayons; these statues; the clear brandybowl;
The ashtray where a girl sleeps, curling among flowers;
This flask of tall glass, green, where a vine begins
Whose bines circle the other girl brown as a cypress knee.
Then, pictures, emerging on the walls:
Bathers; a landscape; a still life with a vase;
To the left, a golden blonde, lain in magentas with flowers scattering
        like stars;
Opposite, top right, these terra cotta women, living, in their world of
        living's colors;
Between, but yearning toward them, the sailor on his red café chair,
        dark blue, self-absorbed.
These stay, exact,
Within the belly of these walls that burn,
That must hum like the domed electric web
Within which, at the carnival, small cars bump and turn,
Toward which, for strength, they reach their iron hands:
Like the heavens' walls of flame that the old magi could see;
Or those ethereal clouds of energy
From which all constellations form,
Within whose love they turn.
They stand here real and ultimate.
But there is no one here.

This poem took me by surprise. Nothing ever comes easily to me; a poem often takes six or eight years. Worse, it usually takes at least one major and total revision—a complete change of mind about the poem's meaning, the material included, the metrical form. To do this even once is very difficult and painful to me; sometimes I have to do it two or three times for a single poem. Besides, for some time I had been working on poems about painful, intimate family affairs. Now, suddenly, a poem had come to me all at once, almost painlessly. I decided to give up, once and for all, my masochism; from that day on, I'd write only poems about paintings and have life easy.

Like most such resolutions, this overlooked only one factor: my psyche. I couldn't find anything I was really interested in. I looked at hundreds of pictures, read dozens of books. Months passed. "What's the matter," I accused myself, "don't you *like* pleasure?" One day at Yaddo, I laid down my book of post-Impressionists to play a game of Ping-Pong. Josephine Herbst, that marvelous lady, picked up my book, leafed about in it, and suddenly exclaimed, "Good Lord! Look at this horrid, tough old woman—and this poor girl! She's simply being turned into wallpaper!"

She was looking at "The Mother and Sister of the Artist" by Édouard Vuillard. I was stuck, once again, with a painful, domestic subject. And far from coming easily and painlessly, my poem on this painting took so very long and cost me so many total revisions that I cannot begin to recount the process. It nearly drove me wild.

Sadly, I had no Adult Education course now; whose brain was I to pick? I knew a child—one who had been raised by her grandmother until she was four years old, then came into a household of some friends of mine. They told me that she had been a terrible feeding problem, would eat nothing; when she came to them, she was thin, drained, lusterless. Much later, I realized that she had looked almost exactly like the girl in Vuillard's painting.

One day I showed her a print of the picture and asked what she thought of it. "It's all right," she said. So I asked her to really look.

After a long time, she pointed to the old woman and said, "Well, she looks like *she* gets enough to eat!"

I'd gone to the right person. I only then noticed the plate sitting beside the mother on the table, empty except for a few greasy scraps apparently remaining after she had finished and pushed the plate away. One of the chief formal structures of the painting is created by the line of those three white circles, the plate and the two faces. Again, this apparent equation of plate and face must say something about the devouring relationship between the woman and her daughter.

But the presence of that plate is scarcely the only reason the mother looks well fed. The little girl and I decided that, sitting there so squat and direct, hand on hip, staring straight at you, she looks like a quarterback. There certainly was no question who was in control there. In terrible contrast, the daughter looks frail, pale, hesitant, almost backing out of the room, out of the world. With her big brown dress cuffs, she looks as if she had been chained to the wall. And— as Josephine Herbst had noticed—her dress is done in exactly the same colors as the wall behind her; we have the illusion that she *is* vanishing into the wall.

Besides this illusion, the perspective is boldly warped and distorted. For instance, the baseboard and ceiling lines are drastically raked so that the whole room seems to be draining down into the mother. Further, the chest behind her seems to be leaning forward—almost as if the mother were carrying that huge chest. And it was my young friend who noticed that the chest has no knobs.

In contrast to Matisse's picture, this is a tiny canvas. Matisse's picture is immense, which lends much to its almost cosmic expansiveness. Vuillard's is just a bit more than 16" × 18"; a tiny pocket of evil on the wall. Critics have long spoken of Vuillard as a decorative painter like Bonnard. I have come to feel this is almost entirely wrong, that he is instead the creator of a world of terrifying domestic drama. A world where people sit around a sunny breakfast table, yet one of them has no face. A world where little girls standing in the park huddle together over their dollies protectively, looking balefully toward their dark mothers in the distance. A world where chests may have no knobs, might go empty at will, where people may be starved, chained, or changed into wallpaper. The world, in short, of the average living room.

If my poem about "The Red Studio" had been about transforming matter into energy, this poem seemed to go off at a tangent. It also was concerned with containment—but here the containment of the daughter by the old woman. Here, again, was a blank space at the center of the painting—the black, empty pit of the mother's body. This girl, too, was being transformed—not from matter into energy, but from living matter into dead; from moving, energetic matter impelled by its own aims and patterns, transformed into her mother's wallpaper, into the fixed and proper walls of her own containment.

"The Red Studio" was dangerous in having too much life, too much energy; that was hardly the problem here. "The Red Studio" had swallowed up its painter in order to give birth to his paintings. Here, too, the girl was being swallowed alive by the walls of a room but in order to give birth to nothing, or perhaps, to undo the fact of her having got born at all. Or to give birth not to paintings but to wallpaper—Vuillard's mother was, after all, a textile designer. After living with her all his life, he left orders that his diary must remain sealed for eighty years after his death.

As I noted before, this poem went through almost endless revisions before I could finish it. A mere record of these blunders would scarcely be interesting. The one significant point is that here, as in "The Red Studio," I could not finish the poem until I had found a dramatic occasion. Again, that occasion proved to be a visit to the room, but in this case, the poem is not just a report of that visit, but rather a set of instructions for it. If Matisse's room seemed frightening because no one was in it, this room seemed much more fearful just

73

because it was so full of humans with their hungers and passions. Like the average living room, no one could hope to come back alive without a full set of instructions to be followed with strictest care.

VUILLARD: "THE MOTHER AND SISTER OF THE ARTIST"
(Instructions for the Visit)

Admire, when you come here, the glimmering hair
Of the girl; praise her pale
Complexion. Think well of her dress
Though that is somewhat out of fashion.
Don't try to take her hand, but smile for
Her hesitant gentleness.
Say the old woman is looking strong
Today; such hardiness. Remark,
Perhaps, how she has dressed herself black
Like a priest, and wears that sufficient air
That does become the righteous.
As you approach, she will push back
Her chair, shove away her plate
And wait,
Sitting squat and direct, before
The red mahogany chest
Massive as some great
Safe; will wait,
By the table and her greasy plate,
The bone half-chewed, her wine half-drained;
She will wait. And fix her steady
Eyes on you—the straight stare
Of an old politician.
Try once to meet her eyes. But fail.
Let your sight
Drift—yet never as if hunting for
The keys (you keep imagining) hung
By her belt. (They are not there.)
Watch, perhaps, that massive chest—the way

It tries to lean
Forward, toward her, till it seems to rest
Its whole household's weight
Of linens and clothing and provisions
All on her stiff back.
It might be strapped there like the monstrous pack
Of some enchanted pedlar. Dense, self-contained,
Like mercury in a ball,
She can support this without strain,
Yet she grows smaller, wrinkling
Like a potato, parched as dung;
It cramps her like a fist.
Ask no one why the chest
Has no knobs. Betray
No least suspicion
The necessities within
Could vanish at her
Will. Try not to think
That as she feeds, gains
Specific gravity,
She shrinks, light-
less as the world's
Hard core
And the per-
spective drains
In her.
Finally, above all,
You must not ever see,
Or let slip one hint you can see,
On the other side, the girl's
Cuffs, like cordovan restraints;
Forget her bony, tentative wrist,
The half-fed, worrying eyes, and how
She backs out, bows, and tries to bow
Out of the scene, grows too ethereal

To make a shape inside her dress
And the dress itself is beginning already
To sublime itself away like a vapor
That merges into the empty twinkling
Of the air and of the bright wallpaper.

The third painting brought me face to face again with the problem which was rapidly becoming the central theme of this group of poems —the transformation of matter into energy. This is one of the water lily series—"Les Nympheas" by Claude Monet; it is the great, gray, scumbly, twenty-foot-long canvas now in the Museum of Modern Art in New York City. (This canvas reproduces so poorly that I must give a print of another painting from the same series.)

This picture is itself so undefined, so gray, rough and scumbly, that if you walked into the room from the wrong angle, you might well think it was no painting at all—merely that the wall on that side was a little rough and dirty. Still, if at first it looks like nothing at all, it may end up looking like everything at all.

You may know that Monet turned the whole garden at his country house, Giverney, into water so he could make this series of water lily pictures. This seems to be an early morning scene, hazy and vaporous. We seem to be looking down onto the misty surface of the water, perhaps from the little bridge that spanned the garden, perhaps from a small boat. Gradually, a few shapes emerge: some irises, a few water lilies riding on the surface. And yet, there, beneath the lilies, we see clouds. They must, of course, actually be overhead, behind us, yet since they are reflected in the water we see them as under the lilies. Then, from beneath these clouds one can see (or imagine he sees) the green of underwater plants, floating or lying near the bottom. It is a very strange perspective on the world—water lilies over the clouds, clouds over the water plants—almost as if one stood an island universe up on edge and then did it in saggital section.

The line perspective of the picture, too (or perhaps its mass perspective) very actively draws you into the center of the picture, into the vortex of these gray waters. Sitting before it for long hours at the museum, I often had the sensation that if I did not get up and leave the room, the guards might well come in and find me missing. Just as Matisse seemed to have been swallowed up by his room, so I—trying to absorb this picture—might be absorbed by it. Perhaps it was hungrier than I was. I sat before it like some small animal fascinated by an approaching cat—it so obviously wanted me, so truly loved me.

I came to feel that the real effort of this painting is to yield oneself to a world of sensation and experience. That, of course, is the task Monet set himself: to strip and divest himself of every intellectual preconception or emotional armoring which might keep him from experiencing the world. In his own words, he would become a machine to record sensory data. Above all, that meant the light. For the light was his first and only subject.

Starting from certain ideas of the optical physicists, Helmholtz and Rood, ideas about the nature of radiant phenomena, Monet set out to record in paint only and precisely the light reflected from or emanating from objects. To do that, he had to divest himself of every conventional preconception about those objects; he must scarcely know that objects exist. Looking at an apple, he must not know that it is red or green or brown, that it is useful or delicious, that it is good or evil. He must only record the light, the color that comes to his eye. If, in a particular early morning light, that apple looked flat and lavender, that and only that must be recorded.

This is why he did the great series paintings: the haystacks, the poplars, the water lilies. Those objects are not really his subject; his subject is the light, not an object but an energy. And since painting is a slow, difficult process, while the light is inconstant, ever-shifting, evanescant, he could only hope it might "sit for him" a half hour or so at a time. So, when he went out to look at, say, poplars, he would take along a 4:00 painting, a 4:30 painting, a 5:00 painting, etc. And as the light changed he would put aside each picture in turn, hoping to return the next day when the light might at least be similar.

As a result, the objects in his paintings tend to disappear, to be dissolved into the light coming from from them. Matter, then, *is* transformed into energy—into the energized surface of the canvas.

We see a similar, but much less profound, phenomenon in the paintings of Renoir. There, however, we are concerned with lesser physical delights, the skin of pears and peaches, the glowing flesh of young girls. I have nothing against the flesh of young girls. Except that my concern with it is trivial and likely to be self-indulgent. Monet's task is to penetrate, to enter a universe of radiances, to become not an object moving among objects, but an energy moving among other energies, fluid like them and so partaking of them. This implies a yielding up of the self and so is terrifying and bleak for all its radiance.

It was not without great actual cost. There are terrible stories of the aged Monet coming to the breakfast table to ask what color a certain plate was. When he was told it was blue, he would smash down his fist in anguish: "But I see it yellow!" He, who had dedicated his life to purest seeing, had developed cataracts and could not see. A little like Beethoven going deaf—as if breaking down so much social convention involved enormous guilts which a man could only pay off by attacking himself in his own creative center. Monet's cataracts apparently caused that extreme violence of color in some of his late paintings—paintings whose violence has been very influential in our own day. Unable any longer to see color, he must have been trying to restore on canvas the colors he remembered or imagined there—doing just what he had dedicated himself never to do. Yet, very late, he had a successful operation, recovered his sight, and could once again record the light around him. And, oddly enough, though he was always very rigorous in culling his own work—he said that others burn piles of leaves every autumn, he burned piles of paintings—he never repudiated the work of this period when his vision had failed.

The depth of Monet's dedication to this revolutionary drive to see made him one of our true giants. Only now do we begin to see how crucial he has been to the whole development of our culture. In many ways, the Impressionist painters, and above all their master and genius, Monet, led the attack on form and matter which touched off the whole revolution in the arts, sciences, all the intellectual disciplines. In the meantime, analogous tendencies were spreading through all areas of our lives—governmental forms, political and religious beliefs, our conception of matter, our conception of human personality. Under the impetus of these drives, the last century of Western civilization has been one of almost unbelievable invention and creativity in the arts and sciences. At the same time, under the force of those same drives, the texture and quality of human life and society has changed at an equally incredible rate.

Not the least marvel of this period, I think, will be the career of Claude Monet. And this, I think, is a painting about that career, about the effort to break down the armoring of the self and its beliefs and ideas, so that one might become an energy among energies, open to the flux of experience, absorbing and being absorbed by sensation.

MONET: "LES NYMPHEAS"

The eyelids glowing, some chill morning.
O world half-known through opening, twilit lids
   Before the vague face clenches into light;
O universal waters like a cloud,
   Like those first clouds of half-created matter;
O all things rising, rising like the fumes
   From waters falling, O forever falling;
Infinite, the skeletal shells that fall, relinquished,
   The snowsoft sift of the diatoms, like selves
Downdrifting age upon age through milky oceans;
   O slow downdrifting of the atoms;
O island nebulae and O the nebulous islands
   Wandering these mists like falsefires, which are true,
Bobbing like milkweed, like warm lanterns bobbing
   Through the snowfilled windless air, blinking and passing

As we pass into the memory of women
   Who are passing. Within those depths
What ravening? What devouring rage?
   How shall our living know its ends of yielding?
These things have taken me as the mouth an orange—
   That acrid sweet juice entering every cell;
And I am shared out. I become these things:
   These lilies, if these things *are* waterlilies
Which are dancers growing dim across no floor;
   These mayflies; whirled dust orbiting in the sun;
This blossoming diffused as rushlights; galactic vapors;
   Fluorescence into which we pass and penetrate;
O soft as the thighs of women;
   O radiance, into which I go on dying. . . .

The next painting—"The Execution of the Emperor Maximilian" by Édouard Manet—took me on a closely related side journey. The standard critical comment about Manet deals with the "dissolution of subject matter"—the way one's interest is diverted from any story being told by the picture, even from any person or object being depicted; one is concerned with the paint surface itself and the style of its creation. This is true of a great deal of Manet's work, yet for this particular painting, a fairly early one, it is only partly so. Not only is the subject matter partly present, the spectator cannot help trying to bring even more of it back. You can neither ignore the subject, nor can you define an attitude toward it. This makes the painting very uncomfortable, above all detached and chill; something one cannot help resenting. When it was first shown, it caused something akin to riots.

Like many of Manet's best canvases, this one is based on an earlier masterpiece—"The Executions of the 3rd of May" by Goya. If we turn to that picture, it becomes obvious that the chill of Manet's picture was very consciously sought for and achieved.

Comparing the two, I am reminded of Auerbach's comments on the different handling of scenes in the Bible and in Homer. In the Bible, a scene is shaped and pared, hot with suspense, above all spotlighted to enforce upon a reader one and only one interpretation, to take captive his mind and soul. Homer, on the other hand (like Manet, here), is cool, detached, unhurried, full of irrelevant detail included for its own sake, or for the sake of justice of vision. Above all, there is no central spotlighting; everything happens in a cool impartial light which plays equally over all the landscape; no particular view is enforced on the audience. We are freed—something we always find disquieting.

Goya's picture must be one of the hottest, most melodramatic in the world. At the center, in a great focus of light, kneel the victims in heroic attitudes of anguish, defiance, prayer, pleading, horror. At the right, loom the dark hulking shapes of the soldiers, their heavy hats, packs, and shoulders bent over the rifles as if they could hurt their victims more by leaning on the guns. To be shot like this is an honor and a delight—the fulfillment of every child's masochistic fantasies. To be killed by such a bunch of hulking bullies, meanwhile kneeling there passive, noble, and pathetic in the glare of searchlights, while "the whole world watches"—it is all any child could ask.

To die as the victims in Manet's painting do is not quite so satisfying, so comforting. Manet's picture incidentally is in Mannheim; we do have however, in Boston, a preliminary sketch he did for this painting. In it, some of Goya's heat remains: the soldiers seem somewhat threatening, the victims somewhat present and center-lighted, a strange suggestion of landscape reaching out beyond.

In the finished canvas, however, all heat and melodrama have vanished. The victims are relegated to a corner ill-defined and half obscured by smoke. It would be easy to dispute even which victim *is* Maximilian. No doubt he *should* be in the middle and that man *has* a lighter complexion. But we can scarcely make out his features at all and why should he wear, of *all* things, a sombrero?

Not only are the victims not spotlighted, the whole scene is swept with a focusless flat light. There *is* some hint of a pleasant vista in the background, yet all real sense of perspective is cut off by the flat rock wall behind the victims. Most surprising, the shadows do not even seem to fall all in the same direction; there seems to be a multiplicity of light sources.

As for the soldiers, they seem almost feminine, relaxed, and comical. Why in the world should they be wearing such musical comedy outfits? We know from photographs, in fact, that the real firing squad wore rumpled khaki fatigues. Why should the Habsburg, Maximilian, wear a sombrero while his Mexican executioners wear European dress uniforms? Unlike his sketchy handling of the victims, Manet has lavished on these soldiers every elegance and precision of style. In fact, the most defined face in the picture is that of the soldier on the right, of whose name and function we are ignorant, and who is doing something inexplicable: at the very moment his mates are killing their emperor, he appears to be inspecting or loading his gun.

In the meantime, those with most cause to be concerned—the peons peering over the wall—sprawl about every which way and may not even be interested; one may be covering her ears; one is fanning herself like the stereotyped Spanish seductress. Still another does seem to be shouting and perhaps gesturing but we have no idea whether this is protest, cheering, or neither. The handling of these figures is even rougher than that of the victims. In fact the three groups are treated in such different styles they might be from three different paintings, different universes.

The mere choice of the subject in this painting suggests some relation to the cluster of revolutionary ideas we have been discussing. The death of Maximilian caused a furor throughout Europe. Juárez was bombarded with telegrams, letters, pleas, and threats. And the Habsburgs did attempt to rescue Maximilian—their secret agents would probably have safely rescued him, but he refused to escape. No doubt the Habsburgs knew that his death would give them an appearance of weakness which would in turn weaken them. This, indeed, proved true. Maximilian's death in many ways prefigured the general collapse of the Habsburgs and so of the European ruling families as of the European colonial empires.

Thus we are witnessing another aspect of the same dissolution of centrality—the simple destruction of a ruler, of a central authority. To judge by the picture, he has already lost importance to such an extent that he cannot even command the central spot in his own execution. That place has been taken over by a faceless crowd of common soldiers through the simple fact of their greater firepower. Just as in Matisse's studio we found ourselves asking "Where's the painter?" so here at the death of Maximilian we find ourselves asking "Where's the Emperor? Where's the ruler? Who's in charge?"

Again, in the uncentered lighting and the apparent diversity of shadows, we see another aspect of the loss of central authority—philosophically, the rise of individualism, of democracy, of relativism. If we cannot say that each figure here carries his own inner light—like a Quaker—we can almost say that each carries his own shadow.

There is a further loss of perspective caused by that rock wall. Here, as in the Vuillard painting, we see a victim somehow chained to a wall and being changed into it. But there is a real difference in that this wall is outdoors. Vuillard's wall showed that the girl had no world but the world of her voracious family. Here, we know there is a wider world, we even have a glimpse of a distant, idyllic landscape in the upper left. Yet we are completely cut off from it. We can imagine some further visita; we cannot reach it. In some essential way, then, no act can have any further significance, any further reach or perspective. A man is killed and that ends it—nothing proceeds therefrom. Lacking perspective, any act lacks ultimate meaning. We are dealing, then, with the breakdown of philosophical matter, the loss of religious centrality, which was going on in this same period.

At a much later time, I became conscious that just as Goya's picture very deliberately recalls a crucifixion scene, so this picture both recalls and parodies such a scene. Thus, Maximilian's sombrero comes to

83

have a peculiar rightness, for it exists as a sort of comic parody of a halo. Further, on close inspection, we find in the palms of the general on the left, marks curiously like Christ's stigmata. Not only are we dealing with the death of an emperor (and an emperor, incidentally, with many delusions of his own divinity), but we are dealing with the decay and death of Christianity, under the attacks of higher criticism, science, Protestantism, and secular power. We may even be suggesting the death of all religion; indeed, throughout most of our civilization it has indeed perished before firing squads, and before the onslaughts of faceless individualism; the religious figure has been replaced by the detached and unquestioning technician who, like the lone soldier on the right, seems more interested in his machine and how it works than in the violence happening around him.

We like to think that because we listen to Beethoven or look at Picasso without a sense of outrage, that shows that we understand them better than those who at first violently rejected them; it may well mean the opposite. For surely, the shock of those works was intended by their authors; unless we learn to re-create in ourselves the shock people felt at some of Beethoven's chords, some of Picasso's colors, we cannot experience those works at all.

My problem in writing about this painting was to somehow re-create some of the shock that attended its first appearance, the climate of violent "hot" opinions which everyone held about Maximilian's death and which made the coldness of Manet's picture so unnerving to them. To do this, I split my poem into sections. The main body of the poem describes the scene in all its cold matter-of-factness in a very prosy, matter-of-fact sort of verse—saying much what a puzzled viewer might say to himself on seeing the picture for the first time. Yet sandwiched in, here and there, are sections of highly poetical prose—highly colored opinions about Maximilian, meant to sound like snippets from partisan newspapers, biographies, or histories. These snippets are always correct in their facts but, I think, often mistaken in their high-flown emotional interpretations of Maximilian's life and death. The prosy verse sections, on the other hand, are sometimes mistaken in their facts, but seem to me more truthful in their cold and detached quality, which seems more faithful not only to this painting but also to our cold and ultimately meaningless universe.

Goya's painting showed how we feel about the world, the world where, above all, we feel crucified and see our own death as the most significant event of all time. Manet's picture shows us how the world *is*. It suggests that in the very act of destroying central authority we have shown ourselves the ultimate meaninglessness of any death, including our own. Small wonder people felt so affronted by the picture, or that they would willingly accept any kind of madness or belief rather than so bleak a truth.

MANET: "THE EXECUTION OF THE EMPEROR MAXIMILIAN"

> "Aim well, muchachos; aim right
> here," he pointed to his heart.
> With face turned upward, he
> waited, grave but calm.

These dapper soldiers, seen shooting the Emperor
  Just now, stand with heels in, toes out, like ballet girls
But not so tense. Chiefly, we're forced to be aware
  How splendid their spats and long white saber-holsters
Gleam. They should deduce this is some crucial affair
  In view of their natty uniforms and dress gear,
Yet one of them has turned up late, naturally,
  For this, which should be the true peak of his career.
He stands aside, cocking his rifle, carefully.
  Still, politics may not mean much to him. Perhaps,
Since he looks less like a penguin or some old gaudy
  Dressform, since he sports a white band on a red cap,
Who knows?—he may be an officer who'll give the body
  The *coup de grâce*. All the grace, themselves, they could conceive,
The men peer down their long sight lines like some long shot

At billiards—some shot men might hope they could achieve
Yet they would scarcely be disgraced if they should not.

> Miramón and Mejía fell at once.
> A second volley was required for
> Maximilian who had wished to be
> shot in the body so that his
> mother might see his face.

Scumbly, vague, the half-formed heads of these peasants stare
    Up over the background, which is a flat rock wall.
Some yawn, some sprawl on their elbows, and some rest their
    Heads on their crossed arms. They peer down like men gone dull
With heat and flies watching some tenth-rate matadors
    Practice, or angels bored with all these martyrs. True,
One waves and does look like he's yelling, yet of course
    That might mean triumph, outrage, or mere shock. Who
Will ever know? Maybe he thinks he knows someone
    Or just wants it known he's here. Caught by the drums
And dress gear, they don't even know the names; they wait
    For marvels, for a sign. Surely someone must come
Declare significance, solve how these things relate
    To freedom, to their life's course, to eternity.
Random and dusty, their clustering faces are
    Crumbled like rocks in the wall, from which they could be
An outgrowth—cool, distant, irrelevant as stars.

> The mutilated body was given full
> funereal honors by the Habsburgs,
> whose general downfall it prefigured.
> On the place of execution, moreover,
> was erected a small chapel to further
> his remembrance on earth and his
> forgiveness in heaven.

Still, for Maximilian, all perspective lines
    End in this flat rock wall. Some may find, in the distance,

An inkling of quiet streams, or pine-shadowed lanes;
    Just the same, we're cut off from all true hope of vistas
As men down a mine-shaft. The peasants, too, detached,
    Held back of this blank wall from their Emperor's passion;
And the soldiers, though close, we know their aim goes past
    Their victims, each fixed in his own plane of existence,
His own style—though they die, each in his own style and fashion.
    And if their Emperor holds his appointed place,
He's bleached out like some child's two-penny crucifixion;
    Stands in an impartial iconoclastic light
That will not hint where you might best direct your sight—
    At the unspotlighted center, just this blank space
That rifles cross; elsewhere, a baffling contradiction
    Of shadows as if each man smuggled strange forces
Into Mexico, and moved from his own light sources. . . .

When the fraudulent French plebiscite
failed to convince Maximilian he had
been elected by the peons, Napoleon
threatened to offer the crown to
some other candidate.

. . . Yet for Maximilian, who hoped he could unite
    The Old World and the New under one ordinance—
Unfortunately his own—bind the Divine Right
    Of Habsburgs with half-chewed liberal sentiments,
Link the True Church to the freely divisive mind,
    Shape a fixed aim from all his own diversities,
Who in his wardrobe joined all the races of mankind;
    For Maximilian, whose wife Carlotta endured
A lifetime mad with loss (or with some love disease
    He'd brought her from Brazil) confined to a convent
Where, though losing her worst fears, she always referred
    To him as Emperor of all the Firmament;
The Emperor who dreamed that one day he might stand
    At the top of some broad magnificent staircase

Vouchsafing from that height of infinite command
  One smile of infinite condescension and grace
On the human beings gathered around its base. . . .

> It was as if some ne'er-do-well had
> found at last his true vocation; as
> martyr and sacrificial victim, he
> has seldom been surpassed.

. . . Still, for Maximilian . . . still, for the man who stands
  In the midst of his own life—or, to be exact,
Off to one side of his dying—he holds together
  Just these two who chose death with him; he holds their hands.
And they're almost obscured by the smoke. Then, in fact,
  Which IS the man? No doubt he should stand at the center,
Yet who gets shot in a frock coat and sombrero?
  In that man's bland face we see nothing, not that firm
Nobility which we demand, and *do* discern
  In this stranger by the wall, or can find elsewhere
Only in this bearded soldier of whom we know
  Nothing. Who knows? Perhaps it's this one, standing there
Spread-legged, whose clenched free hand flaps up like a doll's,
  Whose face twists upward in effort or possibly
Pain, as his chest's opened out by the rifleballs,
  His brain unties, atoms start hurtling out, blind, free,
And he, whoever he was, is all finished being.

> Born, July 6, 1832; brother of
> Franz Josef I, Emperor of Austria.
> 1854, naval administrator; 1857,
> viceroy to the Lombardo-Venetian
> kingdom; 1864, Emperor of Mexico.
> Died, 1867.

I come, then, to my last poem—the one I started with, "The Starry Night" by Vincent van Gogh. As I began studying other Van Gogh paintings all across the country, together with the great collection of his letters which was just then becoming available in English, I began to see that the themes and motifs of this painting were truly the obsessions of his life, that the disorder and violence so frightening to my lady student were far more terrifying to the painter himself.

One obvious example of this fear is the picture of "Vincent's House at Arles," so bright, sunny, tidy, except for the threatening upheaval in the street below. Or the related "Road Menders," where the whole street is torn up, as if by some immense catastrophe, yet out of which springs a row of vigorous, sinewy plane trees—figures of astonishing power. One thinks of the famous "Boats on the Beach at Saintes-Maries" where only the gaily colored, well-made boats preserve a touch of man's craft and order in a fiercely chaotic world. Again, one thinks of that "Self-Portrait" where Vincent's dark blue coat is filled with tiny golden specks like bright sparks, or like the smaller stars of "The Starry Night"; this, in turn, recalls other portraits—that of Dr. Rey or "La Berceuse" where the background is a violent wallpaper whose flowers seem to be exploding like that terrible sky. Again, one thinks of all those landscapes where vegetation seems about to engulf the world in a sea of fertility. Finally, there are those very last paintings like the famous "Crows in the Wheatfields," or "Château D'Auvers" where great crows (or are they only shadows?) burst from the trees like a detonation; or the terrifying "Ears of Wheat" where all perspective is lost and the viewer apparently overwhelmed and buried in the rush of vegetation. All of this must be intimately related to the fact, pointed out by V. W. van Gogh, that Vincent's attacks coincided with the announcement of the engagement of his brother Theo (upon whom Vincent was dependent), with the marriage, the announcement that a baby was expected, and, finally, with the birth of that baby. In any case, all his life Van Gogh lived with great disorder, even violence —as many artists must if they are to keep fertility and energy in their work. Yet, much as he sought those great powers, he must have dreaded that they might escape and destroy all in their path.

This theme, then, was intimately involved with the theme of matter and energy which I've been concerned with all along. Closely tied with this, however, is a second theme which has been present in all the pictures I've been discussing, but which only now rose to the surface—an extremely ambivalent feeling toward a womblike containment: on the one hand a fierce desire to escape; on the other, a desire to be captured and contained. All his life, Vincent painted pictures of his father's church at Zundert or of later substitutes for it: other church spires; in Paris, windmills; in the still lifes, a candle. All his life, he painted pictures of motherhood—the culmination of which is in "La Berceuse." Again, we might note the rigid containment of "Vincent's Bedroom at Arles" or even more, the massive containing walls and corridors of "A Passage at St. Paul's Hospital."

In order to dramatize this split between order and disorder in "The Starry Night," I once again decided to use a form having alternate styles, two styles which would oppose each other. For the sections of the poem describing the little town, I tried to make a very simple, blocked, solid style to imitate the qualities of the town. For the sky, the mountains, the cypress before the town, I would use something much wilder, a style as scattered and slapdash as the handling of the great wild sky in the painting. Thus you look first at the town, then at the sky, again at the town, then to the mountains, once more at the town, and then to the cypress. Yet this seemed too "regular," too easy, so I took a great many quotations from Van Gogh's letters and simply scattershot them through the poem—let them break up the syntax and movement, the sense, though they do this most notably in the wilder movements.

Finally, this all seemed too arbitrary, too conscious and contrived. So I decided to add yet another formal factor, but one which would control the poem at a much deeper level, a level of sound which would not be present in the reader's (or listener's) conscious thoughts but which would give the poem, I hoped, a kind of music. What this music would mean I of course didn't know—that is exactly what seemed hopeful about it.

Here I borrowed a device from Walt Whitman. Many of his poems use a sort of theme and variations device, especially in the handling of rhythm. The first line would state a rhythm either once or twice, usually twice:

> A line in long array || where they wind betwixt green islands
> I see before me now || a travelling army halting
> Out of the cradle || endlessly rocking

The rest of the poem then proceeds to work variations on this theme, sophisticating, complicating, lengthening it—sometimes going so far that one feels he has surely lost it, but finally coming back to it to resolve and complete the poem.

I took as my theme, not a rhythm, but a set of sounds and tried to let my poem grow out of and around variations on these sounds. As in D'Indy's "Ishtar Variations," however, this theme is not stated till the end. In this way, I hoped that by giving all sorts of variations first before stating the theme, that the theme would ring in the hearer's ear and have something like the effect of "rightness" we get elsewhere through rhyme.

The theme itself, the last words of the poem, are Van Gogh's own last words,

"Zóó heen kan gaan."

It is touching that he spoke this, not in French, but in Flemish, the language of his home and childhood.

Vincent, a patient in the mental hospital at Saint-Rémy, had shot himself in the head while painting out in the fields. He lingered for several days; these are his last words, reported by his devoted brother, Theo. It is a strange, fragmentary utterance, which might mean "This is the way to go," "I'd like to die like this," or even "I want to go home."

Van Gogh: "The Starry Night"

Only the little
town
remains   beyond
all shock and dazzle
only this little
still stands
calm.

Row on row, the gray frame cottages, small
Barns and sheds of an old Dutch town;
Plane over plane, the village roofs in order,
One by one, contained and ordered lives;
Aging in place, the weathered walls gone
Gray, grown ancient beyond memory.

what flowers were blossoming, how the fruit
trees bore, had the nightingale been heard
yet, the text of Father's sermon

The squared shapes of doorframes, and bright windows;
Angle above angle, a slate ascent of roofs;
Stone upon stone, like broad stairs or the
Planes of a determined head, convergent
On this still dead center, the village chapel
Tiny as a child's toy

There is something about Father
narrow-minded, icy-cold, like iron

The village chapel, tiny as a child's toy
And as far. Pale as quartz crystals,
Its salients and the keen blue spire
Slim as a needle transfixed in the horizon

Firm in the high winds, high breakers, this
Still eye to the hurricane, this lighthouse

> *How could I possibly be in any way of any*
> *use to anyone? I am good for something!*

In which no light shines.

Through the high zones uncontained
    the uncontaining heavens
  Metaphysics cannot hold
      hump shove swirling blood rising as
  the nipples too come swollen shuddery
        behind the clenched lids, blind
tracers   *chaos in a goblet*   opening
    like a zinnia bed   and chancres   swamp mouths
      outspattering eleven
    fixed stars   one sunburst moon
Midspasm   midheavens   the spiral galaxy
    tumbled in trails of vapor
       Art for Art
      The war still raging while the high gods
    copulate on Garganos
        the holy ground burst
     into flower and a golden dew fell
 Energy for Energy
ethereal first mists   light dusts
    Chaos contains no glass
      of our caliber
  gathering into force and matter
    obliterating to be whole again
    be one.

> *Giotto and Cimabue live in an obeliscal*
> *society, solidly framed, architecturally constructed.*

93

Row on row, plane over plane, the reddish brown
Houses with stepped gables and high stoops.
One by one, the thoughtless comfortable lives
Like steps in an argument, pigs at their dam;
Side by side in one another's lee, huddled
Against weather, against doubt, passion, hope

> *Every individual a stone and*
> *the stones clung together*

The narrow lanes beneath the eaves-troughs,
Hedge rows between the houses and dark
Trees; behind, and laid out side by side,
The kitchen gardens with their heavy odors
Where dew sits chilly on the cabbage leaves
And a bird might sing.

> *And if no actual obelisk of too*
> *pyramidal a tragedy, no rain of frogs*

Down those dark lanes you will never see
A lantern move or any shadow sway,
No dog howl and your ear will never know
The footfall of a prowler or some lover's tread,
Nor any wanderer, long gone,

> *four great crises when I did not know what*
> *I said, what I wanted, even what I did.*

who cannot return.

> *In spring, a caged bird feels strongly*
> *there is something he should be doing.*
> *But what was it? He gets vague ideas.*
> *The children say, but he has everything*
> *he wants.*

Beyond the town, blue mountains rising
   range over range over range
Sometimes just as waves break
   on sullen, hopeless cliffs
              upthrusting
   its salt mass into the sky
   in the public square milling chanting obscenities
      ton on broken ton of stone
      the black earth hovering *I feel a*
        storm of desire to
        embrace something
great ragged crests lumbering in   murderous
   as the seasons   bluer than the years
      the first rocks rattling
through the windows   scattered gunfire
   all you have always held is a lie
Painting   and much screwing are not
   compatible; man   the crowd
   pounds   on and on   blood battering its walls
the feathery surf   first spies   already
     prowling up around the gray
     outbuildings and the orchards
     the unthinkable is also true
      becomes ambitious as soon
    as he becomes impotent a spume
  of ancient vacuum shuddering to
     reclaim its child
to embrace   something   a woman   a sort
    of domestic hen
    so pale
the gardens of olives   gardens
  of agony   frothing
    about its feet in foam.

the hollow dreams of revolutionaries . . .
they would wail in despair if once they
forgot the easy satisfaction of their
instincts, raising them to the unappeased
sufferings of the passions.

Down those dark lanes which you can never see
    Shines only so much light:
Eleven windows and one opened door—crystals
    Under tons of ore, clear garnets, warm;
Through those windows you can never see, and yet
    You always wonder who may waken there,
Who sits up late over a pipe, sits to hold
    A pious, worn book between worn hands,
Who sits up late together and will talk, will talk
    The night away, planning the garden for
Next year, the necessary furnitures,
    Who works there, shreds the cabbages,
Darns some coarse fabric by a hanging lamp,
    Who may have gotten out of bed to calm
Their children fitfully sleeping, each
    In his own bed, one by one another,
Who goes to curry and bed down the patient beasts
    Warm in their old pens. But nothing moves
In those dark streets which you can never see,
    No one is walking or will ever walk there
Now, and you will never know

          One vast tree
        between you and the town:
         one cypress   mocks
      the thin blue spire   licking up
           like flame
             the green metabolism

of this forest sword
driving you from the town

I have sown a little garden of poppies,
sweet peas and mignonette. Now we must
wait and see what comes of it.

Still, though the little town, how peacefully
It lies under the watchful eyes of that
Fierce heaven.

We take death to reach a star.

Nothing moves there yet, and yet
How separate, how floating like a raft, like
Seaweed drifting outward on the tide, already
Dim, half-gone,

And the poor baby, too, whom I had
cared for as if he were my own

diminishing into
Some middle distance of the past.

some canvases that will retain their
calm even in the catastrophe

and still so calm
and still
so still

Zóó heen kan gaan

Four Studies in the Moderns

"That Anguish of Concreteness"—
Theodore Roethke's Career

The career of Theodore Roethke remains one of the most remarkable achievements of a period whose creative vigor will surely astonish succeeding ages. Coming near the end of a great revolution in the arts and sciences (which I have discussed at length earlier in "Poems about Paintings" and "A Poem's Becoming"), his career is like a history in miniature of that artistic revolt. His work not only managed to recapitulate this culture's war against form and matter, he pushed that attack several new steps forward. Yet, coming after the futile social revolutions which rose from the same drives and so accompanied the artistic one, he also summed up our peculiar inability to capitalize on our astounding achievements—our flight from freedom, from the accesses of power we have released. I see this in his withdrawal into metaphysics, his flight from his own experimental drive, his own voice, his freedom. I must view this career, then, with an astonished awe, yet with sadness.

Roethke's struggle with form first revealed itself in his changing attitudes toward verse form and toward rhetorical and stylistic convention. This is typical: the general revolution against form and matter first found large-scale expression in the breaking down of artistic forms by the Impressionist painters and Symbolist poets.

Roethke's first book, *Open House,* seems surprisingly old-fashioned and prerevolutionary. The poems are open and easily graspable; the metric quite regular and conventional. There is even a romantic lyricism which verges on sentimentality and ladies' verse. Here is a typical example:

> O my sister remember the stars the tears the trains
> The woods in spring the leaves the scented lanes
> Recall the gradual dark the snow's unmeasured fall
> The naked fields the cloud's immaculate folds
> Recount each childhood pleasure: the skies of azure
> The pageantry of wings the eye's bright treasure.
>
> Keep faith with present joys refuse to choose
> Defer the vice of flesh the irrevocable choice
> Cherish the eyes the proud incredible poise
> Walk boldly my sister but do not deign to give
> Remain secure from pain preserve thy hate thy heart.
> *"To My Sister"*

This was followed, however, by *The Lost Son and Other Poems*— almost entirely in free verse. A marked prosiness, too, came into the language texture, bringing very real successes. Here appeared many favorite Roethke poems—"Frau Bauman, Frau Schmidt and Frau Schwartze," "Root Cellar," "Weed Puller," "Dolor," "The Minimal," and "Big Wind," which ends in a beautiful balance between lyricism and prosiness:

> . . . she rode it out,
> That old rose house,
> She hove into the teeth of it,
> The core and pith of that ugly storm,

Ploughing with her stiff prow,
Bucking into the wind-waves
That broke over the whole of her,
Flailing her sides with spray,
Flinging long strings of wet across the roof-top,
Finally veering, wearing themselves out, merely
Whistling thinly under the wind-vents;
She sailed until the calm morning,
Carrying her full cargo of roses.

Also in that book, however, were poems which predicted the direction of Roethke's third book, *Praise to the End!*—a plunge into the wildest and most experimental poetry of the period. Though the poem quoted above is in free verse, we scarcely notice that. The verse flows easily and expressively, underlining the immediate meaning, drawing little attention to itself. It is nearly incredible that the same man could have written, in his next book:

Believe me, knot of gristle, I bleed like a tree;
I dream of nothing but boards;
I could love a duck.

Such music in a skin!
A bird sings in the bush of your bones.
Tufty, the water's loose.
Bring me a finger. This dirt's lonesome for grass.
                    "Give Way, Ye Gates"

Even after the wildest surrealists, that voice sounds new and astonishing; it could be no one but Roethke. It is an achieved style, carrying much meaning, and touching only tangentially other voices we have heard in poetry.

What's this? A dish for fat lips.
Who says? A nameless stranger.
Is he a bird or a tree? Not everyone can tell.

> Water recedes to the crying of spiders.
> An old scow bumps over black rocks.
> A cracked pod calls.
>
> Mother me out of here. What more will the bones allow?
> Will the sea give the wind suck? A toad folds into a stone.
> These flowers are all fangs. Comfort me, fury.
> Wake me, witch, we'll do the dance of rotten sticks.
>
> *"The Shape of the Fire"*

Even now, many years since those poems appeared, I do not feel that I really understand them, or feel certain how ultimately successful they are.

Yet that is not the point. The point, I think, is that Roethke had opened out before himself an incredible landscape. He had regressed into areas of the psyche where the powerful thoughts and feelings of the child—the raw materials and driving power of our later lives—remain under the layers of rationale and of civilized purpose. The explorations made possible by this book alone could have engaged a lifetime. Yet Roethke never seriously entered the area again.

It is not surprising that Roethke might at this point need to step back and regather his forces. He did just that in the group of "New Poems" which first appeared in *The Waking* and which were later called "Shorter Poems, 1951–53" in *Words for the Wind.* Here Roethke returned to the more open lyricism of his earlier verse and gave us, again, several markedly successful poems—"A Light Breather," "Old Lady's Winter Words," and the beautiful "Elegy for Jane." Yet one had a feeling that he was marking time, seeking a new direction.

In *Words for the Wind,* Roethke's collected poems, the new direction appeared. It was a shock. There had been hints that Roethke was interested in Yeats's voice, hints that he might follow the general shift in twentieth-century verse by following wild experimentation with a new formalism. No one could have expected that *Words for the Wind* would contain a series of sixteen "Love Poems" and a sequence, "The

Dying Man," all in a voice almost indistinguishable from Yeats's. Roethke, who had invented the most raw and original voice of all our period, was now writing in the voice of another man, and that, perhaps, the most formal and elegant voice of the period.

Yet, also in that book appeared "Meditations of an Old Woman," which suggested still another new direction, and promised, I felt, astonishing new achievements. This poem shows a different influence, but one which seemed much less confining—the Eliot of *Four Quartets*. Perhaps there was also some influence of Richmond Lattimore's translation of *The Iliad:*

> As when silt drifts and sifts down through muddy
>   pond-water,
> Settling in small beads around weeds and sunken branches,
> And one crab, tentative, hunches himself before moving
>   along the bottom,
> Grotesque, awkward, his extended eyes looking at nothing
>   in particular,
> Only a few bubbles loosening from the ill-matched tentacles,
> The tail and smaller legs slipping and sliding slowly
>   backward—
> So the spirit tries for another life,
> Another way and place in which to continue;
> Or a salmon, tired, moving up a shallow stream,
> Nudges into a back-eddy, a sandy inlet,
> Bumping against sticks and bottom-stones, then swinging
> Around, back into the tiny maincurrent, the rush of
>   brownish-white water,
> Still swimming forward—
> So, I suppose, the spirit journeys.
>
>   *"First Meditation"*

Here, at any rate, was a language free from the constrictions of verse movement, free to use all the cadences of prose, yet able to collect as much power and authority as any formal verse:

I think of the self-involved:
The ritualists of the mirror, the lonely drinkers,
The minions of benzedrine and paraldehyde,
And those who submerge themselves deliberately in trivia,
Women who become their possessions,
Shapes stiffening into metal,
Match-makers, arrangers of picnics—
What do their lives mean,
And the lives of their children?—
The young, brow-beaten early into a baleful silence,
Frozen by a father's lip, a mother's failure to answer.
Have they seen, ever, the sharp bones of the poor?
Or known, once, the soul's authentic hunger,
Those cat-like immaculate creatures
For whom the world works?

"Fourth Meditation"

Once again, Roethke seemed on the border of a universe of poetic achievement—a work which might approach the breadth of Whitman.

Theodore Roethe had died before his next book of poems appeared. *The Far Field* opens with a poem called "The Longing" which harks back to those passages in the earlier book which had promised—both in statement and in vigor of style—further journeys, new explorations; "All journeys, I think, are the same: / The movement is forward, after a few wavers . . ." but now there is a sense of failure, or failure of desire:

On things asleep, no balm:
A kingdom of stinks and sighs,
Fetor of cockroaches, dead fish, petroleum, . . .
The great trees no longer shimmer;
Not even the soot dances.

And the spirit fails to move forward,
But shrinks into a half-life, less than itself,

> Falls back, a slug, a loose worm
> Ready for any crevice,
> An eyeless starer.

That note is struck repeatedly through the "North American Sequence," with which the book opens. Although there are assertions of new explorations: "I dream of journeys repeatedly: . . ."

> Old men should be explorers?
> I'll be an Indian.
> Iroquois.

we come away with an opposed sense:

> The self persists like a dying star,
> In sleep, afraid. . . .

> I dabble my toes in the brackish foam sliding forward,
> Then retire to a rock higher up on the cliff-side. . . .

> The river turns on itself,
> The tree retreats into its own shadow. . . .

> I long for the imperishable quiet at the heart of form; . . .

> The lost self changes,
> Turning toward the sea,
> A sea-shape turning around,—
> An old man with his feet before the fire,
> In robes of green, in garments of adieu.

Here, as elsewhere in the book, Roethke accurately predicts his own death, clearly longing for it.

These poems, recording that withdrawal, also, I think, suffer from it. The language grows imprecise with pain, or with growing numbness and half-sleep as an escape from pain. It seems less a regression to capture something and re-create it, than a regression for its own sake, to lose something and uncreate it.

Metrically, too, one has a sense of discouragement and withdrawal.

Many of Roethke's earlier cadences are repeated: the whip-cracking of the third book, the easy free verse of the second book. In this book, the shorter and slighter poems—"The Geranium," "The Lizard," "The Meadow Mouse"—seem most fully realized. The more ambitious poems seem far less successful. This is not to call them failures —they would make a considerable career for many a lesser man. But I, at least, do not feel that they equal Roethke's finest achievements.

What had happened? To investigate that we must go back through Roethke's work and trace out something of his war against form on a different level. And this is a much more causal level— probably causal to Roethke, and certainly causal to the great war against form in our era—the revolt of the sexes against each other and themselves and, in our time, the revolt of the child against the parent. Here, we must investigate not the technical form of Roethke's poems, but rather their statements about his own human form.

Most of Roethke's best earlier poems record a desperate effort "To be something else, yet still to be!," to be "somewhere else," to "find the thing he almost was," to be "king of another condition." As he said it earliest, "I hate my epidermal dress"; as he said it last, "How body from spirit slowly does unwind / Until we are pure spirit at the end." We see his struggle against his own form, shape, and size in all those poems about regression into animal shape—the sloth, the slug, the insect. Or the continual attempt to lose his large human form in an identity with *small* forms:

> . . . the little
> Sleepers, numb nudgers in cold dimensions,
> Beetles in caves, newts, stone-deaf fishes,
> Lice tethered to long limp subterranean weeds,
> Squirmers in bogs,
> And bacterial creepers. . . .
> *"The Minimal"*

This struggle against his own form reached what seemed a sort of triumph in those journey poems where he investigated the landscape as a woman, in the earlier love poems, and in the numerous poems where he spoke *as* a woman. In the earlier love poems, he did affirm a shape; not his own, but the woman's: "She came toward me in the flowing air, / A shape of change, encircled by its fire," or again: "The shapes a bright container can contain!" This containment must have seemed an answer—to lose one's shape, to *be* the woman through sexual entrance: "Is she what I become? / Is this my final Face?" and: "I . . . see and suffer myself / In another being, at last." This idea was repeated over and over. Yet ecstatic as these poems were, there were two disturbing elements. The woman was not affirmed as herself, a person in her own right, but rather as a symbol of all being, or as something the poet might become. And the affirmation was not made in Roethke's voice, but in Yeats's.

The love poems in the final book are considerably changed. Some ecstasy survives: "Who'd look when he could feel? / She'd more sides than a seal," but even this poem suggests a parting or failure:

> The deep shade gathers night;
> She changed with changing light.
>
> We met to leave again
> That time we broke from time;
> A cold air brought its rain,
> The singing of a stem.
> She sang a final song;
> Light listened when she sang.
>
> *"Light Listened"*

Here and elsewhere—e.g., "The Long Waters" and "The Sequel"—there seems to be a farewell to that ecstasy, a turning away, or turning inward from the discovery that this could not satisfy the hunger. I do not suggest that any specific love had turned sour or grown cold, but rather that love had perhaps been asked to perform a transformation, to appease a hunger, which no love possibly could satisfy.

What appears dominant in the last book is a desire to escape *all* form and shape, to lose all awareness of otherness, not through entrance to woman as lover, but through re-entrance into eternity conceived as womb, into water as woman, into earth as goddess-mother. This is the burden of "The Long Waters":

> A single wave comes in like the neck of a great swan
> Swimming slowly, its back ruffled by the light cross-winds,
> To a tree lying flat, its crown half broken. . . .
>
> I, who came back from the depths laughing too loudly,
> Become another thing;
> My eyes extend beyond the farthest bloom of the waves;
> I lose and find myself in the long water;
> I am gathered together once more;
> I embrace the world.

and of the "Meditation at Oyster River":

> Now, in this waning of light,
> I rock with the motion of morning;
> In the cradle of all that is,
> I'm lulled into half-sleep
> By the lapping of water,
> Cries of the sandpiper.
> Water's my will, and my way,
> And the spirit runs, intermittently,
> In and out of the small waves, . . .

His new visitant is the child:

> I see in the advancing and retreating waters
> The shape that came from my sleep, weeping:
> The eternal one, the child, the swaying vine branch,

> The numinous ring around the opening flower,
> The friend that runs before me on the windy headlands,
> Neither voice nor vision.
>
> *"The Long Waters"*

When, in these last poems, Roethke identifies with an animal, that is only as it tends to represent the child, the baby or fetus. He speaks to "The Lizard":

> He too has eaten well—
> I can see that by the distended pulsing middle;
> And his world and mine are the same,
> The Mediterranean sun shining on us, equally, . . .

and even more, "The Meadow Mouse" which he keeps and treats as, by sympathetic magic, he would be treated:

> Now he's eaten his three kinds of cheese and drunk
>   from his bottle-cap watering-trough—
> So much he just lies in one corner,
> His tail curled under him, his belly big
> As his head; . . .

and when the mouse grows up enough to run away, Roethke sees again his approaching death:

> I think of the nestling fallen into the deep grass,
> The turtle gasping in the dusty rubble of the highway,
> The paralytic stunned in the tub, and the water rising,—
> All things innocent, hapless, forsaken.

In poem after poem, he sees the water rising, the water "moving forward," himself "at a standstill."

This standstill, however, is actively sought and defended. The desire to lose one's own form has taken on a religious rationale to support itself. Where Roethke's earlier free-verse poems were nearly always pure explorations, his more ambitious free-verse poems now

111

try more and more to incorporate a fixed and predetermined religious and irrational certainty:

> Do we move toward God, or merely another condition? . . .
>
> The shade speaks slowly:
> "Adore and draw near.
> Who knows this—
> Knows all."
>
> *"The Abyss"*

This is related to the earlier Symbolists' search for a state of being, a religious stasis, as an escape from this world of form and becoming. The poem aims to create a stasis wherein a person is one with all things; that is, where all matter is dissolved. This is related, too, to Roethke's search for pure space as an escape from time. That has been strong in the poems for some time, but now it is easier to see why he identifies space with pure being:

> Space struggled with time;
> The gong of midnight struck
> The naked absolute.
> Sound, silence sang as one.
>
> *"The Moment"*

Our only experience of identity with all space, of omnipresence, is in the womb; our first experience of time brings the mother's breast which may be withdrawn and so force one to recognize external objects, to give up the narcissistic sense of omnipresence and omnipotence, that unity with all objects which Roethke constantly seeks: ". . . the terrible hunger for objects quails me."

This, in turn, helps explain both Roethke's praise of madness (since reason forces the acceptance of external forms and objects) and the poems' increasing mysticism. For instance, in his *New World Writing* remarks on "In a Dark Time," he correctly describes the following as an androgynous act: "The mind enters itself, and God the mind, / And one is One, free in the tearing wind," but also insists that this is a search for God and, moreover, a "dictated" poem. This clarifies, also, the identification of rage with the heart, the true self. Rage is looked upon as a noble quality since it is a rage against the forms of this world, a continued allegiance to one's fantasy of life in the womb.

This intensely creative rejection of form has great destructive possibilities. On the one hand, we have a search for form; on the other (and probably causal to it), a rejection of form which may result in a rejection of all forms, including any form which one might achieve. The balance between these opposed feelings has changed in Roethke's later poems both because of the introduction of borrowed cadences and because of the religious and mystical rationale. Eliot's ideas and Yeats's cadences have rushed in to fill the vacuum of the father-model which might have suggested a shape to become, and so might have made this world bearable. Yet such a model Roethke either could not find or could not accept.

Surely the marvelous thing about Yeats was his unceasing appetite for this world—that is, his unceasing dissatisfaction with all systems of ideas about this world. He created far vaster systems than any of the other Symbolists, yet he never took them seriously. All the ladders —the political fantasies, the metaphysical systems, the reasonable constructs—all are grand, yet Yeats finally "lay down where all the ladders start: / In the foul rag and bone shop of the heart." That is why we love his poems—they hold no stay against confusion, no sedation against the fearful pains and joys. More and more, Roethke's late poems seem to have lost their appetite, their tolerance for that anguish of concreteness.

In a sense, this combination of one man's voice and another man's ideas has given too much form—or too much comforting certainty.

Roethke's formal poems had always celebrated some kind of lyrical certainty, but that was most frequently a certainty about the nature of one's feelings. Now, rejection of earthly forms has become, itself, a rationale, a convention, a form. As the ideas, the metrical shapes and cadencings all grow firmer, however, the language becomes strangely decayed—or at any rate, fixed and self-imitating. The constant terms of Roethke's earlier poems—the rose, the flame, the shadow, the light, the stalk, the wind—are almost emblems. But as all emblems of an absolute have the same ultimate meaning, so all these terms come more and more to mean the same thing. The words tend to dissolve; the poem is more of a musical rite than a linguistic or dramatic one. That is neither good nor bad in itself, but unless the poem's music is very new and original, a slackness and expectability enters into the poem.

The result here is a little obsessive, like a fantasy. The voice says the same things over and over, always reaching the same predetermined meaning, though with slightly different words each time. But meantime, the voice gets smaller and smaller, like "The phoebe's slow retreating from its song," or like an unhappy child chanting small charms to itself, talking itself to sleep.

Roethke wrote a book of poems for children—*"I Am!" Says the Lamb*—which appeared in 1961. The first poem in that book is "The Kitty-Cat Bird":

> The Kitty-Cat Bird, he sat on a Fence.
> Said the Wren, your Song isn't worth 10¢.
> You're a Fake, you're a Fraud, you're a Hor-rid Pretense!
> —Said the Wren to the Kitty-Cat Bird.
>
> You've too many Tunes, and none of them Good:
> I wish you would act like a bird really should,
> Or stay by yourself down deep in the wood,
> —Said the Wren to the Kitty-Cat Bird.

You mew like a Cat, you grate like a Jay:
You squeak like a Mouse that's lost in the Hay,
I wouldn't be You for even a day,
—Said the Wren to the Kitty-Cat Bird.

The Kitty-Cat Bird, he moped and he cried.
Then a real cat came with a Mouth so Wide,
That the Kitty-Cat Bird just hopped inside;
"At last I'm myself!"—and he up and died
—Did the Kitty—the Kitty-Cat Bird.

You'd better not laugh; and don't say, "Pooh!"
Until you have thought this Sad Tale through:
Be sure that whatever you are is you
—Or you'll end like the Kitty-Cat Bird.

I wonder how many lovers of Roethke's poetry have read that to their children, perhaps at bedtime, unsuspecting of its horrors? Or of its prophecy? Who could have guessed that Roethke—who meant so much to us—could think so badly of himself? Or might issue a warning to the children which he himself was unable to heed?

But that is too fearsome a place to end. Earlier, Roethke gave us another animal picture of himself, of his certainties, and of his journey into sleep—"The Sloth":

In moving-slow he has no Peer.
You ask him something in his Ear;
He thinks about it for a Year;

And, then, before he says a Word
There, upside down (unlike a Bird),
He will assume that you have Heard—

A most Ex-as-per-at-ing Lug.
But should you call his manner Smug,
He'll sigh and give his Branch a Hug;

115

> Then off again to Sleep he goes,
> Still swaying gently by his Toes,
> And you just *know* he knows he knows.

Perhaps he does. Surely, after enduring so much uncertainty and anguish, he *deserves* to know. After offering so much for *our* knowledge, he deserves to sleep well.

Master's in the Verse Patch:
John Crowe Ransom

Our poets have a way of blooming late, often after a long sterile period. We have exciting enough early works, splendid last works, but little work of maturity—precisely that period when we might have expected the greatest work. In their middle years our poets often cannot write at all, or, as a substitute for some wisdom we cannot find, will flee to theorizing, philosophy, and literary dogmatism. Often, only the approach of death can shock us from the trance of our life; we come to terms with it more courageously. The artistic problems stem from the problem with love and passion.

The problem is a problem: only a fool would think he knew an answer. How could one be a first-rate artist without offending, deeply, those he most loves? First, by the mere offense of being first-rate. That, with the envy it arouses, quite commonly costs one those dearest to him. All differences, inequalities, seem unjust and odious. We have been encouraged to be feminine or childish, while our women have been encouraged to compete and to dominate. But like most executives, they dominate not through ability but through will—a quality often rising from envy at what one takes for a *lack* of ability in one's self. Every sign of ability in others will be a very real injury. And that injury is likely to be all the greater coming from an artist, since his life involves keeping open the passions, which may be neither humane nor loyal. Meantime, the violence and faithlessness of our passions are only likely to be increased by our desire to be dominated and diminished, our childishness, which resents any loved one and will use its own faithlessness as a subtle and civilized weapon.

Not that many of us would care to reinstate the *droit du seigneur,* or to go back to an age when the male was valued for a brute physical force which we abhor. Yet it certainly seems that we have carried horrid democracy a bit far. Since the great revolutions of the nineteenth century—the Industrial Revolution and the artistic and intellectual revolutions which accompanied it—there has been no masculine, ordering force worth fighting against. In the arts, as in society, we see aimless revolt followed by aimless revolt. After the women went, then the children; the dogs appear to have their revolt fairly well under way; the vegetables are likely next. Nothing is really produced, since these rebellions are directed against powers which do not exist, and carried out by those who are lacking in either ability or purpose. We have half-men, half-women, half-adults, half-children, and nothing first-rate anywhere. It is not to be expected that poets, any more than the rest of us, could escape the problem.

Cruel as this sounds, Hardy was probably the luckiest—his wife died while he had many years to lament, to record the fierce subtleties of their marital techniques, to learn how much she *had* meant, yet marry his secretary and go on with his poems. Tactless and proud as she was, his first wife had perhaps found a way to sacrifice herself into those poems so far greater (as she must really have known) than any she could herself write—a way to escape from, yet aid, a work too great to live with. This suggests both a nobility and a despair quite beyond anything Hardy credited her with, and quite beyond any reasonable demand.

Like Hardy, Eliot outlived a demented first wife. Unlike him, he sought comfort in religion, in rejection of the world of sense experience. When he successfully remarried late, one could only rejoice at the renewed zest his bearing so clearly showed. Hopes for his work, however, were disappointed; he never recovered the enormous powers of his earliest poems. On the other hand, he never became an idea-monger, as had Pound.

Frost outlived his wife, yet for all his brilliance, was never able to make the reappraisal. Perhaps the struggle had gone too far, left too much wreckage and guilt. His earlier poems are the glory of our period—yet he never fulfilled their promise. If Cummings's feelings had reached their fullest at twenty-five, Frost's had reached theirs at forty. When he said "How awful, yet I must . . ." he was a poet; when he says "I must, since it's right . . ." he is only a danger.

Williams truly loved his wife yet spent years trying to injure her. Then, however, he could come back to her. Few have his magnanimity, which could forgive even someone he had so deeply wounded. After years of sterile literary dogmatism, it is to his wife that he comes back in his last great poem, "Of Asphodel"—the flower that tells of his enduring love.

Stevens married a professional model whose face appears on the Liberty dime. To him, love must have been only another expensive ornament, like philosophy or aesthetic theory, to decorate an essentially meaningless world, another wreath for the abyss. In his old age, after *his* years of literary philosophizing, he comes back to no particular woman, but only to a "heavenly desired . . . sleek among the tintinnabula" who alone could offset the grayness of age and the shadow of trees like wrecked umbrellas. He returns to no garden, but to a greenhouse—now battered and in need of paint.

Thomas was perhaps the unluckiest, or the weakest. He had no middle age, much less whatever wisdom it might offer. He died recording the loveless lusts we associate with adolescence, the pure-sex-in-the-pants which appeals so to those with pure-sex-in-the-head. He

119

does not lament his own age and loss, but his father's; he leaves his wife as ruined victor, to write what she can.

In Ransom we see something different from any of these—a man who has made a deep commitment and firmly stood by it, at whatever price. Whether we can be glad is beside the point. We must hold our peace before great dedication and the great loss that always means. There are gains, too—we have, now, a new poem just when we had given up hope for it. And it is a thoroughly remarkable poem—one that not only records this problem of love and creativity, but, in that very act, partially transcends it.

MASTER'S IN THE GARDEN AGAIN
To the memory of Thomas Hardy

I

Evening comes early, and soon discovers
Exchange between these conjugate lovers.

"Conrad! dear man, surprise! aren't you bold
To be sitting so late in your sodden garden?"

"Woman! intrusion! does this promise well?
I'm nursing my knees, they are not very cold.
Have you known the fall of the year when it fell?
Indeed it's a garden, but if you will pardon,
The health of a garden is reason's burden."

"Conrad! your feet are dripping in muck,
The neuralgia will settle in your own neck,
And whose health is it that catches an asthma?
Come in from foul weather for pity's sake!"

"No," says the thinker. "Concede. I am here,
Keeping guard of my garden and minding miasma.
You're lonely, my loony? Your house is up there.
Go and wait. If you won't, I'll go jump in the
    lake."

II

And the master's back has not uncurved
Nor the autumn's blow for an instant swerved.

Autumn days in our section
Are the most used-up thing on earth
(Or in the waters under the earth)
Having no more color nor predilection
Than cornstalks too wet for the fire
And black leaves pitched onto the byre.

The show is of death. There is no defection.

III

He will play out his mood before he takes food.

By the bob of the Power the dark skies lower,
By the bite of Its frost the children were lost
Who hurt no one where they shone in the sun,
But the valiant heart knows a better part
Than to do with an "O did It lay them low,
But we're a poor sinner just going to dinner."

See the tell-tale art of the champion heart.

Here's temple and brow, which frown like the law.
If the arm lies low, yet the rage looks high.
The accusing eye? that's a fierce round O.
The offense was raw, says the fix in the jaw.
We'll raise a rare row! we'll heave a brave blow!

A pantomime blow, if it damns him to do,
A yell mumming too. But it's gay garden now,
Play sweeter than pray, that the darkened be gay.

Herman Broch (in his introduction to Rachel Bespaloff's book *On the Iliad*) defines the style of old-age as an *abstractism* which impoverishes its vocabulary in order to enrich its syntactical relationships. It no longer collects the brilliant *atoms* of "world content," but rather expresses its relationships, its structure. Thus, though it tends to share the scientist's concern for abstract universal structure, its productions come closer to the abstractism of myth.

This seems apt, and a proper distinction between this and Ransom's earlier poems. This is a poem of relationships; it, as a result, invites commentary as the earlier poems never did. Those first poems quite defeat criticism—one can only point to them, with perhaps a few sentences of explication, and say, "See? He's done it again!"

Even this poem's initial technical problem is one of relationship—how to use a passage from the earlier "Conrad in Twilight," now that that poem's situation has come to have more meaning with the passage of time:

> Autumn days in our section
> Are the most used-up thing on earth
> (Or in the waters under the earth)
> Having no more color nor predilection
> Than cornstalks too wet for the fire,
> A ribbon rotting on the byre,
> A man's face as weathered as straw
> By the summer's flare and winter's flaw.

This, the ending of the original poem, was never quite satisfactory. In itself it is remarkable—few poets could have handled dactyls (or anapests) so fluently, placing extra accents so skillfully to avoid the deadly dactylic bounce. But coming at the end of "Conrad in Twilight," a light and breezy poem, and sinking it into a kind of depression and flat despair, the passage was shocking and never quite right.

Ransom's answer now is not to lessen the contrasts, but rather to make them more extreme. He surrounds his original death-dull passage with the gayest and brightest sights and sounds. He even marks the sections off with numbers so that we cannot miss the contrast. It is a little like a classical musical form: the first section is a light and high-comical scolding match between husband and wife; the second, the more serious passage already quoted, which raises the specter of death impinging on Conrad; the last section, tonally like the first, but with an underlying grimness, a dramatization of that "show" which "is of death." The last section is a little like the one of those Mahler scherzi where everything is so splendidly gay but for that *memento mori,* that one sour clarinet; or like children in their Halloween costumes—gay and death-haunted, sacrificial.

Not that there is no attention to vocabulary and detail in the poem. Who else could have written that third line? After two regular dactylic lines to set the scene and tone, enter the wife:

"Conrad! Dear man, surprise! aren't you bold . . ."

So metrically canny, yet so humanly alive! There is so much wife in that line, one can hardly stand it. It is as if a whole flock of bright birds had burst into the room, quarreling for territories. Fluttering and fluting, affectionate and affected, maddeningly charming, the pitches rise, fall, slide, state incredible themes.

And once begun, this jocular brilliance never leaves the poem. Again, the husband's half-joking gruffness:

Woman! Intrusion! Does this promise well?"

Or the continual play of echoes and sound effects: "sodden . . . garden . . . pardon . . . burden . . . guard of my garden." Or the constant hovering on the brink of absurd and delicious puns: "asthma . . . miasma."

Yet these local pleasures are not like the brilliance of vocabulary in Ransom's earlier poems. They are not meant to define this atom of experience, but to conflict with it. They must provide a gaiety to balance the tragic grimness of the poem's situation and theme, yet must never become too attractive in themselves.

The only thing in the poem much reminiscent of the earlier vocabulary is in the Latinism of "conjugate lovers," and I'm not sure but that it is a mistake. For me, at least, "eldering lovers," which one of the intermediate versions had in that place, is better. Most of Ransom's other revisions have tended to cut down the brilliance of the individual line so that the archetypical structure of the whole poem could more fully be realized. Consider these lines with their counterparts in the printed poem:

> Women! intrusion! is this done well?
> ....
>
> Conrad your feet are dipping in muck,
> ....
>
> Come in to your ever and loving pipe
> ....
>
> So, my loony and only, my wanton and wife,
> You may take yourself off, a while, my dear.

It must not have been easy to give those up. Yet, here again the gains are clear.

Consider the title: "Master's in the Garden Again." Master? What does that mean? Of course, it's something a servant might say about the head of the household as she runs to report to her real master— that is, her mistress. Therein, one of the ironies. The master himself recognizes that he is scarcely master of the house:

> You're lonely, my loony? Your house is up there.

Again, by a fine ambiguity, "Master" is just the term we might apply to a child in the family. "The Master, Conrad" is someone very different from "Master Conrad." In his rage, the old man is less like Oedipus or Lear than like a willful child intent on his play, refusing his mother's demands that he wear rubbers, that he keep warm and dry, that he eat his meals. Just as a child may feel that the only way to preserve its identity against a devouring mother is to refuse to eat. "No!—that proves I'm alive! I'll finish my game." And typically, in his helplessness his only weapon against the woman is to damage himself: to stay out in the cold longer, or finally to throw himself in the lake.

Then, she'll be sorry. No question but that she would; or that *he* would be sorry if she didn't come down and ask him to come in. For she must be like the constantly importunate, constantly rejected mother—which is both a cause and an effect of his helpless rage. True, in one sense, Conrad is like an Old Testament prophet, a Lear, an Oedipus, raging against those forces which he has come to resemble and which will destroy him. In this sense, too, he is the Master. But we must first see him as an old man who plays the role of a child, who, in turn, plays the role of Lear or Oedipus.

The game in which he plays that role, of course, is Art. For he must also be seen as the master artist, the Maestro. If his "show is of death" yet the management of that show is "reason's burden." Conrad is "the thinker" on guard against "miasma" and his own "loony." And it is precisely in this area that his lady attacks him—suggesting that he hasn't sense enough to come in out of the damp.

Yet, for all its concern with reason, the poem is very much more about passion. In the first version of the poem, the garden was described as "the ghost of a Forest of Arden." Good enough: not only the place of nature and exile from human unkindness,

Here feel we but the penalty of Adam,
The season's difference; as, the icy fang
And churlish chiding of the winter's wind

but also the place where the young lovers meet and kiss and make love. In the new poem, however, such predilections have been transformed almost entirely into something less threatening—rage. For the poem could scarcely have been written until that transformation was possible. Rage is more easily turned back against the self, or turned against those one sees as all-powerful or impregnable. Neither could the poem be written until the two antagonistic forces, death and woman, could be identified. One of these forces is introduced in each of the first two sections; in the last section, Conrad moves to action, but only because he can identify these two forces. This is clearest in

> By the bob of the Power the dark skies lower,
> By the bite of Its frost the children were lost,

As a Limiting Power upon Life, woman and death are one. Just as it bobs, so she bobs down from her house, lowering, and calling her children home. Naughty, they will play out their games—fierce and grotesque games—the games of Art and Prophecy—games which demonstrate the blankness of the world which has formed and controlled them. "The accusing eye? that's a fierce round O." And that eye, that rage, looks high—to her house or to the skies, to the Power which dwells there and has defeated the old man, laid his arm low, and now scolding affectionately, calls him home to a final surrender. This is only an inversion of our common tendency to see death as a mother, the grave as a womb.

Just as Oedipus's ultimate identity with his Fate is never seen in any surrender on his part, but rather in an implacable rage which shows him to be essentially like that implacable Fate and basically part of it, so here Conrad's refusal to enter the house, his insistence on acting out his self-directed rage and accusation, proclaim his essential oneness with the Powers. His temple and brow frown like the law; it is clear that his laws are woman and death. In that sense, there is no defection, all appearances to the contrary. If he, momentarily, refuses to come in, he will eventually go and be glad enough for the messenger's visit. It shows a constant, almost divine concern for his wellbeing. And his rage shows, finally, his lack of freedom from her.

Stanley Kunitz recently reminded us of Goethe's dictum that all Art lies in Limit, reminding us himself, however, that the artist must always try those limits to the utmost. No doubt most of us accept too readily limits which comfort us emotionally, a world comformable to a childish demand for a universe much concerned with our welfare.

Still, who would accept a world of open rage, of unlimited passion? If we are too childish to be Oedipus, we are also too compassionate. Though this dilemma has itself limited the size and scope of this poem, yet the poem has defined, at the same time, that dilemma—the gain and loss, the passion and compassion, those stools between which life occurs. This seems to me a triumph.

So, in the Garden of his Art, the Master plays out a late performance; one equally composed of protest and reconciliation. For if House and Garden are separated, both still stand. If Master and Woman will never be closer, they will never be farther. If the Gardens have been long shut, we villagers must know there have been sufficient reasons. Today, Master's in his verse patch again and his formal gardens are open to the public; who can be less than grateful?

A Rocking Horse: The Symbol,
the Pattern, the Way to Live

"Daddy! Daddy!" he cried to his father.
"Daddy, look what they are doing!
Daddy, they're beating the poor little horse!"
—CRIME AND PUNISHMENT

Lawrence may seem the least meticulous of serious writers; nonetheless, in "The Rocking-Horse Winner" he has given us something close to the perfect story. It has been anthologized, analyzed by New Critics, and force-fed to innumerable undergraduates. J. Arthur Rank has filmed it. Yet no one has seriously investigated the story's chief structural feature, the symbolic extensions of the rocking-horse itself, and I feel that in ignoring several meaning-areas of this story we ignore some of Lawrence's most stimulating thought.

Though the reach of the symbol is overwhelming, in some sense the story is "about" its literal, narrative level: the life of the family that chooses money instead of some more stable value, that takes money as its nexus of affection.* The first fault apparently lay with the mother.

*Since this essay was first published, I have received a copy of George R. Turner's unpublished essay, "Princess on a Rocking Horse." Professor Turner shows that the story is closely based on the life of Sir Charles Brooke's family. Sir Charles, the Rajah of Sarawak, usually absent on official duties, lavished expensive presents on his chil-

128

The story opens:

> There was a woman who was beautiful, who started with all the advantages, yet she had no luck. She married for love, and the love turned to dust. She had bonny children, yet she felt they had been thrust upon her, and she could not love them . . . at the center of her heart was a hard little place that could not feel love, not for anybody.

We never learn much more about her problems, about *why* her love turned dust. But the rhyming verb "thrust" is shrewdly chosen and placed; knowing Lawrence, we may well guess that Hester's dissatisfaction is, at least in large part, sexual. We needn't say that the sexual factor is the sole or even primary cause of her frigidity, but it is usually a major expression and index of it, and becomes causal. Lawrence wrote in an amazing letter to John Middleton Murry:

> A woman unsatisfied must have luxuries. But a woman who loves a man would sleep on a board . . . You've tried to satisfy Katherine with what you could earn for her, give her: and she will only be satisfied with what you *are*.

There could scarcely be a more apt description of Hester's situation. As for her husband, we cannot even guess what he *is;* he gives too few clues. Failing to supply the luxuries that both he and his wife demand, he has withdrawn, ceased to exist. The one thing he could always give —himself, the person he is—seems part of a discarded currency. The mother, the father, finally the boy, each in turn has withdrawn his

---

dren, yet harped constantly on the family's poverty. These money troubles were in part caused by his own extravagant betting, though he apparently concealed this from his family during his lifetime. His wife, Lady Sylvia (the sister of Lawrence's dear friend Dorothy Brett—who appears as "Uncle Oscar"), apparently despised him. It was their daughter, Leonora Brooke, "Princess Gold" of Sarawak, who actually did pool her bets with a family servant. She did indeed own an expensive, much-loved rocking horse. Further, she actually picked Sansovino to win the Ascot Gold Cup, though she cannot now recall any of the other horses. The rocking horse, however, had no part in the placing of her bets.

vital emotions and affections from commitment in and to the family. Withdrawing, they have denied their own needs, the one thing that could be "known" and "sure." They have, instead, committed their lives to an external, money, and so to "luck," since all externals are finally beyond control and cannot be really known. Thus, it is Paul's attempt to bring an external into his control by knowledge which destroys him. It is a failure of definition.

The father's withdrawal, of course, leaves a gap which encourages Paul in a natural Oedipal urge to replace him. And money becomes the medium of that replacement. So the money in the story must be taken literally, but is also a symbolic substitute for love and affection (since it has that meaning to the characters themselves), and ultimately for sperm. We know that money is not, to Paul, a good in itself —it is only a way to win his mother's affection, "compel her attention," show her that *he* is lucky though his father is not. That money has no real use for Hester either becomes only too clear in that crucial scene where Paul sends her the birthday present of five thousand pounds hoping to alleviate her problems, relax the household, and so release her affections. His present only makes her colder, harder, more luxurious, and:

> the voices in the house, behind the sprays of mimosa and almond blossom, and from under the piles of iridescent cushions, simply trilled and screamed in a sort of ecstasy: "There *must* be more money! Oh-h-h; there *must* be more money. Oh, now, now-w! Now-w-w—there must be more money;—more than ever!"

The mother and father have driven themselves to provide the mother with what she, actually, needs least. And she has squandered it, one would guess, precisely to show her scorn for it and for the husband who provides it. Money as a symbolic substitute has only sharpened the craving it was meant to satisfy; the family has set up a vicious circle which will finally close upon Paul.

As several critics have noted, the story resembles many well-known

130

fairy tales or magical stories in which the hero bargains with evil powers for personal advantages or forbidden knowledge. These bargains are always "rigged" so that the hero, after his apparent triumphs, will lose in the end—this being, in itself, the standard "moral." Gordon and Tate sum up their interpretation: "the boy, Paul, has invoked strange gods and pays the penalty with his death." Robert Gorham Davis goes on to point out that many witches supposedly rode hobby-horses of one sort or another (e.g., the witch's broom) to rock themselves into a magical and prophetic trance. When he rides, Paul's eyes glare blue and strange, he will speak to no one, his sisters fear him. He stares into the horse's wooden face: "Its red mouth was slightly open, its big eye was wide and glassy-bright." More and more engrossed in his doom as the story progresses, he becomes "wild-eyed and strange . . . his big blue eyes blazing with a sort of madness." We hear again and again of the uncanny blaze of his eyes until finally, at his collapse, they are "like blue stones." Clearly enough, he is held in some self-induced prophetic frenzy, a line of meaning carefully developed by the story. When Paul first asserts to his mother that he is "lucky," he claims that God told him so. This seems pure invention, yet may well be a kind of *hubris,* considering the conversation that had just passed with his mother:

> "Nobody ever knows why one person is lucky and another unlucky."
> "Don't they? Nobody at all? Does nobody know?"
> "Perhaps God. But He never tells."

Whether Paul really believes that God told him so, he certainly does become lucky. And others come to believe that superhuman powers are involved. Bassett thinks of "Master Paul" as a seer and takes an explicitly worshipful tone toward him. He grows "serious as a church" and twice tells Uncle Oscar in a "secret, religious voice . . . 'It's as if he had it from heaven.' " These hints of occultism culminate in Uncle Oscar's benediction:

"My God, Hester, you're eighty-odd thousand to the good, and a poor devil of a son to the bad. But poor devil, poor devil, he's best gone out of a life where he rides his rocking-horse to find a winner."

So, in some sense, Paul *is* demonic, yet a poor devil; though he has compacted with evil, his intentions were good and he has destroyed only himself. At first metaphorically, in the end literally, he has committed suicide. But that may be, finally, the essence of evil.

It is clear, then, that the story is talking about some sort of religious perversion. But *what* sort? Who are the strange gods: how does Paul serve them and receive their information? We must return here, I think, to the problem of knowledge and intellection. Paul is destroyed, we have said, by his desire to "know." It is not only that he has chosen wrong ways of knowing or wrong things to know. The evil is that he *has* chosen to know, to live by intellection. Lawrence wrote, in a letter to Ernest Collings:

> My great religion is a belief in the blood, the flesh, as being wiser than the intellect. We can go wrong in our minds. But what our blood feels and believes and says, is always true. *The intellect is only a bit and bridle.* What do I care about knowledge. . . . I conceive a man's body as a kind of flame . . . and the intellect is just the light that is shed on to the things around. . . . A flame isn't a flame because it lights up two, or twenty objects on a table. It's a flame because it is itself. And we have forgotten ourselves. . . . The real way of living is to answer to one's wants. Not "I want to light up with my intelligence as many things as possible" but ". . . I want that liberty, I want that woman, I want that pound of peaches, I want to go to sleep, I want to go to the pub and have a good time, I want to look a beastly swell today, I want to kiss that girl, I want to insult that man."

(I have italicized the bit and bridle metaphor to underscore an immediate relationship to the rocking-horse of the story.)

Not one member of this family really knows his wants. Like most idealists, they have ignored the most important part of the command

Know thyself, and so cannot deal with their most important problem, their own needs. To know one's needs is really to know one's own limits, hence one's definition. Lawrence's notion of living by "feeling" or "blood" (as opposed to "knowledge," "mind," or "personality") may be most easily understood, perhaps, as living according to what you *are,* not what you think you should be made over into; knowing yourself, not external standards. Thus, what Lawrence calls "feeling" could well be glossed as "knowing one's wants." Paul's family, lacking true knowledge of themselves, have turned their light, their intellect, outward, hoping to control the external world. The mother, refusing to clarify what her emotions really *are,* hopes to control herself and her world by acting "gentle and anxious for her children." She tries to be or act what she thinks she should be, not taking adequate notice of what she is and needs. She acts from precepts about motherhood, not from recognition of her own will, self-respect for her own motherhood. Thus, the apparent contradiction between Hester's coldness, the "hard . . . center of her heart," and, on the other hand, "all her tormented motherhood flooding upon her" when Paul collapses near the end of the story. Some deep source of affection has apparently lain hidden (and so tormented) in her, all along; it was her business to find and release it sooner. Similarly, Paul has a need for affection which he does not, and perhaps cannot, understand or manage. Like his mother, he is trying to cover this lack of self-knowledge with knowledge about the external world, which he hopes will bring him a fortune, and so affection.

Paul is, so, a symbol of civilized man, whipping himself on in a nervous endless "mechanical gallop," an "arrested prance," in chase of something which will destroy him if he ever catches it, and which he never really wanted anyway. He is the scientist, teacher, theorist, who must always know about the outside world so that he can manipulate it to what he believes is his advantage. Paradoxically, such knowledge comes to him only in isolation, in withdrawal from the physical world, so that his intellect may operate upon it unimpeded. And such control of the world as he can gain is useless because he has lost the knowledge of what he wants, what he is.

This, then, is another aspect of the general problem treated by the story. A still more specific form of withdrawal and domination is suggested by the names of the horses on which Paul bets. Those names —like the names of the characters—are a terrible temptation to ingenuity. One should certainly be wary of them. Yet two of them seem related to each other and strongly suggest another area into which the story's basic pattern extends. Paul's first winner, Singhalese, and his last, Malabar, have names which refer to British colonial regions of India. (A third name, Mirza, suggests "Mirzapur"—still another colonial region. But that is surely stretching things.) India is obviously one of the focal points of the modern disease of colonial empire; for years Malabar and Singhalese were winners for British stockholders and for the British people in general. The British, like any colonial power or large government or corporation, have gambled upon and tried to control peoples and materials which they never see and with which they never have any vital physical contacts. (Lawrence's essay "Men Must Work and Women as Well" is significant here.) They have lived by the work of others, one of the chief evils of which is that their own physical energies have no outlet and are turned into dissatisfactions and pseudo-needs which must be filled with more and more luxuries. And so long as they "knew," placed their bets right, they were rich, were able to afford more and more dissatisfactions. A similar process destroyed Spain: a similar process destroyed Paul.

Though these last several areas of discussion are only tenuously present, most readers would agree, I think, that the rocking-horse reaches symbolically toward such meanings: into family economy and relations, into the occult, into the modern intellectual spirit, into the financial and imperial manipulations of the modern state. But surely the sexual area is more basic to the story—is, indeed, the basic area in which begins the pattern of living which the rocking-horse symbolizes. It is precisely this area of the story and its interpretation which has been ignored, perhaps intentionally, by other commentators. Oddly enough, Lawrence himself has left an almost complete gloss of this aspect of the story in his amazing, infuriating, and brilliant article "Pornography and Obscenity." There, Lawrence defines pornography not as art which stimulates sexual desire, but rather as art which contrives to make sex ugly (if only by excluding it) and so leads the observer away from sexual intercourse and toward masturbation. He continues:

> When the grey ones wail that the young man and young woman went and had sexual intercourse, they are bewailing the fact that the young man and the young woman didn't go separately and masturbate. Sex must go somewhere, especially in young people. So, in our glorious civilization, it goes in masturbation. And the mass of our popular literature, the bulk of our popular amusements just exists to provoke masturbation. . . . The moral guardians who are prepared to censor all open and plain portrayal of sex must now be made to give their only justification: We prefer that the people shall masturbate.

Even a brief reading of the essay should convince one that Paul's mysterious ecstasy is not only religious, but sexual and onanistic. That is Paul's "secret of secrets." Just as the riding of a horse is an obvious symbol for the sex act, and "riding" was once the common sexual verb, so the rocking-horse stands for the child's imitation of the sex act, for the riding which goes nowhere.

We note in the passage quoted above that Lawrence thinks of masturbation chiefly as a substitute for some sort of intercourse. Similarly in the story:

> "Surely, you're too big for a rocking-horse!" his mother had remonstrated.

"Well, you see, mother, till I can have a *real* horse, I like to have some sort of animal about," had been his quaint answer.

This is one of several doctrinal points where the reader will likely disagree with Lawrence. Nonetheless, the idea was prevalent at the time of writing and is common enough today that most men probably still think of masturbation chiefly as a sex substitute. And like the money substitute mentioned before, it can only famish the craving it is thought to ease. So we find another area in which the characters of the story don't know what they need; another and narrower vicious circle.

The tightening of that circle, the destruction of Paul, is carefully defined; here, one feels both agreement with Lawrence's thought and a strong admiration for his delineation of the process:

> He went off by himself, vaguely, in a childish way, seeking for the clue to "luck." Absorbed, taking no heed of other people, he went about with a sort of stealth, seeking inwardly for luck.

Stealth becomes more and more a part of Paul. We hear again and again of his secret, his "secret within a secret," we hear his talk with Uncle Oscar:

> "I shouldn't like mother to know I was lucky," said the boy.
>
> "Why not, son?"
>
> "She'd stop me."
>
> "I don't think she would."
>
> "Oh!"—and the boy writhed in an odd way—"I *don't* want her to know, uncle."

We may quote here a passage from "Pornography and Obscenity":

> Masturbation is the one thoroughly secret act of the human being, more secret even than excrementation.

Naturally, any act accompanied by such stealth is damaging to the personality and to its view of itself. It involves an explicit denial of the self, a refusal to affirm the self and its acts (an imaginative suicide) and consequently a partial divorce from reality. But this is only part of that same general process of isolation. In the essay, Lawrence says:

> Most of the responses are dead, most of the awareness is dead, nearly all the constructive activity is dead, and all that remains is a sort of a shell, a half empty creature fatally self-preoccupied and incapable of either giving or taking. . . . And this is masturbation's result. Enclosed within the vicious circle of the self, with no vital contacts outside, the self becomes emptier and emptier, till it is almost a nullus, a nothingness.

This is the process dramatized by the story. Paul draws back from his family, bit by bit, until he becomes strange and fearful to his sisters and will speak to no one, has grown beyond the nurse and has no real contact with his parents. Even Uncle Oscar feels uncomfortable around him. Finally he has moved his rocking-horse away from the family and taken it with him "to his own bedroom at the top of the house."

Lawrence believes that man's isolation is an unavoidable part of his definition as a human being—yet he needs all the contact he can possibly find. In his essay on Poe, Lawrence writes:

> Love is the mysterious vital attraction which draws things together, closer, closer together. For this reason sex is the actual crisis of love. For in sex the two blood-systems, in the male and female, concentrate and come into contact, the merest film intervening. Yet if the intervening film breaks down, it is death . . .
>
> In sensual love, it is the two blood-systems, the man's and the woman's, which sweep up into pure contact, and almost *fuse*. Almost mingle. Never quite. There is always the finest imaginable wall between the two blood waves, through which pass unknown vibrations, forces, but through which the blood itself must never break, or it means bleeding.

Sex, then, is man's closest link to other human beings and to the "unknown," his surest link into humanity, and it is this that Paul and his family have foresworn in their willful isolation. And this isolation

137

is more than physical. Again in "Pornography and Obscenity," we find:

> The great danger of masturbation lies in its merely exhaustive nature. In sexual intercourse, there is a give and take. A new stimulus enters as the native stimulus departs. Something quite new is added as the old surcharge is removed. And this is so in all sexual intercourse where two creatures are concerned, even in the homosexual intercourse. But in masturbation there is nothing but loss. There is no reciprocity. There is merely the spending away of a certain force, and no return. The body remains, in a sense, a corpse, after the act of self-abuse.

To what extent Lawrence thinks this reciprocity, this give and take, to be physical, I am not sure; I *am* sure it could easily be exaggerated. Lawrence makes a sharp distinction between the physical and the material. At any rate, it seems to me that the most important aspect of this sexual give-and-take is certainly emotional and psychological and that the stimulus which enters in sexual intercourse lies in coming to terms with an actual sexual partner who is real and in no wise "ideal." Thus, such a partner will afford both unexpectable pleasures and very real difficulties which must be recognized and overcome. But in masturbation these problems can be avoided. Most psychologists would agree that the most damaging thing about masturbation is that it is almost always accompanied by fantasy about intercourse with some "ideal" partner. Thus, one is led away from reality with its difficulties and unpredictable joys, into the self and its repetitive fantasies. This may seem rather far from the story, but I suggest that this explains the namelessness of the rocking-horse. (It also, of course, suggests shame and is valuable in manipulating the plot.) The real partner has a name which is always the same and stands for a certain configuration of personality with its quirks and glories; the fantasy partner, having no personality, has no name of his or her own but is given the name of such "real" partners as one might wish from week to week.

These, then, are the gods which Paul has invoked. This sexual problem gives, also, a startling range of irony to the religious texture of the story. The "secret within a secret . . . that which had no name" comes to be not only the shame of Paul's masturbation, but also a vicious and astounding parody of the "word within a word" . . . that which cannot be named. It should be clear from the material already quoted, and even more so from a reading of "Pornography and Obscenity," that it is popular religion, Christian idealism, that Lawrence is attacking, for it supports the "purity lie" and leaves masturbation as the only sexual expression, even at times openly condoning it. The strange gods are the familiar ones; the occult heresy is popular Christian piety.

It is not clear how Paul receives knowledge from his onanistic gods. Lawrence himself does not pretend to know *how* this comes about, he only knows that it does exist:

> The only positive effect of masturbation is that it seems to release a certain mental energy, in some people. But it is mental energy which manifests itself always in the same way, in a vicious circle of analysis and impotent criticism, or else a vicious circle of false and easy sympathy, sentimentalities. This sentimentalism and the niggling analysis, often self-analysis, of most of our modern literature, is a sign of self-abuse.

This momentary release of energy is, I take it, equivalent to finding the name of the "winner" in the story. Thus the two great meaning streams of the story, intellection and masturbation, relate. Masturbation stands as the primary area: the withdrawal and stealth, the intellectual participation in the physical, the need to know and magically control the external, the driving of the self into a rigid, "mechanical gallop," the displacement of motive, the whole rejection of self, all begins here. And the pattern, once established, spreads, gradually infecting all the areas of life, familial, economic, political, religious. Here, again, the reader may feel a doctrinal disagreement, suspecting that masturbation is more symptomatic than causal. Such disagreement scarcely touches the story, however, whose business is not to diagnose or cure, but to create a vision of life, which it does with both scope and courage.

I want to quote finally one more passage from the essay "Pornography and Obscenity" to round off the argument and tie up some loose ends, and also simply because of its value, its sincerity. It is a kind of summation of the story's meaning and opens with a sentence roughly equivalent to Uncle Oscar's judgment, "he's best gone out of a life where he rides a rocking-horse to find a winner":

> If my life is merely to go on in a vicious circle of self-enclosure, masturbating self-consciousness, it is worth nothing to me. If my individual life is to be enclosed within the huge corrupt lie of society today, purity and the dirty little secret, then it is worth not much to me. Freedom is a very great reality. But it means, above all things, freedom from lies. It is, first, freedom from myself; from the lie of my all-importance, even to myself; it is freedom from the self-conscious masturbating thing I am, self-enclosed. And second, freedom from the vast lie of the social world, the lie of purity and the dirty little secret. All the other monstrous lies lurk under the cloak of this one primary lie. The monstrous lie of money lurks under the cloak of purity. Kill the purity-lie and the money-lie will be defenseless.
>
> We have to be sufficiently conscious, and self-conscious, to know our own limits and to be aware of the greater urge within us and beyond us. Then we cease to be primarily interested in ourselves. Then we learn to leave ourselves alone, in all the affective centres: not to force our feelings in any way, and never to force our sex. Then we make the great onslaught on the outside lie, the inside lie being settled. And that is freedom and the fight for freedom.

One need scarcely share Lawrence's opinions to admire the honesty and passion of such a statement.

for Kathy

Crime for Punishment:
The Tenor of Part One

*A hurtful act is the transference to
others of the degradation which we
bear in ourselves. That is why we are
inclined to commit such acts as a way
of deliverance.*

—SIMONE WEIL

Late in the novel, when he can live no longer without
confessing, Raskolnikov goes to Sonia to tell her it was he who killed
the old woman money-lender and her sister. For seconds Sonia is
silent with shock and horror. Then, throwing herself to her knees
before him, she cries, "Oh, what have you done to yourself?"*

There can be few moments of more dazzling illumination. Yet, it
takes Raskolnikov only a few seconds to cloud the issue completely,
to tangle both Sonia and himself in a huge web of pseudo-motives: he
wanted to prove himself a superman, beyond authority; he wanted the
old woman's money for a grandiose humanitarian scheme; he wanted
to be independent of his impoverished mother; he merely wanted to
prove that he had "the courage to dare." Though each of these has
its truth, each reveals something of Raskolnikov, none is finally convincing either to the characters or to the author. Unfortunately, Raskolnikov's rationalizations have confused most of his critics almost as

*Part V, Chapter ii. All quotations are from the translation by David Magarshack.

completely as himself.* Raskolnikov never discovers his basic motive; none of the other characters suspect it, excepting only Porfiry, the chief inspector. Porfiry, recognizing Raskolnikov's desire for punishment, first preaches to him the need for confession, then makes that confession possible by setting an example—by dropping his tone of accusation and, himself, confessing first to Raskolnikov:

> "I frankly confess—for if I am to confess I may as well confess everything —that it was I who was the first to suspect you. . . . I'm afraid I've caused you a lot of suffering. . . . I consider you in any case. . . . a most honorable man. . . . I want . . . to show you that I am a man who possesses feelings as well as a conscience. I mean it."†

This change to a tone of dignified sympathy and respect for Raskolnikov is crucial; in making it, Porfiry advances from the role of chief inspector into the roles of the priest and father who can help Raskolnikov regain self-respect through, first, confession and, next, punishment or "suffering." I take it, then, that Raskolnikov's original motive in murder was to achieve punishment.

"Never tell the reader the real motive," said Dostoievsky; how admirably he follows his own precept! He was thoroughly aware that such a motive might exist. In a letter to his publisher, Katkov, he suggested this motive for Raskolnikov:

> . . . I find it difficult to explain my idea. My novel, besides, contains the hint that the punishment laid down by the law frightens the criminal much less than our legislators think, partly because he himself feels the desire to be punished.‡

In the novel itself, Dostoievsky offers this motive for the crimes and confessions of lesser characters. Nikolay the painter (who, like Ras-

---

*From this remark I should exclude Avrahm Yarmolinsky who, in *Dostoievsky: His Life and Art*, hints strongly at the interpretation here offered.

†Part VI, Ch. 2.

‡Quoted by Magarshack in his Introduction to the novel.

kolnikov, comes from Ryazan and is, moreover, a "Raskolnik" or "Old Believer") confesses to Raskolnikov's crime because of a religious compulsion to "accept suffering." Again, an unnamed prisoner, whom Porfiry implicitly compares to Raskolnikov, read his Bible so well that he threw a brick at the governor in order to get more punishment, yet "deliberately missed . . . to make sure he did him no injury."*

Yet, if Dostoievsky is conscious of such motives, why *not* tell the reader? First, he usually reveals the greatest truths when he works by hints and indirections. Second, he would have been specially reticent about stating abstractly and conspicuously an idea which most readers would then have thought merely absurd. Finally, this novel has a very large autobiographical element; he must have felt not only a literary, but a personal reticence.

In the autumn of 1866, when he began work on *Crime and Punishment,* Dostoievsky's circumstances were remarkably like those of his hero. Having unnecessarily assumed great debts, he went to Wiesbaden to gamble. There, he had lost all he had or could borrow. He had pawned his wardrobe and valuables, then had been cheated on an object he especially loved by a woman pawnbroker. When he could not keep up room rent, he was abused by the hotel manager and the waiters who (like the landlady and the maid in the novel) would not deliver any food except tea, "because he didn't deserve it." The servant who watched him at night reported that he had "murder on the mind." Thus, his own Wiesbaden situation, though translated into the terms of his earlier life in St. Petersburg,† is carried directly into the novel as the situation of the student Raskolnikov. There, it is offered as one of the factors leading *him* to murder. Yet, misfortune or

---

*Here Dostoievsky strengthens and openly asserts an interpretation for this incident which he had previously only suggested when handling the same incident for *The House of the Dead.*

†Cf. Alberto Moravia, "The Marx-Dostoievsky Duel," *Encounter,* November, 1956.

poverty occur to most of us with no such fearful result; the crux lies in the protagonist's reaction to his difficulties.

It is hardly surprising, then, that Dostoievsky hesitates to offer, abstractly, a motive which might be so damaging to his reader's (or his own) opinion of himself. Yet, with steady insistence and with overwhelming insight, he does demonstrate and dramatize throughout the novel just such a belief. And, after all, it is the special business of a novel to re-create the texture of living, not necessarily to explain it.

The special business of the first part of *Crime and Punishment* is to re-create the circumstances in which a man will commit murder. If, as most critics suppose, this novel aimed only to show remorse *after* crime, then Part I (events before and during the crime) would be extraneous. Yet the removal of Part I, or even of that portion which precedes the murder, would terribly damage the book. This is true simply because the action of Part I accounts for the murder, its own climax, far better than any of the rationalizations later offered either by the murderer or by the novelist.

Establishing the motive, however, does more than merely account for the murder; in large part, it accounts for the whole structure of the novel. First, nearly all Raskolnikov's later actions depend upon his first great decision—to kill Alyona Ivanovna. Second, only if we understand Raskolnikov do such secondary characters as Marmeladov, Luzhin, and Svidrigaylov fall into perspective. Their torments are not incidental displays of horror, but sidelong analyses of Raskolnikov himself. Third, this motive (the desire to achieve a punishment which will reinstate him as a worthy member of a moral universe)—this motive complements and clarifies the doctrine of suffering put forward by Sonia and Porfiry. Finally, it accounts for Raskolnikov's second great decision, the climax toward which the book so carefully builds. It explains why Raskolnikov cannot commit a perfect crime, why he must blunder, must flirt with capture and, finally, confess. To escape would defeat the very purpose of the murder.

To trace the workings of this motive, I will investigate here the action of Part I. I will follow the strict narrative sequence of the book, interrupting that sequence only when its events can be more clearly understood in the light of later scenes, or of events from Dostoievsky's life. I do hope, however, that these comparisons may also throw light on the meaning of the book as a whole.

The opening scene—Raskolnikov sneaking past the kitchen of his landlady, Pashenka—is more important than one at first suspects. His discomfort—he owes rent for a shabby little fifth-floor room—is of a kind we usually think amusing or trivial. Besides, Raskolnikov himself wants to believe that these actions and feelings are not significant. He tries to tell himself that he is terrified to meet Pashenka merely because he does not want to "listen to all that dreary nonsense which [does] not concern him at all," that he has "lost all interest in matters that [require] his most immediate attention," and, finally, in a kind of comic paranoia, that he is "not in the least afraid of his landlady, whatever plots she might be hatching against him." At first reading, such a view of Pashenka may seem reasonable; by the time one reaches Part III, it becomes palpable nonsense. As Razumikhin will demonstrate, Pashenka is pleasant enough—shy, pliable, even generous, when well-handled. Raskolnikov has chosen not to face her, explain his position, and ask decent treatment. Instead, he hides, aggravates his debt, lets her injure him and pockets the injury in silence. It is, after all, a sort of comfort to be plotted against.

Nonetheless, Raskolnikov cannot convince himself that this "dreary nonsense . . . does not at all concern him." He is obsessed by it. The words "shame" and "fear" recur to him again and again. He has a "sickening sensation of terror which [makes] him feel ashamed. . . . His fear . . . surpris[es] even himself." We must not let him convince us—as he tries to convince himself—that he is indifferent, that he lacks conscience. He has, if anything, too much. At any rate, his conscience drives him the wrong way—away from people, away from any solution. He has withdrawn from everyone, been almost totally "absorbed in himself... lying about all day long in that beastly hole and thinking . . . talking to himself . . . amusing himself by indulging in fantastic dreams." This is partly because he *is* aware of guilt and debt. This debt and his response to it—the first of a long series of similar situations in the book—is a trap into which he is slipping further and further. At this point, we needn't decide how much he has devised his own trap; he is caught and is furious.

The scene which follows on the streets of St. Petersburg develops these conflicting feelings of shame and rage, withdrawal and violence. We notice, first, Raskolnikov's intense isolation, passing through the crowded streets "in a kind of coma," self-absorbed and talking to himself. In any *literal* sense, he is almost entirely cut off from the life around him. Yet, symbolically, he is very much at one with it. "The proximity of the Hay Market, the great number of disorderly houses, and most of all, the working-class population which crammed into these streets and alleyways . . . the unendurable stench from the pubs," the drunkards and prostitutes—convey Raskolnikov's sense of internal corruption. The crowds of people, the "summer stench," the heat and the dusty, stifling air, all suggest his own constriction and compression, the rage and filth shut up inside him. This sense of stifling constriction will continue unrelieved almost to the end of the novel—until the rain breaks during that night when Svidrigaylov is on the brink of suicide, and Raskolnikov on the brink of confession. Here, the squalor he sees is mainly an objectification of his own degradation, the repulsion he shows for those around him, an expression of self-disgust. To resolve this ambivalence in Raskolnikov's view of the street, and his corresponding preference for just such scenes of degradation, would lead us farther afield than we can go at this time.

There is another ambiguity which is more obvious and more pressing. We have never been quite sure whether Raskolnikov acts so stealthily because of shame for his poverty, or because he is doing something disgusting and criminal. This ambiguity becomes specially noticeable when Raskolnikov sees a drunkard, being carried in a "huge empty cart drawn by an enormous dray-horse," who suddenly points at him and shouts, " 'Hey, you there, German hatter!' . . . The young man at once stopped in his tracks and clutched nervously at his hat." We suppose that Raskolnikov, sensitive and refined, is embarrassed by ridicule. Dostoievsky at once corrects us:

> But it was not shame, it was quite another feeling, a feeling that was more like fear, that had overtaken him.
> "I knew it!" he muttered in confusion . . . "it is just such an idiotic thing, such a trivial detail, that could ruin the whole plan! Yes, I'm afraid my hat is too noticeable . . . people might remember it, and there's your clue."

For the first time, we learn that this "rehearsal" of the "plan" does involve something actively criminal. The ambiguity is meaningful; the violence of the murder rises directly from Raskolnikov's sense of personal shame. This chapter's movement from the stealth of shame to that of violence is significant for the same reason.

Slipping past Pashenka, passing like a sleep-walker through the streets, Raskolnikov arrives at the house of the usurer, Alyona Ivanovna. Once again he slips past the caretakers; this time he sneaks *up* the stairs, not *down*. Earlier, we saw him in debt to his landlady; now we see him set up another debt to another woman. But this debt will trap *her*, not him. We must never forget his real purpose in this visit. As he must remind himself, he is not pawning his watch for money, he is putting himself in debt in order to rehearse the murder. No causal relation is stated between the scene at the landlady's and the scene at the pawnbroker's; one is easily felt: Raskolnikov will kill his pawnbroker *partly* in revenge against his landlady; the rage withheld from Pashenka will gather interest and destroy Alyona Ivanovna. Incidentally, this relationship between the landlady and the pawnbroker also partly explains why, later in the novel, immediately after he has killed the pawnbroker, Raskolnikov has a nightmare in which the Assistant Superintendent of Police beats Pashenka. As Nastasya, the maid, tells him:

"That was your blood making a noise inside you. It always does that when it can't come out and it starts getting clotted up in your liver. That's when you start seeing things."

In part, this nightmare is one interpretation of motive for the murder just preceding it: the murder was one way of beating Pashenka. This linkage between the two women will need development later; now we need only note that Raskolnikov is indebted to both and has fantasies of violence against both.

I have remarked that Pashenka is fairly reasonable and generous; whatever may be said of Alyona Ivanovna, she is certainly neither of *those* things. She is, in fact, all the vicious things Raskolnikov would like to think of Pashenka. That may be why he chose her. He knew her bad qualities from the beginning and detested her from the first moment,* yet he decided to do business with her. No one can say whether he could have found a better pawnbroker. This much is certain: it is essential that his victim *be* a pawnbroker, a money-lender, a collector of debts; that she be old, ugly, vicious; that she mistreat her sister, Lisaveta. These qualities "justify" the crime he has so long been planning. In the present scene, she cheats him; gives him an unfair price for a pledge of great sentimental and symbolic value —his only memento of his father, a silver watch with the globe engraved on its back. He can hardly be surprised that she cheats him; he would surely have been surprised—and, perhaps, disappointed— if she had not.

If Chapter 1, then, is a prediction of the violence Raskolnikov will commit, Chapter 2 is a premonition of the passivity he embodies. Having rehearsed the murder, having brought at least one of his

---

*Cf. Chapter 6.

fantasies nearer to realization, his rage is momentarily eased; he feels hungry for company, for humanity. Stepping into a tavern, he sees Marmeladov, and is drawn to him "from the very first moment . . . before a word had been spoken . . . he even explained it as a kind of presentiment." Marmeladov, too, finds Raskolnikov a kindred soul. He launches at once upon a flood of self-hatred and self-pity: his wife is ill, the children hungry; he has lost job after job by drinking, filching the money from his family; the neighbors beat his wife and he dare not interfere; his wife beats him and has driven his daughter, Sonia, to prostitution; Sonia has been forced out of their lodgings. On and on: an astounding self-display of mismanagement, abasement, bathos.

However much we want to weep for Marmeladov, still something in us wants to join with the tavern loungers and jeer. He has so deliberately chosen all his miseries, and chosen them to flaunt before us. He has been offered work and its rewards; he does not want them, deliberately throws them away. Why, then, take a position at all? Why not lie around the house all day, beg or steal, wander away? Such reasonable approaches would save him most of his troubles. This is exactly what's wrong with them. Imagine the loss: if he stopped "trying" to hold a position, no wife would make sacrifices to help him, grow excited and hopeful when he seemed to reform, be happy and affectionate when he brought home his check, then, when he threw away the job and the better life he had dangled under her nose, tear her hair and beat him. Next, if he had not lost the job and his wife's affection, strangers could no longer sympathize with him about his strange compulsion, about his cruel wife. The strangest thing about this compulsion is that even he knows its source:

> "That's why I drink, for it is in drink that I'm trying to find sympathy and compassion. It is not happiness but sorrow that I seek. I drink, sir, that I may suffer, that I may suffer more and more."

He has been most appallingly successful at that.

No doubt his marriage *is* painful. One must agree with Raskol-

FOUR STUDIES IN THE MODERNS

nikov, when he later meets her: she is "certainly . . . not the right sort of wife for Marmeladov." Katerina Ivanovna does not want a husband; she wants someone to blame life on. Her every motion is an accusation against her husband, her neighbors, against the whole world. Later in the book, this will culminate in the grotesque display of herself and her children begging under the windows of the supposedly callous officials who (she will convince herself) have injured and starved her family. But it appears most concisely and far-reachingly in this very chapter, where she delivers her curse: "Damn, damn, damn this life." *She* has been all too successful at that.

At least as subtle a technician as Marmeladov, her methods are destroying her almost as quickly. She has become ill; her consumption (like Anna Petrovna's, in Chekhov's *Ivanov*) may be seen as another accusation of her husband. Whether or not she originally so intended it, her illness certainly has *become* an accusation—both for her, and for Marmeladov:

> "It's her eyes I'm afraid of—her eyes. And also the red spots on her cheeks and—her breathing. Have you ever noticed how people with her illness breathe when—when they are excited?"

This, incidentally, is a literary portrait of Dostoievsky's first wife, who had died of consumption in 1864 after a long illness involving much neglect and blame, and to whom he felt very guilty indeed. It is also worth noting that throughout his life, Dostoievsky often bungled his affairs to punish himself and those around him for various guilts.

The worst sort of wife—for anyone. Yet Marmeladov chose her; and with adequate warning. Her first husband had died, leaving her in the provinces with no way to support her children. Marmeladov, thinking he pitied her, offered to marry her. Instead of being relieved and grateful, she went to the altar "weeping and sobbing and wringing her hands." Surely that would have scared off any man concerned for his own preservation, any man who did not want to crucify himself

150

in a marital contest of injury collecting. If Raskolnikov wanted a bad pawnbroker, Marmeladov certainly wants a bad wife.

He is now very skillfully making her worse—shrewish, parasitic and violent. He knows that his own deepest need is for understanding:

"And He will stretch forth His arm to us, and we shall fall down before Him and we shall weep. And we shall understand all . . . and all will understand, and my wife, too, my wife, will understand. Lord, thy kingdom come!"

Yet he does not ask for understanding, but rather pity:

"Oh, if only she'd take pity on me! For surely, surely, my dear sir, every man ought to have at least one place where people take pity on him!"

That demand for pity amounts to an accusation which in turn, makes her less able to understand. Besides, consider Marmeladov's claims for pity: first, that he has thrown away job after job to torment her; second, that she is a monster. How should she sympathize with *those* complaints? Besides, she must always have been completely absorbed in self-pity, even before those injuries which he actually has heaped upon her. What hope of pity from her? Or of understanding? It is more practical to seek disapproval and punishment; they are her chief stock in trade and, further, his habitual demand:

"I like her to pull me by the hair . . . I'm not afraid of blows. Lord no. For you must know, sir, that far from hurting me, such blows are a real pleasure to me. I can't do without them. It's better like that. Let her beat me."

It takes much abuse to replace even a little affection. If she beats him, he can at least feel punished for his "chronic destitution," for starving his family, cruelly tricking his wife, punished for her flushed cheeks and labored breathing.

Yet, at the very same time, when she beats him he collects a new injustice from her—one which he can display in the taverns and streets to anyone who will listen and perhaps supply a sympathy to confirm his flagrant self-pity. Yet even this does not exhaust the possibilities for manipulating the balance sheet. This new injury and abuse (even though he, quite as much as she, has sought and caused it) may, after enough self-pity has been brought to bear upon it, become an excuse for his next "failure." And so the cycle is perpetuated.

We must never miss the ambivalences of Marmeladov's story; disguised as a confession, it is really a condemnation of his wife, a self-justification. Openly abasing himself and praising her, he deftly paints her as trivial, greedy and vicious. His faults seem mild by comparison, especially when he so readily "confesses" and tries so hard to "excuse" *all* her faults:

> She can't help herself, I'm afraid. It's her character, you see.

No man in his right mind could think that a mitigation!

Marmeladov's techniques center on a nearly invincible parody of Christian humility. If his story fails, if he cannot heap enough coals of forgiveness on his wife, if the tavern louts jeer him, that too can be turned to advantage—can serve as another punishment, another martyrdom to display to his next audience. For he *will* die a martyr. If Raskolnikov will not supply the requisite pity, he will find it—of all places—in Heaven:

> "It's not on earth but up there that they grieve over people and weep, but they never blame them, they never blame them! And that hurts more . . . And He who takes pity on all men will also take pity on me, and He who understands all men and things, He alone, He too, is the judge."

His final self-aggrandizement is to identify his own self-induced and rancorous martyrdom with that of Christ:

> "Behold the man! . . . I don't deserve any pity. I ought to be crucified— crucified, and not pitied. But crucify him, O judge, crucify him, and having

crucified him, have pity on him! Then I, too, will come to you to be crucified; for it's not joy I thirst for, but sorrow and tears!"

They do not seem hard to find. For a year, the marriage had gone well enough. But at the first appearance of trouble, when Marmeladov lost his job because of personnel changes in his office, all the destructive possibilities of the marriage took control. Moving from place to place, their agonies have grown steadily sharper. In this chapter, where we first encounter them, they have been in St. Petersburg sixteen months and have brought themselves to a horrifying pitch of degradation. Within the course of the novel—not more than a few weeks—both will die. First, Marmeladov will step in front of a cart to find the death which even his wife will recognize as "what he asked for." Then she will complete her own destruction by conspicuous suffering and disease. Their deaths are the natural culmination of their techniques; final acts of blame against their world and each other.

Though at first Raskolnikov and Marmeladov seem completely opposite—Raskolnikov, self-aggrandizing, aggressive, murderous; Marmeladov, self-abasing, passive, suicidal—they are ultimately similar. We have already sketched much of the Raskolnikovian element of Marmeladov's character. And Raskolnikov will come, finally, to see in Marmeladov a large part of his own soul, and to be deeply affected by that recognition. But for the moment it is Marmeladov's family which moves him—moves him to pity. As he goes, he leaves them all the change he has in his pocket.

This is the first of Raskolnikov's several attempts to save his self-respect, to prove himself good, through charity. This time, however, any self-approval he might have gained is soured immediately by the recollection that he has no money, that this gift to the Marmeladovs helps to impoverish his own mother and sister. Ironically, his act of charity has only thrown him deeper into the guilt he was trying to escape. He smiles sardonically at the Marmeladovs' victimization of Sonia:

> What a girl! What a gold mine they have found! And they are making jolly good use of it! Took it for granted. Wept bitter tears and got used to it! Man gets used to everything—the beast!

We recall that Marmeladov had frequently called himself a beast. We do not recognize until the next chapter that Raskolnikov is calling himself a beast for victimizing his own family. His judgment upon Marmeladov, his judgment upon Man, is only a reflection of his opinion of himself.

Chapter 3 has several crucial functions. Not the least of these is the interrelating of Chapters 1 and 2, and of their heroes. Even as Raskolnikov and Marmeladov seem at first diametrically opposed, so do the chapters which present them: Raskolnikov's rehearsal of murder seems unrelated to Marmeladov's recital of his self-destruction. In the novel as a whole, murder and suicide are ultimately related by the psychological and religious doctrine that Raskolnikov's hatred of others is only a reflection of his self-hatred, that the murder he commits is actually a blow struck against himself. More immediately these two chapters are related by Chapter 3, which reveals basic similarities between these two men and suggests that underlying (and causal to) Raskolnikov's apparent viciousness lies a deeper passivity and self-destructiveness.

In the tavern the day before, Raskolnikov had heard the bartender shout at Marmeladov:

> "And why ain't you working? . . . why ain't you got a job seeing as how you're a civil servant?"

Next morning, at the beginning of Chapter 3, the maid Nastasya brings Raskolnikov some tea and asks him:

> "Why are you asleep? It's almost ten o'clock. . . . why does a clever man like you lie about like a sack of coals, of no use to himself or anybody else?

You used to give lessons to children before, didn't you? Well, why is it you do nothing now?"

When he answers that he is "doing something . . . working . . . thinking," she only laughs convulsively, just as the drunkards had laughed at Marmeladov. Raskolnikov, however, compares her not only to the drunkards, but to something much more intimate. We have already heard him scolding himself:

> I talk too much because I do nothing . . . Lying about all day long in that beastly hole and thinking . . .

Now he answers Nastasya "reluctantly and sternly . . . as though in answer to his own thoughts," for she has lined up with his conscience against him.

Raskolnikov has just failed, at the end of Chapter 2, in one attempt to save himself from his conscience; his gift to the Marmeladovs backfired. Now, Nastasya's answers are driving him back further, step by step, into a corner:

> "You shouldn't bite the hand that feeds you, sir . . . You don't want to get rich all at once, do you?"

He answers truthfully that he *does* want to get rich all at once; he does not admit the whole truth—that he wants terribly to bite the hand that feeds him and that if he can't get rich all at once, he'd rather starve. It's hard to say those things to one's conscience. Nastasya, at any rate, has made the normal blunder: Raskolnikov, because he felt guilty, hopeless, and helpless, has created a bad situation; now she makes him feel more guilty, hopeless, and helpless *because* of the situation. He will spend the next several chapters trying to answer her charge, trying to prove that he is of some use to someone and to himself. Yet anything Nastasya could say is trivial compared with the weight of guilt she carries into Raskolnikov's room in a letter from his mother.

This letter reveals many similarities between Raskolnikov and Marmeladov. At the same time, it has several more obvious functions. First, it gives the reader much essential information about the forces and events which have brought Raskolnikov to this tormented and murderous state of mind. It also introduces important characters for the rest of the book—Dunia, Luzhin, Svidrigaylov. Beyond this, it has a vital dramatic effect: it not only explains Raskolnikov's past torments; it cruelly tightens these upon him, so impelling him toward the murder.

Raskolnikov has waited two months for this letter; he must expect some of its bad news. Knowing his mother, he must anticipate her self-sacrificing tone, some of her hidden accusations. Yet no doubt he hoped to be spared some of the disgrace, the coals of forgiveness this letter heaps upon him. In comparison, the Marmeladovs' techniques seem childish and clumsy. Like Marmeladov's wife, Raskolnikov's mother accuses everything around her; like Marmeladov, she can do this while using terms of overt approbation. With great finesse, she presents each item of accusation as praise for her son or blame for herself. Thus she never relinquishes a tone of saintly selflessness.

Though this is disguised as admiration for her son, she begins with a demand that he take immediate action, since all depends on him:

> you are our only hope of a better and brighter future.

Then, pretending to accuse herself, she confronts him with his past failures:

> You can't imagine what I felt when I learned that you had left the university some months ago because you hadn't the means to keep yourself and that you had lost your lessons and had no other resources.

Next, apparently excusing her inability to help him, though actually pointing to *his* failure to help *her,* she makes a long list of the debts she and Dunya have incurred for him: she, by borrowing against her widow's pension; Dunya, by borrowing against her wages as the Svidrigaylovs' governess. As a result, she has lived in great hardship, while Dunya has been subjected to the brutalities, then the lustful advances of Svidrigaylov, and finally to his wife's slander. Both debts have been traps; both were contracted for Raskolnikov's sake.

Having reminded him of these past sacrifices, she turns to reveal their new plans: Dunya is now to marry Peter Luzhin, a civil councillor. The duplicity of the mother's tone is especially useful here. Beneath her open defense of Luzhin, she conveys sharp distaste:

> It is true he is forty-five years old, but . . . I daresay women might still find him attractive. He is altogether a highly respectable and dignified man, though perhaps a little morose and overbearing. But quite possibly that is only the first impression he makes on people . . . He said a lot more, for he seems a little vain and he likes people to listen to him, but this is hardly a vice.

If she really wanted to reassure her son, she would scarcely think out loud so often or so pointedly; neither would she make it so clear that she expects him to object to Luzhin:

> And, please, Roddy dear, I must ask you not to judge him too hastily and too heatedly when you meet him . . . as I'm afraid you're all too likely to do . . . I'm saying this, dear, just in case, for I'm quite sure that he will make a good impression on you. And besides to get to know any man properly one must do it gradually . . .

There could scarcely be a surer way to set two men against each other. Again, she conveys a complete lack of hope for happiness in the marriage:

> There is of course no special love either on her side or on his, but Dunya is a clever girl and as nobleminded as an angel, and she will consider it her duty to make her husband happy, and he too will probably do his best to make her happy, at least we have no good reason to doubt it, though I must say the whole thing has happened rather in a hurry.

Raskolnikov's mother goes on immediately to demonstrate that she has very good "reason to doubt it." She knows perfectly well Luzhin's motive in this marriage:

> even before meeting Dunya he had made up his mind to marry some honest girl who had no dowry . . . for, as he explained, a husband should never be under any obligation to his wife for anything, . . . it seemed just to have slipped out in the course of the conversation, so that later he even tried to correct himself and make it sound much nicer.

She is aware, and makes her son aware, that Dunya is being sold into a hopeless slavery where she will be ruled by debt to Luzhin. Not only does the mother expect Dunya to be wretched; she expects no better herself:*

> it would perhaps be much better if I lived on my own after their wedding . . . I am quite sure he will be so nice and considerate as to ask me himself to live with them so as not to be separated from my daughter and that, if he has said nothing about it so far, it is simply because no other arrangement has even occurred to him.

Both she and Dunya, then, are to be sacrificed once more. And she leaves no room for doubt as to where to place the blame for this:

> He has been practising law for many years and . . . he may, therefore, . . . be very useful to you, too, in lots of ways; in fact, Dunya and I have already decided that even now you could start on your career . . . We have even ventured to drop a few words about it to Mr. Luzhin . . . We, of course, were very careful not to say anything about . . . our great hopes that he would help us to advance you some money for your university studies . . . or about your becoming his partner.

This is, in itself, quite enough threat to Raskolnikov's conscience. His sense of indebtedness is already almost unbearable; this new plan will

---

*This is the only detail which I have displaced from its original place in the letter's sequence.

hurl him far deeper still. Worse, there is no faintest hope that this scheme could work. His mother knows this; she lets him know it:

> he did immediately express some doubts as to whether your university studies would leave you much time for work at his office . . . in spite of Mr. Luzhin's present quite understandably evasive attitude . . . Dunya is firmly convinced that she will be able to arrange everything.

The briefest reflection, or the briefest glimpse of Luzhin, would convince anyone of the plan's patent folly. Small wonder Raskolnikov will cry out in the next chapter, "Are they blind, both of them, or don't they notice anything on purpose? And how pleased they are!" He suspects they have chosen a bad plan deliberately to bring down more dependency and guilt upon him; intended or not, that will be the plan's effect. He feels he has already been trapped into debt to his mother and sister; now they, and he through them, are to be indebted to Luzhin. And Luzhin clearly *is* all those things Raskolnikov suspects (rightly or wrongly) about his family—an underhanded tyrant who rules others through the debts he can collect against them.

The marriage arrangements completed, Luzhin has sent for Dunya and Mrs. Raskolnikov to come to St. Petersburg, though giving the barest minimum of help, to humiliate them. (He later recognizes this as his greatest blunder; if he had given them money, he could have controlled them.)* Their imminent arrival is perhaps the worst news of all for Raskolnikov; he will have to face these two women who have been willingly injured by him, and who now seem intent on suffering more for him, deepening the guilt he is frantic to escape. A mere letter from them has brought him all the blame he can bear, not only of the sorts sketched above, but a whole battery of unconscious and disguised reproaches:

*Part V, Chapter 1.

not only do I hate the idea of being in any way a burden to anyone, but I myself want to be entirely independent so long as I still have something to live on, and such children as you and Dunya.

The letter closes, then, with a hint at the fearfulness of Dunya's sacrifice and (as at its beginning) a reminder that all depends upon Raskolnikov:

Love Dunya, Roddy. Love your sister. Love her as she loves you, and remember she loves you very much, much more than herself. She is an angel, and you, Roddy, are all we have in the world, our only hope of a better and brighter future. If only you are happy, we shall be happy.

Small wonder that he hates them both; that he is more wretched than ever, rushing out into the streets "muttering and even talking aloud to himself, to the astonishment of the passersby, many of whom thought he was drunk."

The parallel to Marmeladov is clear and extensive, even to the suggestion of drunkenness. Raskolnikov, too, is being destroyed by accumulated guilt and debt to his dependents, again an older and a younger woman. Marmeladov sold his sick wife's shawl and stockings for drink; Raskolnikov accepted an advance on the pension of his sick and aging mother. Sonia became a prostitute to support the Marmeladovs, so filling the gap of her father's failure; thereupon he, refusing her help, took her earnings for drink. Similarly, Dunya has just escaped a position very like prostitution (governess to the Svidrigaylovs), only to be sold into something even nearer prostitution (marriage to Luzhin); Raskolnikov, refusing to be helped, has left the university and given up his pupils. Both men have refused any intermediate position; if they cannot support their family, they will hang helplessly upon them until they drag them to the ground. At least one of them has deliberately set the standard of success impossibly high so he could retain failure and the position of the dependent child.

This letter, then, clearly relates Raskolnikov and his mother to

Marmeladov and his wife; the mother makes implicitly (and so, much more threateningly) the open accusations of the wife. When he saw Marmeladov beaten by his wife, Raskolnikov must have imagined—and perhaps wished—himself beaten by his mother. But this letter suggests a far more frightening resemblance of the mother to the landlady, Pashenka, and so finally to the pawnbroker, Alyona Ivanovna. For if Raskolnikov has intentionally picked Alyona Ivanovna to stand in the image of Pashenka, he has picked both to stand in the image of his mother. They form a triumvirate of old women, each a widow, each accompanied by a younger woman. From each Raskolnikov has asked and received something; to each he is indebted. They hold his spirit as a pledge. They seem to him tormentors, since it is on their account that he torments himself. When Raskolnikov strikes down the pawnbroker with an ax, he will strike at Pashenka; but he will also strike behind her at the image of his greatest creditor, his mother. Good reason then that, later in the book, when he is ready to face the police and confess to murdering the pawnbroker, but meets instead his mother, alive and ready to accuse him not only for his past failures, but for this new stroke against her as well, he will fall in a dead faint. Good reason, too, that when he recovers and she offers to sit up beside him that night, he cries, "Don't torture me!"

His mother's letter brings Raskolnikov to a very low point—very near the murder. Yet, several torments remain before he will be ready for that. They are provided in Chapter 4. All of Raskolnikov's actions in this chapter seem quite trivial in themselves, but by now very small things can tip the scale. By the end of this chapter he will be ready to turn his back on sanity and kindliness.

The first of his added torments, as he wanders through the streets talking to himself, are self-torments. Her letter has left him in a surprising rage against his mother:

Oh, the cunning woman, . . . Is it possible that her conscience is secretly pricking her for agreeing to sacrifice her daughter to her son? Are they blind both of them, or don't they notice anything on purpose? . . . Well, of course mother can't help being the person she is, but Dunya . . .

Again, he has already commented on Dunya:

No, dear Dunya . . . the ascent to Golgotha is certaintly not so easy. No.

which tacitly compares her with Marmeladov and his ludicrous desire to be crucified. No doubt he is enraged by the accusations buried in the letter, yet even more by his suspicion that they have intentionally planned a bad match so that he will be responsible, so either forcing him to save them, or else proving once and for all what misery he has brought upon them. If true, this would indicate a strong familial resemblance between the techniques of mother and son.

Yet, whatever his suspicions, Raskolnikov's rage is chiefly turned against himself in torments which are only aggravated by his rage against his family:

he kept torturing himself, tormenting himself with these questions, and he seemed even to derive some pleasure from it. Still, all these questions were not new, nor did they . . . occur to him just at that moment; they were old, old questions, questions that had long worried him.

In just the way that his wife's beating had two opposed purposes for Marmeladov, Raskolnikov's worrying has two such purposes. First, it is a punishment for the debts his inaction has already collected. At the same time, it prevents him from taking any action; it is as much a way of "stalling" as is his daydreaming. Clearly, it is collecting new guilt even faster than it can pay off the old:

It was clear that he ought not now to brood or to suffer passively, to waste his time in idle thoughts about how impossible it was to solve those questions, but that he had to do something at once and quickly, too. He had

162

to make up his mind at all costs, do something, anything, or—"Or renounce life altogether!"

"To suffer passively"—that is the crucial accusation. He must no longer rationalize, worry, lie about his room daydreaming of riches or revenge. The background filled in by the letter, Nastasya's accusations, his mother's demands, her coming visit, the impending marriage—all lay on Raskolnikov the need for some immediate action. He has reached one crucial decision:

While I'm alive this marriage will not take place, and to hell with Mr. Luzhin . . . I don't want your sacrifice, Dunya! . . . mother! It shall not be, as long as I live.

He will not permit them to aggravate his debt to them. But this only leads him to a greater dilemma:

He suddenly recollected himself and stopped. . . . It shall not be? And what can you do to prevent it? Will you forbid it? What right have you to do that? What can you promise them in return, to lay claim to such a right? To devote all your future, all your life to them *after* you have finished your course at the university and got yourself a job? We've heard that before, old chap! Those are only words. But what now? You simply have to do something now, do you understand that? And what are you doing now? You're robbing them. . . . How are you going to protect them from the Svidrigaylovs or from Vakrushin, you future millionaire . . .

Once again, he feels unable. It seems absurd to give lessons to children, work at odd jobs, or do translations as does Razumikhin;* that would not begin to cover the debt he feels. But if he rejects these ordinary accomplishments, then the demand for extraordinary achievement is only the greater. He must "get rich all at once." Besides, his refusal to work at some such ordinary job makes his actual need for money (as opposed to his feeling of need for action)

*This becomes explicit only at the beginning of the next chapter, Chapter 5.

163

more severe. He dare not sit out the game any longer; yet he dare not play, either, for he has made the stakes too high to dare any loss.

He has, moreover, lost confidence in himself. Because of his past failures, he now feels not only unable to solve his personal problems, but unworthy to perform any good act. "What right have you to do that?" he asks over and over. This phrase, with its many paraphrases, holds his deepest sense of degradation. All "good" acts are being removed from him; he has no "right" to perform one. Yet if he cannot find one, he must

"renounce life altogether!" he suddenly cried . . .

Immediately upon the heels of that thought comes the recollection of the man who *has* renounced life altogether, who seeks his own destruction:

"Do you realize, . . . sir, what it means when you have nowhere to go to?" he suddenly recalled the question Marmeladov had asked him the night before.

This comparison of himself to Marmeladov is so anguishing that his mind must blot it out, replace it with something at least less painful. That less painful thought is the murder:

Suddenly he gave a start; a thought flashed through his mind, a thought that had also occurred to him the day before . . . he knew, he *felt* that it would most certainly cross his mind and was already waiting for it . . . it was only a dream, but in a sort of new, terrifying and completely unfamiliar guise, and he himself suddenly realized it. The blood rushed to his head and everything went black before his eyes.

Raskolnikov replaces the image of himself as Marmeladov, then, with the image of himself as murderer; and finds a relief in that; if he cannot see himself as good, then he must either see himself as nothing ("renounce life altogether") or else see himself as evil. The latter, of course, is less agonizing. He nearly faints trying to escape the mere thought of the murder; yet, the more horrible that thought, the better;

for his mind must use this violence both to discharge his accumulated rage and to refute its own cruellest accusation of Marmeladov-like passivity and nothingness.

Yet he has one chance to rescue himself. He is on the Horse Guards' Boulevard, giddy with horror; as he tries to clear his vision and stagger toward a seat, he becomes involved in an episode with a drunken teen-aged girl. This episode—at first puzzling and apparently out of place—is of very highest importance. It is Raskolnikov's last opportunity to save his self-respect. When it fails, he will feel that he has no choice but to seek an active evil. First, his refusal to help this girl has a passive destructiveness which casts a new light on his past actions, a light anything but flattering to him; second, it is a step nearer an active destructiveness. For the first time, his feelings of helpless self-hatred will turn toward an open viciousness toward others.

This scene on the boulevard is one of a closely related series running through the novel, which involve either Raskolnikov or Svidrigaylov (in many ways, Raskolnikov's *alter ego*) with younger girls, especially girls who have some air of sexual degradation. These scenes are specially significant as indexes to Raskolnikov's or Svidrigaylov's current view of the world and especially in exploring their ambiguous attitude toward degradation. Many of these scenes will spring into the reader's mind with ease: Raskolnikov with Sonia; Svidrigaylov with Katya, with his fiancée, with Dunya. There are two scenes, however, so closely related to this one, that I want to interrupt the natural flow of the narrative to discuss them before returning to this episode on the boulevard.

I want first to recall that scene near the end of the book where Svidrigaylov, having finally given up Dunya, is sleeping drunkenly in a little attic room, very much like Raskolnikov's attic. There, he suffers three evil and tormented dreams, each more terrifying and archetypal than the one before. In the first, a mouse runs about over his body beneath his clothes. In the second, he sees the coffined body of a young girl he must have sexually assaulted long ago, so causing her suicide. The third dream (after he *thinks* he has wakened) is a close variation of the scene on the Horse Guards Boulevard—Svidrigaylov finds a five-year-old girl who, after being beaten, has fallen asleep on the stairs. Picking her up, he takes her to his room and tenderly puts her to bed. Seeing the feverish flush of her face, he thinks she is drunk, but suddenly decides instead, "It was lust, it was the face of a whore, the shameless face of a French whore." We had not imagined that the old roué, Svidrigaylov, so detested lust, that his libertinism (as revealed in the second dream) rises so directly from his Puritanism, his accusation of the world as evil (as revealed in the final dream). The order of his dreams strongly suggests that Svidrigaylov's own evil is produced directly by his vision of the world as evil. (Similarly, Raskolnikov will kill when he decides the world is too evil to be coped with except by evil.) As he tries to strike the little girl, Svidrigaylov *does* wake, horror-stricken, then goes out at once and shoots himself.

Against this series of nightmares, I want to contrast that scene, much earlier, where Raskolnikov, after the murder and his subsequent illness, goes into the streets looking for company and makes his first steps toward redemption. First, he gives some money to a fifteen-year-old street singer. This is the first of his two "successful" attempts to be charitable; the second happens only when he is on the way to the police station to confess at the end of the novel. (Throughout Part I, Raskolnikov is unable to perform a "successful" charity; he must first have reached some sort of peace with himself and so with the people around him.) Having given the money to the street singer, he tries to start conversations with passersby, then goes to a tavern, looks at a young prostitute named Duklida and says, "What a pretty face." When he gives her some money, he hears her shamed for begging by an older prostitute with a "bruised face and swollen upper lip." He moves at once to his first affirmation: "Live under any circumstances —only to live!"

Let me return, then, to the scene on the Horse Guards Boulevard. Svidrigaylov is specially pertinent here, since at this very moment Raskolnikov is reacting to his first knowledge of him: in her letter, his mother had mentioned him as Dunya's persecutor. He has already asked himself, "How are you going to protect them from the Svidrigaylovs . . . you future millionaire. . . ." Now he introduces the name, himself, into the scene: when he first sees the fat dandy approaching the drunken teen-ager, who has apparently been raped already and then turned loose on the streets, Raskolnikov rushes at him calling, "Hey you! Svidrigaylov! What do you want here?" He obviously identifies the girl, whom he wants to help, with Dunya. Moreover, he *is* able to help her, at least with the aid of the elderly policeman who shortly arrives. Raskolnikov gives the policeman twenty copecks, telling him to get a cab and take the girl home. Suddenly, however, as the policeman is about to do this, Raskolnikov makes a shocking about-face:

> in an instant he became quite a different man. "I say! Hey, there!" he shouted after the policeman . . . "Leave them alone! It's not your business! Let them be! Let him . . . have his fun!"

Once again, he feels:

> Who am I to help her? Have I any right to help anyone? Let them devour each other alive for all I care. What business is it of mine? And what right had I to give away the twenty copecks? They weren't mine, were they?

On the verge of absurdity, he complains that the policeman "walked off with my twenty copecks." From this, he goes on to try to justify his about-face on the "modernistic" grounds that

> It's essential . . . that such a percentage should every year go—that way —to the devil—It's essential so that the others should be kept fresh and healthy and not be interfered with.

Once again he has failed to help; he believes (at least consciously) that this is because he has no money of his own, is dependent. Yet we must not too readily accept his evaluation of the situation. Something is very odd here; after all, Raskolnikov *was* able to help this girl; may even have helped against his will.

The problem of the twenty copecks is a distraction. If Raskolnikov had wanted to help, he could have done so nearly as well without any money at all. Money is hardly the only kind of help, for this girl or anyone else. Raskolnikov himself gets his greatest help from Razumikhin, Porfiry, and Sonia; not one of them offers him a cent. Those characters in the novel who give money to others often injure them with it, and sometimes intentionally: Raskolnikov feels injured by advances of money from his mother, his landlady, the pawnbroker; Svidrigaylov offers money to nearly everyone he meets, but no one dares accept it for fear of being in debt to him; worse, Luzhin again and again "helps" people with money by which he quite consciously intends to trap them—as already noted, he openly defines this as his best strategy. The most extreme example of that, of course, is the gift Luzhin makes to Sonia for no other purpose than to call her a thief.

One could almost sum up this novel as a structure of financial and emotional debts which some try to pay off with charities, others with self-punishments. The charities of Raskolnikov and Svidrigaylov may not be so malevolent as those of Luzhin, yet their motives are badly mixed, and show little real concern for the person supposedly helped. Has Raskolnikov, really, any care for the needs of the girl on the boulevard? Any more than Svidrigaylov has for Dunya's? Not really. All Svidrigaylov wants of Dunya is her virtue—if she loves him, or will submit to him, or even only accept his money, that may prove once and for all that he is not evil—or so he hopes. Similarly, Raskolnikov is using this teen-aged girl to answer the accusations of Nastasya and his mother, to raise his self-appraisal.

The problem for him is that a gift of money may not only fail to help the receiver, but the giver as well. The selfishness is not, in itself, so terribly damaging; the act fails because of its essential displacement. Both Raskolnikov and Svidrigaylov try to use their money in one area to solve a problem which lies elsewhere. Svidrigaylov wants to buy off his conscience; yet even if Dunya should accept his money, his love, his bed, that could not cancel the debt he feels to his wife, to his servant John, to the young girl he must have assaulted. Similarly, Raskolnikov must know that he is demanding an unreasonable return from whatever investment he might make in this teen-aged girl. Since she is only symbolically related to Dunya and his mother, he can do nothing for her which will *drastically* alter his self-evaluation. Yet he needs something drastic, wants "to get rich [emotionally] all at once." So he must realize that this charity is doomed to failure and abandons it and the girl together.

Yet this does not fully account for his turning against the girl; surely not for the viciousness with which he does so. I have suggested that Raskolnikov has failed because of a feeling of shame and guilt, of helplessness and dependency, because of a lack of self-confidence. These are all true, yet there may also be reasons less flattering; he may have encouraged himself to fail. He identifies this drunken girl with Dunya; he wants to help both. He does not help either and claims that this is because he is not able, does not have the right. Yet in this case, that is clearly a rationalization; he has both the right and the ability. This strongly suggests that his past statements have also been rationalizations; that he could have helped Dunya or his mother if he had really wanted to. He knows that by dismissing his students and dropping out of the university, he has injured his family. Perhaps that is why he has done so; like Marmeladov, he has found a way not merely of "passive suffering," but of passively injuring his family when he has a grudge against them. In the way he offers help to this young girl (as to his family), he must be reenacting a part of the way he feels he has been mistreated. By such a method of revenge, he could not only hurt his family, but in the very same act punish himself for so doing, while gaining the secondary benefits of self-pity. This would account, also,

169

for his terrible isolation: those energies which should have been directed outward into ordered action have been withheld and withdrawn, but then have turned against him as self-violence in punishment for his passivity.

To have helped this girl, then, might have worsened his view of himself by questioning his past actions. Again, his conscience has driven him the wrong way: he feels so very guilty that he must continue acting badly or else admit that he *has* been wrong. He has not the basic sense of worth which would let him admit to any particular wrong act. It seems less painful to carry on the tendencies, the self-definition, already started. So he tells the policeman, "It's not your business . . ." just as he has already told himself "It's not your business" whether you pay your landlady, whether you help your family out of their troubles. Yet, in one sense, this episode differs from anything earlier. This is not mere passive destructiveness like giving up his lessons; this has an element of active viciousness. Raskolnikov, trying to escape the figure of Marmeladov, driven to "do something, anything," has made a first step toward that very man he detests and wishes to attack—Svidrigaylov.

He has refused, then, an act whose performance was of greatest importance to his view of himself and of his world. Svidrigaylov would have given the inverted Puritanical rationale that the girl was evil anyway, hence a proper victim; Raskolnikov gives, instead, the "modernistic" rationale that a certain percentage must "go . . . to the devil anyway." This is only a disguised statement of his own (self-encouraged) weakness: i.e., I am helpless to prevent suffering, therefore I may as well join the persecutors, so as to have *some* active role, some escape from being nothing. Later, he will expand this rationale of "scientific percentage" into the "modernist" and "scientific" justification of the murder of Alyona Ivanovna. He now claims that he has not "any right to help anyone . . . to give away twenty copecks," that he is powerless to act in the direction of good; he will shortly commit a hideous murder in a desperate hope of proving that he *has* "the right to possess power"; a power which, he thinks, can only act for evil. Further, just as he did with the pawnbroker, Raskolnikov has tricked the girl on the boulevard so that he can claim that *she* has injured *him* by taking his money. This, in some absurd way, seems to excuse his attempt to injure her. What we have, then, in the boulevard scene, is really a second, and much more dangerous, rehearsal of the murder.

Yet this moment on the very brink of despair is relieved by a single, momentary ray of light and sanity. Raskolnikov suddenly asks himself a singularly pertinent question:

"And where am I going to?" he thought suddenly. "Curious! I came out for something. Came out as soon as I had read the letter. Oh, yes, I was going to Vasilyevsky Island to call on Razumikhin. That's it."

If he had planned to visit Razumikhin, we had not known it; perhaps he had not known it, himself. Yet, after reading his mother's letter, that is clearly what he *should* do. Razumikhin can help him to repair and replace his clothing, get some lessons or translations; can, in general, help him to a practical approach to his difficulties.

Razumikhin's function as a contrast to (and relief from) Raskolnikov is obvious. He has all the external problems of Raskolnikov; none of the internal ones. He, too, has had to leave the university for lack of money. He, however, has responded directly, taking whatever work he could find, then doing it happily and well until he could resume his studies. Both strong and intelligent, he has "managed to keep himself without any outside assistance whatever," so owes no one and has not complicated his problems. He never takes "any of his failures to heart;" has never demanded more of the world than it gives and so has no desire to see himself as a martyr. Again, not demanding much from the world, he does not hear it demanding so much in return; his conscience remains free and untroubled. Simple, frank and outgoing: when angry, he knocks someone down; when chagrined, he bangs his fist into the stove; when spreeing, he is liable to fell policemen. Unlike Raskolnikov, he is "extraordinarily cheerful and com-

171

municative" and even Raskolnikov finds it "hardly possible to be on any but friendly terms with Razumikhin." Above all, he knows who he is, what he wants, what he stands for, and preserves in himself that "sense of dignity" which Raskolnikov so desperately needs.

The names of the two characters tend to define them: "Raskolnikov" suggests that which is divided, either the schismatic in religion (the heretic or "Old Believer") or the schizoid in personality. "Razumikhin" suggests reason, reasonability, efficiency, and practicality, the very qualities he both preaches and exhibits. We may also note that Razumikhin lives on Vasilyevsky Island and that Raskolnikov finds himself headed in that direction at this moment. Vasilyevsky Island is the home of the University, the Academy of Arts, and the Academy of Sciences*; it must have stood in the minds of most Russians as the very center of enlightenment, culture, and reason. It is precisely the place, as Razumikhin is the man, Razkolnikov should seek in these difficulties.

As Chapter 5 opens, however, we discover that Razumikhin has been introduced only to suggest what Raskolnikov is turning against. Even the thought of visiting him suggests to Raskolnikov's bitter and tormented brain "some ominous meaning." It would mean to give up being bitter and tormented, to reverse his strategy and, to some degree, overhaul his personality. It must seem to Raskolnikov, just as it often seemed to Dostoievsky, that the very bases of his personality lay in the unreasonable and cranky; to give up those qualities might, he fears, also make him nothing. It would surely deprive him of the great triumph which he has imagined would prove once and for all his transcendent worth and buy off his conscience:

> Suppose (Razumikhin) does get me some lessons, suppose he even shares his last penny with me, . . . so that I could buy myself a pair of boots and mend my clothes to be able to give lessons, what then? What shall I do with

*Cf. Jessie Coulson's Introduction to her own translation of *Crime and Punishment,* Oxford University Press, 1953.

my few coppers afterwards? Is that what I want? . . . did I really think of putting everything right . . . a solution of all my difficulties in Razumikhin?

Nothing small or partial will do—Raskolnikov is nothing if not proud. He has put off his visit too long; to go now to Razumikhin would mean admitting he has been wrong, must accept other men's way out of his dilemma. He knows that eventually he *must* go to reason and to Razumikhin ("I shall call on Razumikhin, of course") . . . Yet, to save his pride, he must first "solve" his own problem his own way:

> I shall call on him . . . on the day after I've *done* it, after *that* [the murder] has been settled, and when everything is different.

This, in its way, is true enough—he *will* go to Razumikhin after the murder; further, Razumikhin (and reason) will then visit *him*. Again, after the murder everything will be different, yet Raskolnikov must suspect even now that in a more crucial sense everything will be just the same. Nonetheless, he has made his decision. He jumps up, crying, "Will it really happen?" His answer comes, very fittingly, as a nightmare.

So far, in the first four chapters, Dostoievsky has investigated his hero through a few highly significant bits of action and by means of comparisons and contrasts. At the same time, he has laid the groundwork for all the book's structure* by introducing all the important secondary characters, excepting only Porfiry Petrovich, the chief inspector, who obviously cannot enter until after the murder. We have met first, Marmeladov, the key secondary figure of Part I: he has shown to Raskolnikov his own passive masochism, a revelation which, as I have said, is crucial in driving Raskolnikov toward violence. We have also met, though at second hand, Razumikhin, who will step in after the murder and dominate Part II, bringing Raskol-

*A stimulating study by Edward Wasiolek, "On the Structure of *Crime and Punishment*," appeared in the March 1959 issue of PMLA.

nikov to the very verge of confession and redemption. In the letter, we have met Raskolnikov's mother and sister, who will appear just when he is ready to confess (at the end of Part II); they, together with other "accusers"—Porfiry Petrovich and that unnamed workman who calls Raskolnikov "Murderer!"—will hurl Raskolnikov back into the terrible depths of Parts III and IV. We have been told about the book's one true saint, Sonia, and its one true villain, Luzhin—the two characters who will struggle and exert such strong and opposite attractions upon Raskolnikov through Parts IV and V. Finally, we have met Svidrigaylov, who will oppose Porfiry Petrovich as a father-figure in the struggle for Raskolnikov's soul in Part VI. Oddly enough, Svidrigaylov's influence will ultimately be for the good, showing as he so graphically does, the self-destructive agony that falls on the man who tries to explain away his guilt, who will not confess. At the end of the novel proper, the police will hear of Svidrigaylov's death and of Raskolnikov's confession almost at the same moment.

Dostoievsky has planted the seeds, then, from which most of the novel must grow. He has made a preliminary exploration of Raskolnikov and of his torments. Now, after one brief respite, one glimpse of Razumikhin and rationality, he is ready to plunge into the depths of Raskolnikov's agonized mind, into his nightmare of himself. Turning his back on Vasilyevsky Island and on Razumikhin, Raskolnikov has fallen, characteristically, into a deep but troubled sleep. If we have had one momentary ray of light and sanity, the darkness which follows will only be the darker for that.

Raskolnikov's dream may be briefly summed up (with none of its overwhelming horror): Raskolnikov, a boy of seven, is walking with his father to the little church and cemetery where his grandmother and younger brother are buried. On the way they must pass a tavern which has an ominous atmosphere. Out of it, a group of artisans and their women swarm, climbing into a cart which belongs to one of them named Mikolka. Attached to this cart is a weak little old mare which they jeer, curse, and whip, trying to force her into a gallop. When the mare can scarcely pull them, they become wild with rage, dancing about and beating her with whips and sticks. Mikolka, infuriated, kills her with an iron bar. After trying futilely to stop them, the young Raskolnikov finally "put[s] his arms round her dead, blood-stained muzzle and kisse[s] . . . her . . . eyes . . ." Then he suddenly "rushe[s] in a rage at Mikolka with his little fists," but is caught and restrained by his father. When he tries to cry out, he wakens.

Like many dreams, this one has day remnants which offer hints about its meaning; further, these motifs in the dream may carry on into the later development of the novel. Carts, for instance, like trunks and taverns, have considerable textural importance throughout the book. Raskolnikov will later pass through the gates of his victim's house hidden behind one; after the murder, he will very nearly walk under the wheels of a carriage, and will be beaten by its driver who believes (correctly, I think) that he did it on purpose; later Marmeladov *will* fall under the carriage and find there his own death.

We are now more concerned, however, with the carts Raskolnikov has already encountered during the day, those carts from which this dream-cart must derive. Reading that his mother and Dunya would be driven to the railway station in a peasant's cart, he had recalled that he himself used to drive such a cart. Again, we have already noted the scene in Chapter 1 where Raskolnikov was shouted at by a drunkard in an empty cart, "Hey, you there, German hatter!"

That episode first introduced the element of ridicule which in later scenes would be pointed so strongly at Marmeladov and Raskolnikov. The tavern loungers and the neighbors who had jeered at Marmeladov, the wife who beats him, the drunkard who shouted at Raskolnikov, Nastasya with her convulsive laughter—in the dream all are transformed into the mob that swarms, jeering, from the tavern to drive and beat the poor old horse. From this viewpoint, then, the horse represents both Raskolnikov and Marmeladov, being jeered, beaten, and finally killed because they cannot pull the load of their families.

Raskolnikov's dream has reminded him how he, as a little boy

> always liked watching those huge dray-horses with their long manes and thick legs, walking leisurely, with measured steps, and drawing a whole mountain behind them, but without the slightest strain, as though they found it so much easier going with carts than without carts. But now, curiously enough, some peasant's small, lean, greyish-brown mare was harnessed to one of these huge carts, the sort of poor old nag which—he had seen it so often—found it very hard to draw quite an ordinary cart with wood or hay piled on top of it, especially when the cart was stuck in the mud or in a rut, and every time that happened, the peasant flogged her so brutally, sometimes even across the eyes and muzzle, and he felt so sorry, so sorry for the poor old horse that he almost burst into tears, and his mother always used to take him away from the window.

I take this to be a description, first, of the ever-capable Razumikhin (who was introduced only a short time before the dream); then, a description of Raskolnikov, the thin, little feeble mare who "doesn't earn his keep" and is "stuck in the mud." In part, then, the nightmare shows Raskolnikov to himself as a man who simply cannot (or thinks he cannot) pull the huge, vulgar load laid on him and is being derided and beaten because of it. All he can do is to kick with impotent rage at his tormentors. Good reason, then, that when he wakes from his dream, "Every bone in his body seem[s] to ache" and "his eyes [are] burning." He wakes with the physical sensations of having actually undergone the beating he has dreamed of, and which he has been undergoing, emotionally, for many months.

Yet, the dream not only interprets the past where he sees himself as helpless and injured; it also predicts the future, where he hopes to see himself filled with injurious power. His recollection that he used to drive a peasant's cart, like the one his mother and sister will take to the station, suggests that in the dream he may not be the horse, but the driver, Mikolka. Much evidence supports this reading. While the peasants are beating the little mare, someone shouts to Mikolka, "Why don't you strike her with an axe? Despatch her at once!" Like the pawnbroker woman, the old mare is sickly, feeble, and essentially inferior. Though outwardly respectable, she is actually parasitic and certainly "doesn't earn her keep"—in the next chapter, the young student will tell his officer friend that Alyona Ivanovna is "of no use to anyone." When he wakes, Raskolnikov himself immediately assumes that the dream *was* a vision of himself killing her:

> Good God! . . . is it possible that I will really take a hatchet, hit her on the head with it, crack her skull, slither about in warm, sticky blood, break the lock, steal and shake with fear, hide myself all covered in blood and with the hatchet—Good God! Is it possible?

He decides that it is not possible. Yet no one can miss the tone of delight with which he describes these horrors.

We may also note here, incidentally, that Nikolay the painter, who falsely confesses to the murder, is also occasionally called "Mikolka." In the dream, Raskolnikov, disguised as a workman named Mikolka, kills a horse symbolic of a pawnbroker woman; later a painter, also called Mikolka, and who also comes from Ryazan and is a Raskolnik, confesses to Raskolnikov's actual murder of that same woman.

Yet, if Mikolka is identified with Raskolnikov, and the old horse with the pawnbroker, we must not forget that the pawnbroker is always symbolically related to his landlady and his mother. Thus, in the dream, Raskolnikov may be seen to be beating Pashenka, and, more important, his mother. It is she who still pulls the family load, though too old and feeble to do so. It is she who is "just breaking his heart." We should notice the great emphasis upon beating the horse across the eyes; Raskolnikov feels particularly guilty about his mother's knitting shawls and cuffs at night; he fears she may go blind before he can help her. It is he who drives his mother and sister. In this aspect, the dream presents him to himself as already fearful and evil; this, in turn, must help lead him to more active evil in the future.

In one sense, then, Raskolnikov is the horse killed in his dream. In another, he is the brute who kills it. But he is also present in a much more obvious guise—as himself at seven years old. This interpretation is strengthened by several phrases in the dream which echo phrases in the previous episode (the scene on the Horse Guards Boulevard). When, in the earlier scene, he saw the dandy approaching the teen-aged girl,

> Raskolnikov rushed at him with his fists, without stopping to consider that the thick-set gentleman was a match for two men like himself.

Similarly, in the dream, the young Raskolnikov

> rushed in a rage at Mikolka with his little fists.

In the dream, the vision of himself as dependent and helpless is even more exaggerated than in the boulevard scene: he has now become a church-going little boy who must deal with hulking, vicious workmen. Once again the fact that he owns nothing is offered as proof of his helplessness: Mikolka rages, as he beats the mare, "My property . . . Mine . . . My property!" In his dream, Raskolnikov again has "no right to help." Yet this may be as much a hope and an excuse as a fear; having no rights, one has no responsibilities. Thus Raskolnikov need not help the mare—or the girl on the boulevard, or Dunya, or his mother. And though his dream credits him with a heroic attempt, he has been forcibly restrained—on the boulevard, by the policeman; in the dream, by his father who tells him:

> "Come along . . . they're drunk. Having fun, the fools. Come along and don't look. . . . Playing the fool. It's not our business."

This is a startling echo; on the boulevard, Raskolnikov had turned to the policeman and, at the very moment of his shocking change of heart, shouted almost the same words:

> "Leave them alone! It's not your business! Let them be! Let him . . . have his fun! What do you care?"

This echo, when one first notices it, can be misleading—one may be drawn into speculations about whether or not Raskolnikov may, in his childhood, have witnessed a scene like that in the dream, and have heard his father make such a comment. This is of no importance; even if such an event *had* occurred, that would neither excuse nor explain Raskolnikov's actions on the boulevard. To put his own words from that earlier scene into his father's mouth in the dream is, at best, a rationalization, an attempt to give his father's authority to the idea that he had "no right" to help, or to blame his own viciousness upon a supposed callousness in his father.

The deeper purpose of this echo is less simple and less flattering. Twice—once on the boulevard, once in the dream—Raskolnikov has refused help to someone and claimed it was not his business. Both claims are, themselves, echoes of his earlier statement about his own intimate affairs, his "business"—his rent, his debts, his clothing. He has claimed that they, too—those "matters that required his most immediate attention, . . . did not concern him at all." And here again, as in the dream or on the boulevard, the reason "he did not want to bother" about his own business is that this is the best way he can refuse help to others. Thus, these echoes lead us back, once again, to Raskolnikov's relation with his family. This explains why he is restrained from going to the aid of the horse in the dream—it partly represents his mother and sister, and he wishes them to be injured. This is the same factor which restrains the horse, insofar as it represents Raskolnikov himself, and makes him too weak and feeble to pull his cart—and then makes him so furious with himself for having injured others and himself, that he feels like thrashing himself to death.

It is very suggestive that Raskolnikov picks this particular phrase —that his affairs are none of his business—to explain his method of revenge. It makes possible a guess about his grudge against his mother, or at least about particular events which must have irritated and activated a resentment which must be very old and complicated.

179

The only hint we have of a specific grudge concerns Natalia Zarnit-syn, the landlady's invalid daughter, whom Raskolnikov had loved and contracted to marry. We learn of this affair only much later, when Raskolnikov is called to the police station because of his debts to Pashenka.* Still later, we learn that Raskolnikov's mother had apparently raised strong objections, and from her self-pitying account of the affair to Razumikhin, we may judge what tack she took with Raskolnikov:

"I could never rely on his character, not even when he was a boy of fifteen. . . . Why, to take something that happened only recently. I wonder if you know that only a year and a half ago he took it into his head to marry that girl—what was her name?—the daughter of Mrs. Zarnit-syn, his landlady—oh, it was an awful shock to me! . . . Do you think . . . my tears, my appeals, my illness or perhaps even my death from grief, or our poverty would have stopped him? He would have calmly stepped over all the obstacles. But surely, surely, he does care for us a little, doesn't he?"†

The marriage did not take place, apparently because of Natalya's death, and it is not possible to tell how much the mother's interference may have complicated matters. She plainly has acted very possessive and blameful and now feels anything but charitable:

"May God forgive me . . . but I couldn't help being glad when I heard of her death, though I don't know which of them would have ruined which . . ."

Raskolnikov apparently feels the loss of Natalya more than he likes to admit. He certainly resents the mother's possessive interference, the kinds of technique she has used against him. Watching the first awakenings of love between Dunya and Razumikhin, he suddenly breaks in, full of nostalgia and, though he tries to deny it, resentment:

*Part II, Chapter 1.
†Part III, Chapter 2.

".. . do you remember, mother, that I was in love and wanted to get married. . . . I really don't know why I was so attached to her at the time. Because she was always ill, I suppose. If she'd been lame or a hunchback I believe I'd have loved her better still." He smiled wistfully. "Yes,—a sort of spring madness."

"No, it wasn't only spring madness," Dunya said, warmly. . . . Then, completely absorbed in his thoughts, he got up, went up to his mother, kissed her, went back to his seat and sat down.

"You're still in love with her," said Mrs. Raskolnikov, touched.

"Her? Now? Oh, I see, you mean her? No. It's as if it never happened in this world at all. . . . And everything here seems to be happening quite in another world. . . . You, too, seem to be miles away."*

I am certainly not suggesting that Raskolnikov would have been happy with Natalya; there is every reason to think their marriage would have been just about like the Marmeladovs'. I am only pointing out that he must feel deprived of the management of his most intimate affairs, feel that his mother has made his life into her business, not his own. He, in revenge, has learned to frustrate her plans by refusing to "concern himself" with his own affairs. This also would account for the childish possessiveness of Mikolka in the dream. Raskolnikov has permitted the control of his life to pass out of his hands; recalling the incident of Natalya, he even gets up like a dutiful little boy, walks over and kisses his mother, then returns and sits down as if in a trance. Yet, however withdrawn he becomes, some part of his mind must be frantic with rage, must want to shout at her that these things are "Not your business!" that his affairs are "My property! . . . Mine . . . My property!" Thus, in the dreams, he beats his mother to death, mocking her all the while with her own possessiveness.

Further, Raskolnikov seems to have taken a similarly ironical method of revenge in using his mother's accusations: resenting her blamefulness, he sees to it that her worst reproaches come true. He has picked up her phrase that "he would have calmly stepped over all

*Part III, Chapter 3.

181

the obstacles" and has apparently decided to "show her"; his theory for the murder is built upon a claim that the superior man (himself) has a right to "step over certain obstacles," is even entitled "to step over a corpse or wade through blood, . . . to eliminate all obstacles"* if his conscience leads him to do so. We should also recall that Raskolnikov always acts worse under the influence of those who accuse him—his mother and sister, the workman who calls him "Murderer," the Porfiry who torments him, Svidrigaylov who insists on seeing a likeness between them. He can only confess to, and be saved by, those who respect him regardless of whatever evil he may have committed—Sonia, Polya Marmeladov, the changed Porfiry. Throughout the book, Raskolnikov tends to *become* what people tell him he already *is*.

But I have gone far from the dream; let me return to it. I am faced, now, with the problem of resolving these seemingly disparate readings. First of all, where is Raskolnikov in his dream? Is he the horse, the little boy, the father, or the brute Mikolka? The answer must be Yes. All of the characters of the dream are the dreamer. The problem is not to decide who is who, but rather to understand the dreamer's apprehension of the world and of himself.

In these broader terms, the dream's meaning is quite clear. The dream shows Raskolnikov to himself as a man too feeble in drawing his burdens, but entirely too strong in punishing himself for his weakness. He is stuck on a treadmill of guilt and rage where he beats himself to death for being stuck. All the energies which might have been used to pull his load are instead being used in a sort of drunken, joyous cruelty. The dream presents a world where all "good" characters are either weak or victimized. (The dream contains but disguises the fact that they have chosen their weakness or victimization.) Meantime, "the worst are full of passionate intensity." The only active role

*Part III, Chapter 5.

belongs to the destroyers. This dream, then, is a way for Raskolnikov to tell himself he must choose either murder or suicide.

Under this vision of his world and his alternatives lies the dream's sexual implications. This is clearly a "primal scene"—the child's view of the sex act. Jealous of the parents' relation and unwilling to see it in affectional terms, he is only too likely to create an image of the sex act suffused with the violence of his own emotions. To persuade oneself that the act of love consists of such cruelty can only warp one's view of the world as a whole. This has not previously concerned us because Part I shows us little of Raskolnikov's relations with women. On the other hand, this image of sex is of extreme importance in his sadomasochistic view of all human relations, the need to destroy or be destroyed.

If the dreamer is everywhere present in his dream, however, then Raskolnikov is not merely choosing between killing and being killed. If he is both Mikolka and the mare, then in some sense he is both killer and killed. Though he chooses the murder to externalize and be rid of his problem, he never succeeds in this—he is always basically identified with the pawnbroker he murders. We have already noted that he picked Alyona Ivanovna as exemplifying the worst qualities of his mother—debt collecting and tyranny. But we have also shown that he shares many of those qualities—especially the techniques of intentional mismanagement so as to blame others and collect debts against them. These are the qualities he wants to punish and annihilate in himself. Thus, he has chosen Alyona Ivanovna to stand not only as a scapegoat for his mother, but much more important, for himself. Though outwardly respectable because she earns a living, she is at least as much a parasite as he is. In Chapter 3, Nastasya had said that he was "of no use to himself or anyone else." In Chapter 5 which follows, the young student will tell his officer friend that the pawnbroker is "no use to anyone," and Raskolnikov will recognize this as a reflection of his own thoughts. In a world, then, where he sees no alternatives but murder or suicide, Raskolnikov has carefully picked out Alyona Ivanovna to take the punishment he feels he should level at himself. I return to my initial quotation from *Gravity and Grace* by Simone Weil:

> A hurtful act is the transference to others of the degradation which we bear in ourselves. That is why we are inclined to commit such acts as a way of deliverance.

The fact that Raskolnikov wakes with the assumption that the dream meant murder:

> Good God! . . . is it possible that I will really take a hatchet, hit her on the head . . .

instead of the only other alternative, suicide, indicates what choice he has made.

In the bases of his mind, then, he has reached the first of his two great decisions. He believes he has decided not to kill the pawnbroker; he is wrong. He is, in fact, unable to reach any conscious decision, for the unconscious areas have taken over in a desperate, though blind, effort to prove himself worthy of life. From this point on, he is less and less able to control or understand his actions. He cannot imagine why he goes home so indirectly, detouring through the Hay Market where he encounters Lisaveta, or why

> such a decisive, and, at the same time, such an entirely accidental meeting in the Hay Market (where he had no business to be at all) occurred just at that hour and even at that minute of his life. . . . It was as though it had happened on purpose, as though the meeting had been specially arranged for him!

It was. The meeting may be "entirely accidental" so far as Lisaveta's part in it is concerned. He, however, has deliberately placed himself where he could run into her. It is luck that he happens to find her today; but if not today, then sooner or later.

Having "accidentally" encountered Lisaveta, and "accidentally" learned that she will be away—and her sister home alone—the next evening at seven, Raskolnikov returned to his house and "entered his room like a man sentenced to death." For good reason; we have already seen how closely he identifies with his chosen victim.

> He thought of nothing, and indeed he was quite incapable of thinking; but he suddenly felt with all his being that he no longer possessed any freedom of reasoning or of will, and that everything was suddenly and irrevocably settled.

From this point on, he acts under compulsion; his conscious mind has yielded to forces it does not recognize. Thus we reach a great irony; in the murder, the very act meant to prove he is active, he feels entirely as if compelled by forces outside himself. The only act which could have felt "active" would be some direct action taking command of his problems. The murder itself is, in the long run, an act of the deepest passivity.

Even though the unconscious mind has gained control, the conscious mind must still be reckoned with, must be convinced that the murder is a proper act. Chapter 6, which is concerned with other preparations for the murder, demonstrates the workings of this most important preparation. At the same time, this permits us to investigate the motive which underlies all those motives we have discussed. Here, by revealing Raskolnikov's desire to make his preparations badly and get caught, his determination to blunder, Dostoievsky can lay the groundwork for Raskolnikov's second great decision—the decision to confess.

The conscious mind can be assuaged only by bringing the murder under some noble-sounding rationalization. The outlines of this rationalization are sketched in by a flashback where Raskolnikov recalls a student called Pokorev telling an Army officer that one might kill Alyona Ivanovna as a humanitarian project. He argues that he could:

> "gladly murder that damned old woman and rob her of all she has . . . kill her, take her money, and with its help devote [himself] to the service of

185

humanity and the good of all. Well, don't you think that one little crime could be expiated and wiped out by thousands of good deeds? . . . One death in exchange for a hundred lives—why it's a simple sum in arithmetic!"

When reminded that this is a matter of "human nature," not of arithmetic, he replies:

"even human nature can be improved and set on the right path, for otherwise we should all drown in a sea of prejudices. Otherwise there wouldn't have been a single great man."

Raskolnikov, also a student, recognizes in Pokorev his own thoughts. We meet this rationalization in its fuller form much later in the book, when Porfiry produces Raskolnikov's essay, *On Crime*. This essay recounts Pokorev's ideas of the humanitarian criminal, but greatly expands the idea, only suggested by Pokorev, of the superman. Raskolnikov argues in his article that men fall into two types: the vast, sluggish mass who must be led, as opposed to the "great" men, the leaders who try to improve mankind's lot, or at least do *something* with it. The supermen show themselves by their ability to step across any lines of already existing authority. The masses fear and mistrust them, may outlaw or even kill them. The superman must expect this and must yet dare, for if successful, he will become an object of veneration.

On first reading, one is surprised by this essay which seems to introduce a completely new motive for the murder; it is only the old motive inverted. Raskolnikov suspects that he is a sub-man, unworthy of notice, so invents a theory to prove himself superior to all, above authority; he suspects himself of being completely incapable of action, so invents a theory to prove himself capable of the grandest actions; he suspects himself of being a parasite upon his mother and sister, so invents a theory to prove himself a benefactor to all mankind.

Thus, at the end of this chapter when Raskolnikov has completed his preparations, we will see there the grotesque spectacle—by no means so uncommon as one could wish—of a man walking through

the public streets on his way to commit a hideous murder, but specu-
lating, as he goes, about what improvements he might make in the
public gardens when he comes into power:

> Walking past Yussupov Park, he became entirely absorbed in the question
> of improving its amenities by high-playing fountains, and he could not help
> thinking that they would improve the air in all the squares marvellously.
> Gradually he came to the conclusion that if the Summer Gardens were
> extended to Mars Square and even joined on the Mikhailovsky Palace
> Gardens, it would be a most wonderful improvement for the town.

Such a passage, of course, brings Raskolnikov into line with the heroes
of Dostoievsky's political novels, especially with Stavrogin and his
group of young revolutionaries in *The Possessed*. The characters of
both novels tend to be young people actually or effectively deprived
of fathers, tormented by newfound freedoms and inactivity, driven
into violence by unresolved guilts. Both are likely to confuse aimless
violence, rebelliousness, or criminality with political action.

Many writers have commented on Raskolnikov's relation to these
precursers of the Russian Revolution; few have noted, I think, how
Raskolnikov's story has become a parable and prediction of that
Revolution. The historical revolutionary, also, indulged himself in a
brief and highly sexualized orgy of murder and terror, wiping out a
few older people, most of them relatively useless though relatively
harmless. Then he sentenced himself and all his society to prison for
forty years or so. Only then could he feel free—of his guilts, of the
violence he too well knew he embodied. Raskolnikov' and his story
may indeed stand as exemplifying the history of revolutionaries and
their actions in the Western World ever since the French Revolution.

This is not to judge whether or not Raskolnikov might become a
statesman; he might very well make just such improvements as he
envisages. He seems more likely to dedicate himself to the welfare of
humanity than most politicians one can recall—revolutionary or conservative. His only serious miscalculation about his overstepping of

authority concerns his motive in so doing; he has no real intention of making such improvements. Yet he continually hovers about this truth. He recognizes that people in general may not seek such amenities:

> Why was it, he wondered, that in all the large cities people seemed inclined to congregate, not by any means out of sheer necessity, just in those parts where there were neither gardens nor fountains, but dirt, bad smells, and every kind of abomination?

Then he notices his own preference for poverty, even degradation:

> He then remembered his own walks in the Hay Market, and for a moment he seemed to wake up. "What silly nonsense!" he thought. "No, much better not to think of anything at all."

Better not indeed; he might recognize his own urge which is carrying him at this moment, not toward power and aggrandizement, but toward degradation and abasement.

This problem opens the motive basic to all those we have discussed. Once Raskolnikov's unconscious has convinced his conscious mind that murder is permissible, even noble, the conscious mind must set about making the physical preparations. Yet, even as it does so, it realizes that its chief problem will be to protect itself against the deeper motives of the unconscious mind—its desire that Raskolnikov should be caught:

> he had been greatly interested in the question why almost every crime was so easily solved . . . the main reason for it lay not so much in the physical impossibility of concealing a crime as in the criminal himself; the criminal himself, at least almost every criminal, is subject at the moment of the crime to a kind of break-down of his reasoning faculties and of his will-power, which are replaced by an amazingly childish carelessness just at the moment when he is most in need of caution and reason.

Raskolnikov knows, even before he commits the crime, that once again he will defeat himself. He knows, then, at some level of his mind, that he will be trying to get caught, that there is a purpose to his "childish carelessness." The only plausible purpose is a desire for punishment. Thus, before he ever commits the crime, he knows that he belongs, and wishes to belong, not to the class of "great men" who may overstep, but to the class of "ordinary" people who, should they ever mistake themselves for advanced people or "destroyers" and get out of hand,

> "you won't even have to employ anyone to thrash them—for, being extremely law-abiding by nature, they will thrash themselves: some of them will perform this service for one another, while others will administer the thrashing to themselves with their own hands. In addition, they impose all sorts of public penances upon themselves, and the result is both beautiful and edifying. In short, you needn't worry. It's a law of nature."*

It may well be asked what Raskolnikov hopes to gain from so severe a punishment. The answer, I think, may be divided into four parts. First, he needs to feel adequately punished for his past wrongs, cleared of the deep sense of shame which has dogged him throughout Part I. This sense of shame is so severe that, as René Fülop-Miller rightly observes, Raskolnikov has a nightmare in the Epilogue where he sees his own degradation as a great plague that spreads over and infects the whole European continent. He must somehow cleanse his view of himself and of his world. He later admits that he already knew that the sacrifice of Alyona Ivanovna, which was supposed to accomplish this, would fail:

> finally, I am a louse, . . . because I myself am perhaps worse and nastier than the louse I killed, and I knew *beforehand* that I would say that to myself *after* killing her!†

Yet, knowing this, he went on with the murder, for it was not really the murder, but its consequences which held out hope to him.

*Part III, Chapter 5.
†Part III, Chapter 6.

Second, he must want punishment as a proof that he is not negligible, like a child who would rather be whipped than ignored. In *The Need for Roots,* Simone Weil has written:

> Just as the only way of showing respect for somebody suffering from hunger is to give him something to eat, so the only way of showing respect for somebody who has placed himself outside the law is to reinstate him inside the law by subjecting him to the punishment ordained by the law.

And, in *The House of the Dead,* Dostoievsky himself has written of the convicts in the prison at Omsk:

> This general tone was apparent externally in a certain peculiar personal dignity of which almost every inmate of the prison was acutely conscious. It was as though the status of a convict, of a condemned prisoner, was a sort of rank, and an honourable one, too.

Punishment may be one form of respect, then; at best, it may show the criminal that those in authority still hold some hope for him; at worst, it shows him that he is enough of a person to have some effect, if only in angering those in authority.

Third, and as an extension of this, Raskolnikov must want a punishment which will force him into line with his own conscience. In a sense, his problem is to accept his mother's morality, while giving up her conflicting technique. Unsupported by any external force, his conscience's accusations are driving him to act always worse and worse. He must find an authority so overwhelming, even vicious, that he will have to knuckle under to it and stop, once and for all, his painful rebellion. Simone Weil, again, has written in *Gravity and Grace:*

> The powerful, if they carry oppression beyond a certain point, necessarily end by making themselves *adored* by their slaves. For the thought of being under absolute compulsion, the plaything of another, is unendurable for a human being. Hence, if every way of escape from this constraint is taken from him, there is nothing left for him to do but to persuade himself that

he does the things he is forced to do willingly, that is to say, to substitute *devotion* for *obedience.*

It is just such a devotion, such an obedience, that he desires; none other will assure him of being as good as he demands of himself. Thus, no leniency on the part of the state is tolerable. When, during his last interview, Porfiry Petrovich offers him a lighter sentence if he will confess, Raskolnikov at once replies that he does not want any reduction of sentence; Porfiry admits that he had suspected as much all along.*

Finally, Raskolnikov wants not only to be forcibly made a worthy citizen, but most especially he wants to be defined as a loved and worthy child in a God-centered, family-style universe. That universe must be founded upon moral law, and that moral law enforced by the fatherly punishing arm of the state. Raskolnikov is exactly like a child who deliberately disobeys to find out if the rules really exist, if behavior has limits, if his family lives inside solid walls. It is no use to ignore such disobedience, the child will only force attention, make his defiance conspicuous. He will not be happy until he has received the punishment, the assurance, that he wants. This explains Porfiry's emphasis, in the later chapters, on the idea of definition:

> "You see, if, for instance, I were to put my suspect under lock and key a little too soon, I may, as it were, lend him some moral support. . . . I'd give him, as it were, a definite status, I'd, as it were, satisfy him psychologically and set his mind at rest, so that he'd slip through my fingers and retire into his shell."†

Raskolnikov is like the ex-convict Kuzma, in Chekhov's story "An Encounter" who, if not punished and reviled for his misdeeds, is faced by the awful prospect of an empty universe where "anything is possible" and where no god-father enforces justice or order upon mankind.

*Part VI, Chapter 2.
†Part IV, Chapter 5.

So it is that Dostoievsky, in *The Diary of a Writer,* warns the new jurors about their leniency:

> by prison and penal servitude, perhaps, you would have saved half of them. You would have assuaged, and not burdened, them. Self-purification through suffering is easier, I tell you. . . . You are merely planting cynicism in their souls. . . . You infuse into their souls incredulity in the popular truth, in the truth of God; you are leaving them confused. . . .

It may seem strange that Dostoievsky, who had himself been a convict, should urge jurors to send more people to prison. But one might recall the paradoxical development of Dostoievsky's political and religious thought. Nearly all his adult life he was given to compulsive gambling and mismanagement of his affairs; this has often been interpreted as a form of onanism and self-punishment. Much of the guilt he felt emanated from the time that his tyrannical father was killed by rebelling serfs—a time which coincided with the period when Dostoievsky was, himself, feeling most rebellious.* Finally, nearly everyone knows how Dostoievsky was later arrested among a group of liberal thinkers and mildly revolutionary literati, sentenced to death, led to the scaffold with a group of other "condemned" men (all of whom had already been pardoned) then, at the last minute, "saved" and his sentence commuted to four years' hard labor in Siberia and four more years as a common soldier. Anyone would expect that the severity of this sentence and the deliberate cruelty of the mock execution (one of the prisoners never fully regained sanity)—that all this would set Dostoievsky once and for all against the established Czarist regime. Quite the opposite happened. From the moment of his imprisonment, Dostoievsky began moving, year by year, toward an ever more conservative political position, an ever more servile attitude toward the Little Father, the Czar. At the same time, he became more and more an orthodox Christian and more convinced of the mission

*Cf. e.g., Freud, *Dostoevsky and Parricide.*

of the Czarist state as the bearer of true Christianity to the world. He himself claimed in a letter to Dr. Yanovsky that his period in Siberia had cured him of a mental derangement. I would recommend to the reader, once again, that passage just quoted from Simone Weil, which began, "The powerful, if they carry oppression beyond a certain point, necessarily end by making themselves *adored*. . . ." Or one might compare that superb scene in *Great Expectations* where the vicious and tyrannical Mrs. Joe, after long suspense, finally confronts old Orlick who had struck her down and half killed her with his blacksmith's hammer. She politely requests him to sit down and take tea with her.

Thus it is that, to Dostoievsky, those characters who are sick or handicapped—the invalid Natalya, the near-idiot Lisaveta, the crippled and stuttering Kapernaumovs—seem to be specially godly and blessed. The crushing hand of god has already been laid upon them; they have received His attention, "accepted suffering" (which is synonymous, here, with punishment) in advance, and so are blessed.

This also explains how Dostoievsky can feel that the criminal may be the most earnest God-seeker; the naughty child may be the most earnest parent-seeker. In Raskolnikov's awful nightmare, the murder symbolized there is only an interruption of his journey toward the church. In another sense, it is another way of making part of that journey. Several times, Raskolnikov vigorously asserts that he does believe in God; his crime is one way of provoking God to declare himself. Again, Raskolnikov is a law student. He has chosen a very dear school—the experience of punishment and law. Though there *are* many other schools of universal moral law, none are too convincing. What Raskolnikov most anxiously wants to learn is that "you can't get away with it"—whatever it is. He gets the answer he wants; it does seem a shame, however, that he has to work so hard to see that the answer comes out right.

And how very hard he *does* work, trying to get caught. He begins with his usual method of sabotaging his plans—day-dreaming; he lies half-asleep in his room fantasying about oases in the desert and sands of gold, until it is well past six o'clock, so that he is rushed in his preparations and late in arriving. This late arrival leads directly to the murder of Lisaveta. Then again, he has made no *real* preparations. He has counted the number of steps to Alyona Ivanovna's house, invented a sling to carry the ax under his coat, prepared a needle and thread; yet he has taken no care to see that he could find an ax, nor, what is worse, that he could return it, unseen, after the murder. Neither has he made any plans for getting out of his own house, or into Alyona Ivanovna's, unnoticed. Hardly conducive to the "perfect crime." Then again, as he walks through the street, glancing at no one and trying to

> make himself as inconspicuous as possible . . . he remembered his hat. "Good God! and I had the money the day before yesterday and I didn't think of getting a cap!" He swore loudly.

We should not forget that he *did* think of getting a cap; it was the first thing he thought of when the drunkard in the cart called him a "German hatter."

It is true that Raskolnikov has found an ax, that he does get into Alyona Ivanovna's house unnoticed, screened by a passing cart, he does get up the stairs without meeting anyone, but this is all a matter of chance. Unfortunately, his "luck" holds.

As Chapter 7 opens, Raskolnikov continues making blunder after blunder, while "luck" carries him through the murder and his escape. Though the murder scene itself is uncanny and hideous, it is, at the same time, terribly ludicrous. No one has ever bungled so completely and so successfully.

After Alyona Ivanovna has been kind enough to look aside long enough for Raskolnikov to extricate his ax from the sling and murder her, we watch him rushing about the apartment, acting less reasonable with each moment that passes. First he tries the chest of drawers, then rushes back to be sure the old woman is dead—this time getting blood all over his hands and the ax. Then he returns to the chest,

> but he kept making mistakes; for instance, he would see that a key did not fit, but he kept trying it.

Next, having wasted much time, he forgets the decisions he had already reached:

> Suddenly he remembered the big key with the notches in the bit which was hanging there with the other small keys, and he realized that it could not possibly belong to the chest of drawers (the same idea had occurred to him the last time) but to some trunk or box . . .

Having got the trunk from under the bed and opened it, he begins to wipe the blood from his hands on the red trimmings of clothes, explaining this with the most insane logic:

> "It's red, and blood doesn't show so much on red," he thought to himself, but suddenly he came to his senses with a start. "Good Lord, am I going off my head?" he thought in a panic.

Here, he is interrupted by the entrance of Lisaveta. Having killed her, he very nearly loses all control:

> Raskolnikov almost lost his head. He picked up her bundle, threw it down again, and rushed out into the passage.

Then he comes back, but not to prepare his escape. As if he had not lost enough time already, he now falls

> into a kind of brown study or even reverie; there were moments when he seemed to forget everything, or . . . to start worrying about something that did not matter.

He does finally rouse himself enough to try to wash his hands and the hatchet, both of which are covered with Lisaveta's blood. Yet even while he knows that he is doing a poor job of this, he cannot make himself do better:

> He realized . . . that his examination was too perfunctory, and that there might be something that would attract attention which had escaped his notice.

At this point, he has the very sensible reflection that he is possibly not in control of himself, that he was "not able to do anything to protect himself, and that, generally, he most probably should not be doing what he was doing now. . . ." Yet an even more shocking recognition awaits him:

> He stood there unable to believe his own eyes: the door, the front door, leading from the passage to the stairs, the same door before which he had so recently stood ringing the bell and through which he had come in, stood open, at least five inches open! Neither locked nor even latched all that time!

He has committed the "perfect crime" with the front door standing open; everyone in the apartment house could have been watching him.

Yet the only person who did come through that open door was Lisaveta. Why? In a narrative sense, this second murder may seem accidental and arbitrary. Yet no one can deny that the second murder "feels right" in the novel. In the first place, it is symbolically "right" in the Christian morality of the story. It shows how wrong Raskolnikov was in taking murder as a "mathematical problem"—in thinking he could overstep the moral law in one single instance, thereafter devoting himself to the welfare of mankind. Evil leads to evil; killing a woman he hates, he has placed himself where he must kill another woman he admires and pities.

There is, however, a symbology far under this, which is related to Sonia's beautiful question: "What have you done to yourself?" As I have pointed out, when he killed the pawnbroker woman, Raskolnikov was striking against that part of himself which is most like

Alyona Ivanovna, like his mother, like Pashenka—that part which is idle, passive, debt-collecting, "not worth its keep." His irrational hatred of Alyona Ivanovna is clearly a reflection of his refusal to confess the qualities he has shared with her.

Yet he can never escape those qualities except by confessing them. In killing Alyona Ivanovna, he has not obliterated the worst part of his personality; as the narrator in Dostoievsky's story "White Nights" says, in committing a crime, the criminal "has destroyed what is best in him. . . ."* Thus it is that the simple, gentle Lisaveta (symbolically tied to Dunya, Sonia, and all the best qualities of Raskolnikov) must wander in to fall under the ax. Once dead, she does not rise again. The pawnbroker is another matter; by killing her, Raskolnikov has merely perpetuated everything usurious, cruel, and tyrannical in his own personality. Refusing to stay dead, she will rise up and live in Raskolnikov's mind; we meet her there all too soon again in that nightmare where Raskolnikov hits her again and again with the ax, yet she will not die. He bends down and finds that she has been laughing at him the whole time. The murder has made him more like her, not less; "What have you done to yourself," indeed!

This, too, suggests something about the sexual symbology of the murder scene and helps account for part of its uncanny phosphorescent glow. The murder itself has the appearance of an act of sexual aggression against the pawnbroker as a mother-figure. Raskolnikov's opening of the trunks, his theft of the purse "full to bursting," his fumbling with the keys:

> the moment he began fitting the keys into the drawers, the moment he heard their jingling, a sort of spasm passed over him. . . . He . . . picked up the keys and again began trying them. But for some reason . . . the keys would not fit in any of the locks. . . . he kept making mistakes; . . . he would see a key did not fit, but he kept trying it. Suddenly he remembered the

---

*A canceled passage quoted in the Introduction to David Magarshack's translation of *Crime and Punishment.*

197

big key with the notches in the bit which was hanging there with the other small keys . . .

All these details seem strongly sexual. Yet, because of Raskolnikov's deep identification with Alyona Ivanovna, the murder must finally be seen not as an act of sexual violence directed against another; but rather as an act of self-destruction and "self-abuse." If sex is seen as an aggressive and harmful act, then this form of aggression, too, may be turned against the self. Thus, a desire to commit some sexual violence against the mother, or some substitute figure, might be turned into sexual self-assault, into a blameful rape upon the self. For Raskolnikov, the loss of Natalya Zarnitsyn must be very important: even though one cannot imagine any great sexuality in either Natalya or Raskolnikov, to lose her might still *symbolize* an important sexual privation and so might generate new aggressive sexuality which might, then, be turned back against the self. This onanistic pattern underlying the crime must partly account for the way Raskolnikov throws away the stolen money and articles, or hides them beneath a stone beside a urinal.* This, too, helps explain that little scene just after the murder when Raskolnikov puts himself more obviously in the victim's role, as well as his actions upon leaving the building: first he wanders "accidentally" under a passing carriage, then is whipped by the driver (who may be compared with Mikolka of the nightmare); a passing woman and her daughter take pity on him and charitably give him 20 copecks. He throws the money into the river.†

Thus, however much the murder appears an act directed toward the outside world, Raskolnikov sees his victim—like everything else in the world—only in terms of himself. And within minutes of murdering her, he will assume the same positions and attitudes which she had taken before. As soon as he realizes that the door is open,

---

*Dostoievsky's second wife, Anna, reported that after they had been married a week, he took her to see the actual stone.

†Part II, Chapter 2.

He rushe[s] to the door and bolt[s] it.

"But what am I doing? I must get out of here! I must get out!"

There is no out except through confession. No sooner does he step into the hall than he hears footsteps—all the way from the ground floor —and knows at once that they are coming "to the old woman." Raskolnikov darts back into the room just in time, latches the door, again, and stands breathless, clutching his hatchet.

> They were now opposite each other, with only the door between them, just as he and the old woman had been a short while ago when only the door separated them and he was listening intently.

Outside the door stands Koch, "a big fat man . . . a man of authority," who is joined at once by a younger man, "a future public prosecutor." "The whole thing was like a nightmare" to Raskolnikov; he experiences these men as figures of his own creation and conscience. That is why, as he stands listening to them approach:

> he felt as though he were turned to stone, as though it were all happening in a dream, where you are chased by a murderer who is getting nearer and nearer, but you are unable to stir, you seem to be rooted to the ground, unable even to lift your arm.

He is pursued by a murderer—the only one he knows. And he would like, terribly, to surrender to those who can save him from himself:

> the thought occurred to him suddenly a few times to put an end to it all by shouting to them from behind the door. And, at times, he felt like starting cursing and taunting them, while they were still unable to open the door. "Oh, if only one could get it over quickly!" flashed through his mind.

"Get it over quickly!" He knows all along what he will have, eventually, to do. Yet he was never one to cut short his own suffering.

By the most fantastic set of coincidences and accidents, he will escape and get back to his landlady's house, manage to return the ax and get into his room. But only to prolong his agony. As soon as he can get on his feet again, he will be back, ringing the bell, looking around the room, asking about the blood, mercilessly torturing himself. Then, too, he will be flirting with the police, hinting to them, dropping clues all over St. Petersburg. He will be in a perfect agony every time their suspicion seems to turn from him. And when, finally, Sonia and Porfiry have brought him to see what he has done to himself and Svidrigaylov has shown him the logical next step, suicide, then at last he will stop, turn, go to the police who could not come to him, and confess.

Four Studies in the Classics

Moonshine and Sunny Beams:
Ruminations on
A Midsummer Night's Dream

"*A Midsummer Night's Dream!*" exclaims one early editor. "Who is the dreamer? The poet, any of the characters of the drama, or the spectators?"

Well carped, critic! Let's go on from there. Not only who is dreaming; who gets dreamed? Surely a dream, or a play, must be "about" someone. In this dream, we find four separate groups of characters derived from different periods of history, far-flung areas of the world, diverse literary and mythological backgrounds, opposed levels of reality. Can we decide which group is central to the play's concern? Mightn't we even ask for a central character?

And is it really too much to ask what the dream means? What most critics tell us about this play would apply to the dreariest hackwork. No one would perform a play that means so little—neither Peter Brook, the Comédie Français, nor Podunk Junior High. Yet all those troupes *have* been performing this airy flummery for 350 years and with almost unmitigated success. What has this play been imparting to so many actors, so many audiences, all these years?

203

Until Jan Kott came along and said some really interesting things about this play, it seemed almost impossible to give a performance lacking in all interest. Should we not question this play's secret workings, lest some well-meaning director snap up our speculations, turn them into overt and conscious motifs for his production, and ruin the thing once and for all?

I. The Rulers

Scholars tell us that *A Midsummer Night's Dream* was probably first written and produced to celebrate a wedding in the British royal family. If there is little hard evidence for that, it does seem to fit our feeling about the play. Its first scene opens on just such a royal pair, Theseus of Athens and Hippolyta of the Amazons, planning their own marriage. And if marriage implies a joining of opposites, Theseus and Hippolyta have assuredly been opposed:

> Hippolyta, I wooed thee with my sword
> And won thy love doing thee injuries;
> But I will wed thee in another key
> With pomp, with triumph, and with revelling.

Modern practice, of course, has changed all that. To have the fighting all settled before the wedding must have left them little to look forward to; we'd be bored.

And if that seems old-fashioned, it seems downright quaint for Theseus and Hippolyta, each of whom has quite a past, to forgo sex until after the ceremony. We moderns have reversed that, too. If we fail to stay chaste before the wedding, we frequently make up for that afterward.

Still, in most things, Theseus seems old-fashioned. He governs by right of conquest and by ability to rule. No wonder he seems half-mythical! He even obeys the laws he enforces on his subjects. No sooner has he announced his wedding plans and his determination to restrain his lusts until that time, than in rushes Egeus with his daughter Hermia, to accuse her and her two suitors of a wilful desire to break Athens's marriage laws. Most of us sympathize with Hermia, yet we see a justice in Theseus's rule. Suppose we thought he and Hippolyta were slipping off now and then to make out on the sly?

All the better then, if Theseus is upright as well as erect; restraint is valuable, especially when it channels great force:

> . . . . but O, methinks how slow
> This old moon wanes; she lingers my desires
> Like to a step-dame, or a dowager,
> Long withering out a young man's revenue

His desires for Hippolyta, then, are strong; yet his telling of them sounds strangely rancorous. Hippolyta's reply seems almost threatening:

> Four days will quickly steep themselves in night
> Four nights will quickly dream away the time;
> And then the moon, like to a silver bow
> New bent in heaven, shall behold the night
> Of our solemnities.

Even lusts so high-strung needn't be imaged as weaponry. Both rulers seem to have slipped back into recollections of that war between them which we had hoped was finished.

Who are these two we have come together to join? Surely, Theseus stands for the model ruler and male, the man of conquest as of conquests, who is yet capable of noble commitment. If his rule is just and central, so is reason's rule in him. When he later comes to the forest, his hounds baying musically, he gives an admirable picture of the animal forces trained and held in harmonious order. The hunter's bow (which elsewhere stood for Diana's chastity or for sexual attack) now is turned to useful sport. Such controlled sport, such harmony, he must induce in himself as in the Lovers, those who look to him as their authority.

Hippolyta? She is an Amazon. Spenser's Radigund makes her role clear enough: the warrior woman whose single aim is to defeat and enslave the male. As the story goes, all Amazons cut off one breast lest it be injured by the bowstring—that is, partly defeminized themselves to better fight the male. Still, we imagine Amazons were thoroughly democratic; would as readily subject the male to surgery. So the sexes would be more equal, yet the woman would rule. Hippolyta, seen here in defeat, has none of these fiercer qualities. True, she seems to get the last word in arguments; yet she is both right and uninsistent, an engaging combination. She carries herself with such grace and dignity that we wonder if a woman might be as improved by defeat as some men can.

These two, then, have been fierce enemies; it would be a wonder if no bitterness remained. Their reconciliation, their coming marriage, is indeed a consummation devoutly to be wished. To them, the present moon seems a time of drained resources, of grudging tight-fistedness. How shall we reach a new moon of generosity, of free spending and fulfilled desire—how shall we bring this couple to union? How but by airing and expiating, owning and healing those age-old grudges, the wounds of our long war?

Where better to do that than in our dreams—perhaps in just such a dream as this play? Midsummer Night, after all, was the night when a girl might dream about her future husband. A Midsummer Night's dream, then, tells the truth about our love. Dare we ask it not only to reveal, but also to reconcile us to our love?

II. The Fairies

OBERON   Ill met by moonlight, proud Titania.

TITANIA   What, jealous Oberon? Fairies, skip hence:
I have forsworn his bed and company.

OBERON   Tarry, rash wanton; am not I thy lord?

TITANIA   Then I must be thy lady; but I know
When thou hast stolen away from fairy land,
And in the shape of Corin sat all day,
Playing on pipes of corn, and versing love
To amorous Phillida.

Now *that* has a good modern sound—nothing restrained about the Fairies' rage or their lust. Like Theseus and Hippolyta, they are chaste; theirs, however, is that spiteful abstinence many of us have found in marriage. These Fairies fully display and act out those passions which compel all the couples—though Theseus tries to control them, though the Lovers try to disguise them. The Fairies could almost be a negative and all the other couples its various positive prints.

The Fairies' war echoes another of the problems plaguing Theseus, not only the struggle for dominance between the sexes but also that between parents and children. He has just heard Egeus's claim that his daughter, Hermia, is his property to give in marriage as he wills. The Fairies, too, are struggling for ownership of a child—a "little changeling boy" each wants as a page and follower.

Faced by such problems, Theseus defeated his woman in open conflict; Oberon uses subtlety, magic, stealth. It hardly seems cricket (even among lovers) to win the war by putting your woman to bed with the most bestial creature available:

Be it ounce, or cat, or bear,
Pard, or boar with bristled hair,
In thy eye that shall appear,
When thou wak'st, it is thy dear.
Wake when something vile is near.

207

Bottom may not be all *that* vile; most wives would scarcely thank their husbands for so asinine a lover. Yet, the very queen of Fairies, once her vision has cleared, does almost thank Oberon. How can her humiliation result, not in a deeper rejection of Oberon, but in acceptance? Can he, like Theseus, win his woman's love doing her injuries? Perhaps the ferocity of his strategy flatters her—he must love her very much to fight so fiercely. Or persuades her to surrender quickly before he does *worse*. More likely it shows her something about her own desires and her rejection of her lord—that she would be willingly embowered only with a man who could be made an ass. Or that her love is a love of the ass.

Anyway, Oberon's strategy works; who is to quarrel with success? The Fairies' reconciliation is surely no less desirable than is the rulers' —do we imagine any love can be happy while these Fairies rage? These are love's divinities, parental figures who have guided both Theseus and Hippolyta through all their past loves and must now assure their permanent union. By their own admission, they have caused the world's present coldness and sterility. The seasons are disordered, disease rampant, the rivers rebellious and uncontained; fields are barren, the folds empty, the flocks dying:

> And this same progeny of evils comes
> From our debate, from our dissension;
> We are their parents and original.

In the normal rounds of his practical business, Theseus encounters most of the other characters of the play. He judges and helps reconcile the Lovers; their wedding becomes part of his. The Artisans devise their play just to celebrate that same marriage. For all his hard-nosed narrow-mindedness, he seems a splendidly capable ruler; we expect him to be a good husband. Moreover he has had a considerable hand in straightening out the Lovers, his subjects. On the one hand, he has made it clear to Hermia that he will maintain the laws of Athens; on the other, he has drawn both Egeus and Demetrius aside for "private schooling" in matters that concern them closely. We have seen that his rule is firm and effective.

Yet Theseus never meets the Fairies, those who have guided his past and on whom his future totally depends. How strange that he should not even believe in forces which he has somehow successfully enlisted, and without whose help all his reason and power would be useless.

In Act V, Theseus issues various firm pronouncements on the unreality of love and lovers, plays and players, above all Fairies:

> I never may believe
> These antique fables nor these fairy toys.
> Lovers and madmen have such seething brains,
> Such shaping fantasies, that apprehend
> More than cool reason ever comprehends.

No sooner has he left the stage, though, taking his bride to bed, than those same nonexistent Fairies enter to bless his marriage and make that bed fruitful. Had their quarrel gone on, not only his bed but his household, his state, his world had been barren and fruitless.

No more than Theseus do we believe in Fairies. Yet we see something that he cannot—you had better have them on your side. There is no Oberon. And Titania is his consort.

III. The Lovers

If you ask the Romantic Lovers—Hermia and Lysander, Helena and Demetrius—they don't want to rule each other, only to serve each other. "I am your spaniel. . . ." If you ask the Lovers, they wouldn't think of hurting each other. (There's a fact—they do it without a thought.) If you ask the Lovers, they want only to marry.

But who believes a Lover? They are as full of passion as the Fairies, as full of reason as the rulers. But they use reason not to channel passion, rather to disguise and license it. So they remain wilfully chaste, wilfully sexual. Yet, being so ready to fool themselves, they seldom fool anyone else:

LYSANDER   O take the sense, sweet, of my innocence.
             Love takes the meaning in love's conference. . . .
             Then by your side no bed-room me deny,
             For lying so, Hermia, I do not lie.

HERMIA   Lysander riddles very prettily; . . .
             But, gentle friend, for love and courtesy
             Lie further off, in human modesty.

At times their speeches have more truth than they yet recognize:

             Love looks not with the eyes, but with the mind,
             And therefore is winged Cupid painted blind.
             Nor hath Love's mind of any judgement taste;
             Wings, and no eyes, figure unheedy haste;
             And therefore is Love said to be a child,
             Because in choice he is so oft beguiled.

The Lovers demand to choose Love by their own sight, yet they obviously can't see who they are, what they want, or what they are doing. As the play later shows, they are running around lost in a fog. They think they are trying to get married; to us they seem to be doing the exact opposite.

The law will not let Hermia and Lysander marry, so they plan to run away to the home of his widow aunt. (A very moony aunt she seems, "a dowager of great revenue.") No sooner has Hermia joined him in the woods, eager to marry him, than Lysander becomes curiously unable to find that place where marriage will be so easy; within hours he has fallen desperately in love with someone else. Soon, he is plying Helena with all the frantic endearments he once gave Hermia, meantime treating Hermia as hatefully as Demetrius ever did Helena. Throughout the play the truly hurtful things are always said by someone to the person they most love—Titania to Oberon, Lysander to Hermia, Demetrius to Helena. We are told art imitates life.

Where did all these tangles start, these triangles among our four Lovers? Apparently when Demetrius, having won Helena, turned from her to Hermia, obtaining her father's permission to marry her. Why did he suddenly desire the scornful Hermia, abandoning the willing Helena? Perhaps just because Helena *was* willing? Lysander certainly turned against Hermia precisely at the point he could marry her.

Consider the advantages for Demetrius in this "unhappy" unfulfilled love. Imagine saying to your true love:

> Hang off, thou cat, thou burr! Vile thing, let loose
> Or I will shake thee from me like a serpent!

and getting this answer:

> Why are you grown so rude? What change is this?
> Sweet love . . .

Or better yet, to say:

> I do not and I cannot love you

and then get this reply:

> And even for that do I love you the more . . .
> Use me but as your spaniel, spurn me, strike me,
> Neglect me, lose me; only give me leave,
> Unworthy as I am to follow you.
> What worser place can I beg in your love—
> And yet a place of high respect with me,—
> Than to be used as you use your dog.

What victory has either Oberon or Theseus compared to that? What has marriage compared to that? Suppose Demetrius won either Hermia or Helena—he would have to live with her. He would have

211

to give up self-pity in being deprived of some imagined love, stop rejecting what love is convenient and available. He would have to become an adult; small wonder both he and Lysander postpone it as long as possible. Meantime, each is deeply indulging himself in injuries to the girl he loves:

LYSANDER   What, should I hurt her, strike her, kill her dead?
                     Although I hate her, I'll not harm her so.

HERMIA   What can you do me greater harm than hate?
                     Hate me? Wherefore? O me, what news, my love?

That is almost motive enough in itself.

But meantime, both girls are just as agile in preserving their "single blessedness." In the first scene, Helena hears that Hermia and Lysander are about to elope—that she will be relieved of her rival. Instead of bidding them a fond good riddance, she tells Demetrius of their plans:

> Then to the wood will he tomorrow night
> Pursue her; and for this intelligence,
> If I have thanks, it is a dear expense.
> But herein mean I to enrich my pain,
> To have his sight thither, and back again.

If she ever was as available as Demetrius thought, she must since have learned the pleasures of rejection and abandonment.

Earlier in this scene, she wished she might be translated into Hermia, who is pursued by both men. In the woods, she gets her wish; under Puck's enchantments both men turn ga-ga over her. How does she respond? By refusing both, starting a quarrel with Hermia, then running away. What else can you do if events threaten to impoverish your pain?

As to Hermia, when both men courted her, she chose the one forbidden. Listening to Egeus's long speech, we cannot quite make out whether Hermia wants Lysander because her father insists on Demetrius, or whether her father insists on Demetrius because she wants Lysander. Both may be true. It's worth noting, though, that in the companion play (I cannot think of them separately) Juliet fell in love with Romeo only just after her father gave her to Paris. That, surely, is part of the reason she fell in love with someone else, especially with an enemy of her family. In *this* play, we feel that one of Pyramus's greatest attractions is precisely that he is a family enemy and so forbidden to Thisby. As to Hermia's choice between Lysander and Demetrius, everyone concedes there is no difference between them. How does she tell them apart?—ideally they would be played by identical twins. Lysander has only two discernible advantages: he is not available to Hermia, and he gives her a way to oppose her father.

Only occasionally do we have glimpses of the girls' disdain for their lovers. Hermia gives only a hint:

> Before the time I did Lysander see,
> Seemed Athens as a paradise to me.
> O then, what graces in my love do dwell
> That he hath turned a heaven unto a hell!

Helena's slam against Demetrius is much nearer the surface:

> . . . as he errs, doting on Hermia's eyes,
> So I, admiring of his qualities.
> Things base and vile, holding no quantity,
> Love can transpose to form and dignity.

Except for Hermia's opposition to her father, neither girl shows much desire to directly assault the male. (There will be years and years for that.) On the other hand, before the young men are accepted as husbands, each has proved himself inconstant, trifling and childish. Perhaps the girls need do nothing to humiliate their lovers; Lysander and Demetrius can be counted on to make asses of themselves.

The Rulers then have already fought out their war and wish to be married; the Fairies are married and fighting harder than ever. The

213

Lovers must keep up the pretense of wanting marriage but are actually doing everything to evade it—at least until they have carried their battle to a point where the final outcome is clearly indicated.

IV. The Craftsmen

Like the Lovers, the Artisans live in Theseus's world and must seek resolution there; like the Lovers, they can reach that only by first withdrawing into Oberon's world. The young Lovers now must enter a world of adulthood, marriage, business, reason; in their revulsion, they regress even further into fantasy, childhood, magic. The Artisans also go there, apparently sensing that's the place to learn a role, to discover one's part. So develops one of the major structures of the play —the general migration from the sunlit city into the moonlit forest, then back again.

Just as Theseus never had contact with the Fairies, the world most comparable to his own, so the Lovers have no contact with the Artisans, the world that most reflects theirs. True, they watch the craftsmen perform "Pyramus and Thisby." But only after they have married—it is questionable whether they *are* Lovers then. In any case that's small contact with a world which sheds such light on theirs.

From the first, "Pyramus and Thisby" has been a mockery of Lovers:

FLUTE   (as Thisby) My love! thou art my love, I think.

BOTTOM   (as Pyramus) Think what thou wilt, I am thy lover's grace,
And like Limander am I trusty still.

FLUTE   (as Thisby)
And I like Helen, till the Fates me kill.

Like the Lovers whose names they just echoed (Lysander and Helena), Pyramus and Thisby ran away to meet far from the constraints and divisions of society. There, they found much what the

Lovers found, much what Romeo and Juliet found—that they are certainly not "trusty still," that they are much more likely to kill themselves than to be killed by Fate. All are like the old joke about the spinster and the hen: "Poor dears, they'd rather die!"

That old sexual pun (among a myriad others) is much in evidence here. The artisans not only rehearse "obscenely and courageously," they perform that way as well. Pyramus picks up Thisby's mantle, bloodied by the lion's mouth, and exclaims:

> O wherefore, Nature, didst thou lions frame?
> Since lion vile hath here deflowered my dear:
> Which is—no, no, which was—the fairest Dame
> That lived, that loved, that liked, that looked with cheer.
> Come tears, confound:
> Out sword, and wound
> The pap of Pyramus:
> Ay, that left pap,
> Where heart doth hop;
> Thus die I, thus, thus, thus.
>
> Now am I dead,
> Now am I fled, . . .
>
> Now die, die, die, die, die.

Demetrius sets out to cap the pun:

> No die, but an ace for him; for he is but one.

Then Theseus caps the cap:

> With the help of a surgeon he might yet recover, and prove an ass.

We are reminded, of course, of Bottom's earlier transformation. Yet, much as the court mocks the Craftsmen's acting, this whole playlet remains a mockery of the hammier performances these Lovers just gave with the very substance of their lives.

We are never allowed to forget that the playlet is only a way to pass

215

the time till the Lovers may and must bed each other for the first time. By the end of the play, even Hippolyta (who earlier had soothed Theseus's impatience) seems anxious to get on to bed:

I am a-weary of this Moon; would he would change!

THESEUS . . . in courtesy, in all reason, we must stay the time.

The play's purpose is, in part, to make us more eager for marriage and for bed; it does this partly by its mockery of Romantic Love. At the same time, it helps reveal and expiate our fear of marriage, even of sex itself.

Demetrius calls Snug the Joiner (O sweetly fitting name!):

The very best at a beast, my lord, that e'er I saw.

then says of Bottom and Flute:

A mote will turn the balance, which Pyramus, which Thisby
is the better, he for a man, God warrant us, she for a woman, God
    bless us.

Such ready criticism suggests that he is trying to rise to better performance himself but may be none too sure of his abilities. Still, we must not be overcritical ourselves—he has had a courage lacking in Pyramus or Romeo, has come back from the world of fantasy and settled down to live with the woman he loves. No mean feat, that.

Yet it is not only in their playlet that the Craftsmen provide an ironic view of Love and Lovers; they do that far more richly in their forest scenes. There, we watch Puck tangling and untangling the Lovers; watch him first transform Bottom into an ass, then, with the same herb that charmed the Lovers, put him into the cradle of Titania. Bottom went to the forest when the Lovers did, was enchanted by the same magical powers, was released when they were. He of all people has known the quintessential love experience, has been embraced by the queen of love, gone to the very bottom of the world of passion and

imagination. And he was an ass. And he is an ass. Watching Titania
coo and gurgle over him, we see as nowhere else how

> Things base and vile, holding no quantity,
> Love can transpose to form and dignity.

In some sense, then, all the Lovers have proven an ass in the bower
of divinity.

Bottom, above all, has had the power (a very passive power it must
be) to reenter the world of the child's, even the baby's, sexuality—the
world of Mustardseed and Cobweb, of Mother Squash, Father Peas-
cod, and Baby Peaseblossom. There, without the faintest qualm, he
replaces the "King of shadows." If he does not actually cuckold that
king (we cannot be sure), it is only because he is more interested in
eating. The queen has made every amorous advance to him and he has
come back safe and sound to tell of it. Well, not perhaps to tell of it:

> Man is but an ass if he go about to expound this dream. . . . Methought
> I was, and methought I had. . . . I will get Peter Quince to write a ballad
> of this dream; it shall be called "Bottom's Dream," because it hath no
> bottom and I will sing it in the latter end of the play, before the Duke.

He never does but the clear implication is that it is this experience
which is not only the basic love experience but also the material which
must be translated into the work of art, the experience which makes
"Pyramus and Thisby" possible. In the play's last act, the Artisans
bring back to the city their forest experience; there they wield (however awkwardly) the powers of transformation which they must have
gathered from the Fairies who had transformed them in the woods.

All along, we have seen that the Artisans making their play to
further an Athenian royal wedding clearly image Shakespeare and his
company making *their* play to celebrate an English noble wedding.
Who knows better than Shakespeare what goes into the making of a
play?

V. The Firmament

You could scarcely imagine, unless you had looked into the Furness *Variorum,* what energy critics have spent arguing for the centrality of some one or another of these four worlds. The Lovers, the Fairies, the Rulers—each has its partisans heatedly arguing that their candidate holds the central place while the others only revolve around it, reflecting and illuminating its meaning.

No critic (excepting Dr. Gui, whose penetrating and eccentric analysis appears in the *American Imago*) sees the Artisans as central. Yet actors and directors often make them so. We surely remember their scenes most vividly—the enchanted Bottom in Titania's bower; the hilarious "Pyramus and Thisby"—and those scenes are often extracted to play separately.

I certainly don't intend to take sides here. The mere existence of the dispute lends force to my view—that *none* of these worlds is central. As I see it, all four worlds exist only in their balanced relationship to one another. Just as four dancers, or four groups of dancers, might all be part of a larger pattern, each maintaining relation with the others, none more important than the others. Our four Lovers did, in fact, create just such a dance pattern in their shifting and alternating triangulations. Or to return to the astronomical figure, the play's firmament holds four worlds, one of which has created its own moon —the play within the play. These four worlds form a circle, as twinned stars might in *our* universe, holding each other in orbit around a center which no one of them may permanently occupy. Each world has close narrative contact with two of the others; each remains apart from a fourth. Each, as it passes through the center, gives and takes illumination from all the others—often most strongly from that fourth world opposite to and separate from itself.

This play was written, after all, at a time when centrality was being broken down in all areas—I take as my authority here Hiram Haydn's *The Counter-Renaissance*. There, we may trace the rise of individual-istic philosophies and religions, of capitalist economies, democratic ideas of government; of the child's rights against his parents, the subject's rights against his sovereign, of relativistic views of the world, of reality, of astronomy. Giordano Bruno, that most daringly relativ-istic of thinkers, had been in England only about ten years before the writing of this play. Haydn quotes Bruno:

> Since the horizon forms itself anew around every place occupied by the spectator as its central point, every determination of place must be relative. The universe looks different according to whether we conceive it from the earth, the moon, Venus, the sun, etc. . . .
>
> Why, indeed, may not all the stars be themselves suns, and each new sun appear to itself the center of the universe? Where then are its limits? . . . There must be hundreds of thousands of suns, and about them planets rolling, each one, perhaps, inhabited. . . . Throughout, Nature must be the same, everywhere worlds, everywhere the center, everywhere and nowhere.

From this amazingly modern view, Bruno advances directly to relativity of motion, of time, even of weight.

It is Montaigne, however, who can show us a comparable relativity of manners, morals, of levels of reality. First he points out that such relativity of place and judgment makes all agreement between men impossible:

> men are in agreement about nothing. I mean even the most gifted and ablest scholars, not even that the sky is over our heads.

Yet even if only one man had ever existed, that one could not truly know reality:

> . . . the conception and semblance we form is not the object, but only the impression and the impression and the object are different things. . . .
>
> Now if anyone should want to judge by appearances anyway, to judge

by all appearances is impossible, for they clash with one another by their contradictions and discrepancies. . . . Shall some selected appearances rule the others? . . .

Finally, there is no existence that is constant, either of our being or of that of objects. And we, and our judgement and all mortal things go on flowing and rolling ceaselessly. Thus nothing certain can be established about one thing by another, both the judging and the judged being in continual change and motion.

Such men as Bruno and Montaigne had moved into a world of limitless change, of rolling and flowing, boundaries shifting and re-forming, realities dissolving and illusions becoming real. Shakespeare was a man of his time; not the man least sensitive to forces which were driving others to create and explore new areas of thought and feeling. Most readers would grant that the play implies that all illusions have their reality, all realities their illusion. It is only a step further (though a dangerous one, as Bruno found at the stake) to suggest that no reality is more important, more real, that no one appearance may be selected to rule the others.

One of the peculiar triumphs of Shakespeare's art is to have taken an artistic convention common to his time—the use of subplot—and let it grow until it quite broke down the whole principle of central plot. What is for lesser writers only a useful device, a way to relieve and vary their central story, is for Shakespeare a way to suggest a whole new view of the world.

Such tendencies must have been very deep in Shakespeare's nature. We see it in every aspect of his work—for instance, his use of imagery. In the sonnet cycle we can watch his technique growing into something that reflects his own psyche, his peculiar vision. In the earlier pieces, imagery tends to be confined to rather low-powered metaphors and similes; we always know what is real and what merely compared to it. As Shakespeare's art grows, the components of an image will be drawn from ever more bafflingly diverse areas of experience, ever more complex structures of reality:

220

Not marble, nor the gilded monuments
Of princes, shall outlive this powerful rhyme
. . . you shall shine more bright in these contents
Than unswept stone, besmeared with sluttish time.

Not only is metaphor added to metaphor; the vehicle of the first may be snapped up as the tenor of a second, mounted metaphor:

That time of year thou may'st in me behold
When yellow leaves, or none, or few, do hang
Upon those boughs which shake against the cold,
Bare ruined choirs where late the sweet birds sang.

until we can scarcely say which term is "real" and which only a reflection of it.

In *Rehabilitations,* C. S. Lewis sees a similar urge in Shakespeare's rhetorical practice, contrasting that with Milton's. Milton normally tries to sum up the meaning of his subject in some one description or definitive statement, then lets that stand for better or worse. Shakespeare, on the contrary, tends to come back to his subject again and again—or rather, his characters do. They say things quite as brilliant, as definitive, as anything in Milton. Yet they say them only in the rush and fumble of trying to grasp a reality that seems always elusive, always too broad for summing up. However wonderful their words may be, they never seem to feel them adequate to experience. Again, we find this same drive toward variousness, toward turbulent diversity, in that violent mixing of genres which so disturbed continental critics: realistic scenes collide with highly fanciful stylized scenes; prose rubs shoulders with blank verse or even with tight rhyme; high wit mixes with buffoonery, high tragedy with melodrama. Shakespeare's plays may not, like the Artisans', be "tedious and brief"; they are surely "very tragical mirth. . . . hot ice, and wondrous strange snow." In their despair of imitating this life, they become downright "tragical-comical-historical-pastoral." All conventions are seized on; none is admitted to yield final truth.

221

And this, of course, is intimately part of what makes Shakespeare so bafflingly great. Stepping into the universe of his plays, we are surrounded with characters, with situations, with meanings, various and far-flung as stars on a summer night. We can no more locate the center of this universe than we can fathom its edges. We cannot define the creator from within his creation. We cannot sum up Shakespeare; we only set up housekeeping there.

VI. *Translations*

In the play's first scene, when Hermia is being pursued by both Demetrius and Lysander, Helena says to her:

> Sickness is catching; O were favour so,
> Yours would I catch, fair Hermia, ere I go. . . .
> Were the world mine, Demetrius being bated,
> The rest I'd give to be to you translated.

Soon, she gets her wish: she becomes Hermia; both men pursue her. That, of course, is even less satisfying.

In that same process, Hermia is translated into Helena and finds herself abandoned. Weary from wandering in the forest, she and Lysander had lain down to rest. First, however, she has had to persuade him to lie at a more modest distance. Then, with vows of eternal constancy, they fell asleep. Suddenly Hermia wakes with a nightmare-vision, a dream-within-the-*Dream:*

> Help me, Lysander, help me! do thy best
> To pluck this crawling serpent from my breast!
> Aye me, for pity! what a dream was here!
> Lysander, look how I do quake with fear.
> Methought a serpent eat my heart away,
> And you sat smiling at his cruel prey.

MOONSHINE AND SUNNY BEAMS

Lysander has already abandoned her, chasing after Helena. The dream has shown her her own plight, both in this abandonment where Lysander enjoys her pain, and also in her fear of being preyed upon —a fear which Lysander must have activated by his sly and subtle attempt to seduce her.

Sickness is indeed catching. During the Lovers' near-epidemic Lysander, too, suffers a translation: not into what he wished to be, but into what Egeus said he already was. In the opening scene, it was ironic that Egeus should try to take Hermia from the constant Lysander on the grounds that he was inconstant and feigning, giving her instead to Demetrius, whom we know to be faithless. Yet no sooner have the Lovers fled to the woods than Lysander becomes all Egeus said he was. He even goes Egeus and the Fairies one better: Puck's enchantment may force him to love Helena; to hate and mistreat Hermia is an improvement supplied from his own nature.

Puck's final enchantment, the curing of Demetrius's vision, straightens out all the tangles at once—shows Demetrius that he has always loved Helena and that his pursuit of Hermia was

> . . . an idle gaud
> which in my childhood I did dote upon;
> And all the faith, the virtue of my heart,
> The object and the pleasure of mine eye,
> Is only Helena . . .
> . . . like in sickness did I loathe this food
> But, as in health, come to my natural taste,
> Now I do wish it, love it, long for it,
> And will for evermore be true to it.

This brings the Lovers back where they started before the play began. Except that they may be a little more mature after an experience which reveals so much about themselves. Demetrius is shown who his love is; Lysander, what. He, once so ready to call others "spotted and inconstant," is full of inconstancy. Even more, full of hate and venom which he, like Theseus, must recognize and control. The aim of all these translations, then, is to change something so we can see how it always was.

All the Lovers are shown lost in a fog where they cannot find, cannot recognize each other or themselves. They declare a deathless love for another person, without whom their lives will be desolate; an hour later, they feel exactly the same thing for someone else. As wild beasts wake famished and devour the first prey at hand, so the Lovers wake enchanted and fall in love. It is Love-in-Idleness that enchants them; being of the leisure class, they can indulge their fantasies, can grieve and blame, can enrich their pain. Hardworking people like Peter Quince may dabble with such loves as they dabble in the arts; they haven't the leftover energy or time to let it control their lives.

I have earlier touched on some of the ways that the enchanted Bottom in Titania's bower reveals the truth about Bottom and about the rebellious Titania as well. Those same scenes also show much about the Lovers who undergo a similar enchantment in the same time and place. What happens to Titania and Bottom is obviously related to what happens to the Lovers, and not only in the asininity all display.

If the two young men seem almost identical to each other, the two girls are only slightly more differentiated. They cherish, moreover, a vision of their union in infancy:

> We, Hermia, like two artificial gods,
> Have with our needles created both one flower
> Both on one sampler, sitting on one cushion,
> Both warbling of one song, both in one key;
> As if our hands, our sides, voices and minds
> Had been incorporate. So we grew together,
> Like to a double cherry. . . .

This vision, of which Helena prates so ecstatically, is close kin to that of Bottom in Titania's bower. It is an imagined bower of bliss where, above all, the pains of individuality and separateness are turned to ecstacy in a dream of childish, even babyish, union.

Moving toward maturity and marriage, the Lovers must give up the narcissistic dream of being one with those identical to themselves. As individuals they must learn not only to accept what is different, but even what is opposite. They are growing into a world where things are separate and self-willed, yet where union is still possible:

HERMIA   Methinks I see these things with parted eye
               Where everything seems double.

HELENA   So methinks. And I have found Demetrius like a jewel
               Mine own and not mine own. . . .

DEMETRIUS   . . . . Do you not think
               The Duke was here, and bid us follow him? . . .

LYSANDER   And he did bid us follow to the temple.

DEMETRIUS   Why then, we are awake.

The Lovers, then, are waking from their dream of blissful union (essentially Bottom's dream) and going to the temple and to marriage —a world of differences, of separations, of walls, yet walls that can be penetrated.

The Lovers, making this painful change, have the help of the Artisans who shared their forest experience. In the last act, the Artisans take over from the Fairies the power to transform things so they may be truly seen. Performing "Pyramus and Thisby" they mock their own and the Lovers' flight into moonshine and so help them emerge into the raw and difficult light of day. Truly, Bottom and his friends do not "stand upon points," are poor enough actors. Fearing lest the lion terrorize the Ladies, or that everyone be shocked by Pyramus's suicide, they seem not to discern what in their art is reality and what illusion. Yet, in effect, they perform very well indeed. Theseus does well to honor them, not because of their supposed good will to him (their *real* aim, of course, is self-advancement), but because their play has a salutary effect on the Lovers, helps lead them into Reality.

In the play, the Lovers leave the world of Bottom's dream to enter the world of marriage. Outside the play, lovers made Bottom's dream the aim of marriage. Alas and alack for us all.

VII. *The Fundament*

Bottom was translated into an ass. Like all good translators, Puck must have been quick to leap to a pun. And as any good analyst must be quick to hear a pun, Dr. Gui finds Bottom the central character of the play.

Bottom has a strong urge to take over all roles—not just the Lover and the Lady, but the lion's part as well. He wants to play the tyrant; if there is to be no tyrant, the next best thing is to be the director. While directing the playlet, Peter Quince—whose name echoes Penis Cunt—has continual trouble keeping Bottom in his place.

Bottom himself, almost like a baby, has trouble keeping straight the parts of the body and *their* proper roles:

> The eye of man hath not heard, the ear of man hath not seen, man's hand is not able to taste, his tongue to conceive, nor his heart to report, what my dream was.

Playing Pyramus, he says:

> I see a voice; now will I to the chink
> To spy an I can hear my Thisby's face.

He does not let many things keep their assigned function:

> Sweet moon, I thank thee for thy sunny beams.

226

He is not just undiscriminating; he seems determined to break down all distinctions. He dissolves the meaning of words, often saying the exact opposite of what he means:

> You were best to call them generally, man by man . . .

> . . . there may we rehearse most obscenely and courageously.

> I will aggravate my voice so, that I will roar you as gently as any sucking dove . . .

In our world, doves have voices neither grave nor aggravated; they seldom roar and never suck; in Bottom's world, fish, flesh, and fowl are all one.

> . . . there is not a more fearful wild fowl than your lion living . . .

Bottom so longs to equalize everything that when Quince proposes to write a prologue in eight and six syllable verse (the "fourteeners" then so common), Bottom will not hear of it:

> No, make it two more; let it be written in eight and eight.

Loving equality, he tends to break down social distinctions, too. He never hesitates to correct Demetrius or even Theseus. Unlike other characters of the play, he addresses everyone he meets with a complete democracy of courtesy. In Titania's bower, he has no sense that he is out of place, addressing Titania's pages with the absurdly patronizing familiarity of Le Bourgeois Gentilhomme. There, in the bower of the Fairy Queen, he realizes what must be his dearest dream: the blissful union of the asinine with the sublime, the beastly with the ethereal, the great with the small, the ugly with the beautiful.

This is all thoroughly apt, for in the world of the emotions, anality is the direct counterpart of relativism in philosophy. At bottom, we can scarcely tell male from female; it is the great equalizer which yearns to break down the hierarchies, discredit the phallic and/or superior. Taking over both male and female roles, it is impatient to assume the world.

Theseus and Bottom, then, stand for diametrically opposed ways of life, not only in their social stance but in the whole bases of their natures. Theseus, the phallic male, always of the elite, holds his position simply because he has more (more anything) than others have. Bottom is the Common Man; he has what we all have.

Theseus takes for granted the Artisans' goodwill toward him. To us, he may seem absurdly complacent. Kaiser Wilhelm, after all, was replaced by a saddlemaker; King Alexander by a mill mechanic. Nowadays, Bottom has not only taken over the throne; Theseus could not even get into the legislature—every chair already has an ass. Theseus is no longer Theseus when he seeks the masses' vote; besides, they wouldn't give it to him.

Not believing in Fairies, in the overwhelming powers of the unconscious, Theseus could scarcely suspect what powers Bottom has lain beside. Theseus is very much of the past—a past so ancient it may never have existed.

Yet, as far back as the Bronze Age, perhaps we *can* see a bit of Theseus after all—a hunting society demands the direct and powerful rule of one man; bronze weapons could only be owned by an aristocracy. Bottom is of a time when Artisans, working in a poorer but commoner metal, iron, would give the farmer tools and so a surplus, letting him turn sedentary, anarchic, indulge himself in dreams, would give the masses weapons and so control of the battlefield and ballot box. Bottom directs the present and the future.

One day, I was talking about all this with a dear old friend, Donald Hall. By now, I don't know which ideas came from him and which from me. Suddenly he burst out laughing: "But how predictive! Where did our modern collective and democratic states come from? From the asshole of society; where else?"

VIII. Poets and Parents

Romantic Love, of course, has no very ancient history; it is open to dispute whether even the Romans were romantic. The first time we can isolate and firmly identify this strange virus in the Western World is in the courtly love lyrics of the twelfth-century Renaissance in Provence. Oddly enough, there, too, it is involved with a historical movement which helped break down centrality of rule.

We are only now beginning to suspect that neither the Troubadour's music nor his sentiments were as "pretty" as we had been told. With some justice, we could say that the Troubadour song has only two obsessions: let's go Crusading and kill Moors, or let's go seducing and lay the boss's wife.

After many centuries of terrifying upheaval, the twelfth century was a time when men could once again afford unhappy love, self-pity, betrayal, envy of authority. After all, the local strong-arm chief, the feudal equivalent of Theseus, was no longer so desperately needed for protection against invaders, had become in fact a considerable threat himself. It has been seriously argued that one real purpose of the Crusades was to keep the turbulent and idle aristocracy out of trouble nearer home. Meantime, the lower orders were beginning to envy their power, their freedom, their women.

The courtly love object is always a married woman, usually the wife of the singer's overlord. Most Troubadour songs are much less interested in that lady's excellences (which are praised in habitual, desultory fashion) than in the desire to humiliate, annoy, or deceive her husband. Thus, the singer might satisfy two illicit cravings at once: to get a forbidden woman and, at the same time, exercise a good deal of homosexual fascination. Beyond this were the pleasures of a dual betrayal—offering to the lady that loyalty the singer owed her husband and the Christian deities, then using this false "loyalty" to convince her that she, too, should betray her husband, her feudal lord, her religion. Throughout these songs the husband is known as the jealous one, the thief, the liar. What else can you call a man of whom you are jealous, whose wife you are stealing, to whom you must continually lie?

As prosperity filtered downward during the next two centuries, this tradition spread through the *trouvères* and *minnesänger,* the French *chansons de toile,* and into the folk ballad which apparently began among the French peasantry of the fourteenth century. Throughout this process, the effects of a growing prosperity and security are seen in a growing concern with human wishes and aspirations (not merely actions), with personal psychology, with self-expression, with Love.

No doubt the spread of Romantic Love was hastened by the Albigensian Crusade in which the French obliterated Provence—ostensibly to clean up the vice down there; actually to bring it all back home. One of the chief effects of this Crusade, like most earlier ones, was that a little of Arabic high culture rubbed off on the barbarous Franks and Europeans. Likely enough, the Provençals themselves had picked up Romantic Love (with most of their musical and poetical practices) from brushes with the Moors in earlier Crusades. Those who survived the Albigensian Crusade were scattered all across Europe; no doubt this helped disseminate their type of song, their type of love. Yet surely any tradition that offered such lively music, together with so many opportunities for betrayal, was bound to catch on.

By the seventeenth century, the time of *A Midsummer Night's Dream,* the forces of church and state had managed to change Romantic Love—it had been, in every sense, housebroken. It had moved from the aristocratic warrior classes of the court (which it had helped undermine) into the households of the triumphant middle class. (We should not be surprised that capitalism, value through scarcity, first expressed itself in love.) It remains essential that the lady be unattainable—what's romantic about a woman you can have? But now the lady is single; the obstacle is not her husband, but her father. The aim

MOONSHINE AND SUNNY BEAMS

is not seduction but marriage against opposition. No doubt it must have seemed to the church and state—the initial targets of Romantic Love—that this was a less dangerous line of attack. Indeed, for a time it probably had a salutary effect: it may be argued that the sudden dramatic rise of Western culture over its neighbors was very much furthered and fueled by the tensions Romantic Love fostered between fathers and sons. When this tension could not be directly expressed, one result would be an increase of competition with other males and so a generally higher level of achievement. You can no more write a great play alone than you can run a great mile. You can only have Shakespeare *with* Marlowe and Jonson; Bannister *with* Landy and Chattaway. Such accomplishment usually demands a kind of admiring competition—and so is often more available to those not entirely comfortable with themselves or their loved ones.

In any case, the art form leading this attack against the father as center of authority was no longer the love lyric, but rather the drama. One often feels that half the surviving Renaissance plays portray the struggle of two young people to marry against their parents' opposition. If they can defeat, trick, or thwart those parents, it is automatically assumed they will settle down to love each other forever, all their dreams fulfilled. The play ends in confident assurance that this may be called "a happy ending."

This is one of the reasons it is so fitting that Bottom be an actor —consider the loss if the Craftsmen had decided to form a chorus and sing for Theseus's wedding! Beyond this, to be an actor, a role player, fits in perfectly with the anality, the antisexuality of his nature. The driving aim of an actor has always been to escape his own definition in a borrowed role, above all to escape sexual definition. Theater was greatest when only men played (Renaissance England, ancient Greece); the crowning achievement has always been to play the opposite sex.

This is to say that while actors and dramatists were among the first to demand freedom to control their own sexuality, what they really

231

sought was either the transformation or the obliteration of that sexuality. Thus we can clearly see in them those self-deceptive drives toward freedom which have proved so superbly productive in the hands of the gifted men who could sublimate them into areas such as the creative arts. We can also see the underlying passivity which would make these drives so destructive in the hands of the mob.

Bottom seems to have known all along where fashions in the arts were running, both in our greatest creative geniuses and in our popular travesties of art. The poem did not stop at eight and eight—it finally lost its erect shape altogether, falling into a soft and pliable (at worst, doughy) shape. Music overthrew the phallic hierarchy of the dominant seventh for the artificial communism, the unisex, of the tone row. The same tendencies could be followed out in any of the arts.

No doubt, most of our greatest artistic creations derive a part of their force from profoundly antisexual drives. The phallic artist whom D. H. Lawrence demanded was, after all, only a figment of his fantasies—above all, fantasies of becoming something diametrically opposed to the artist he was. Who can be sure that if he had become as phallic as he wished, he mightn't have stopped all artistic work? Knowing such achievements as Lawrence's or Whitman's, we can only be grateful for those less phallic forces which fostered them. At the same time, we may be horrified at the results of those drives as acted out directly by ordinary men: modern government and modern marriage, glamour and sexlessness, mediocrity and conformity, drugs and television, the paintings everyone can paint, the songs everyone can write.

Who says poetry makes nothing happen? The artist's open rendering of his emotions may have such unpredictable effects on the public that totalitarians from Plato to Stalin have been willing (with some justice) to muzzle or exterminate these unacknowledged and unconscious legislators. Poets and playwrights helped bequeath us a society where we could choose our own mates and settle down to lives of unmatchable wretchedness. A psychoanalyst recently commented that domestic troubles, unhappy love lives, have cost us more misery than all history's wars and famines together. Who can say him nay? It is only one of the ways we are now at the mercy of our pitiless fantasy lives.

Clearly, Egeus is a vengeful old cur, ill-equipped to pick a mate for Hermia. The only person less well equipped is Hermia. No more than anyone else am I willing to give up the right to pick my mate. No more than any other of the freedoms I habitually demand is this likely to make me happy or (unless I am uncommonly lucky) more creative or useful. My personal experience—and I have had too much—has been the exact opposite. To the best of my knowledge, no sensible person has ever tried to show that we Westerners have become either happier or more useful since we started picking our own mates.

Neither do I think Renaissance dramatists are responsible for the wretchedness of our families, the uselessness of our women, the emptiness of our men, the loneliness of our children. The artist's only business, after all, is to depict his passions honestly; the citizen must decide what to do about them. Artists, in fact, showed perfectly clearly how self-deceptive and dangerous those passions were; we preferred not to hear. We at least need not go on feeding ourselves the old lie that what is good for the artist is good for the citizen, or that what either one wants (or thinks he wants) is likely to be good for him. Both might recall what the Athenians knew: if the gods really hate you, they give you just what you're asking for.

IX. Weavers and Revolutionaries

If it is strangely apt that Bottom be an actor, how much more so that he be a weaver. Who can imagine him as anything else—Bottom the Butcher, Bottom the Greengrocer, Bottom the Hostler?

It's not just the name—that a bottom is the spool or base on which weavers wound thread. Not only that it is a sedentary trade, demanding a good deal of *sitzfleisch,* leaving its practitioner time for mooning and fantasizing (even as the Lovers were enchanted by "Love-in-Idleness"). So, as Hazlitt commented, it is right that Bottom be "accordingly represented as conceited, serious and fantastical."

It goes far deeper into our past. Weaving is a craft basal to our history, ingrained to our oldest thinking; it takes us even into our prehumanity—birds can do it, some with surprising skill. It has come to image some of life's most fundamental processes. We say a man's life is spun or woven by the weaving goddesses until his thread is finally cut. As Pyramus, Bottom rants:

> O Fates! come, come:
> Cut thread and thrum,
> Quail, crush, conclude and quell!

In Northern mythology, the Norns weave the loom of war, whose threads are weighted by human skulls. A man and a woman, in marriage and in sex, are seen as weaving the fabric of our life; Theseus says:

> . . . in the temple, by and by, with us
> These couples shall eternally be knit.

We have long used weaving, or related crafts, to represent the building of the body through digestion, or the building of the mind in its cross-lamination, layer on layer. We image the products of that mind, too, as a woven fabric. The radio announcer who late at night (when no one else would buy the time) read sentimental poems to sentimental music was called, of course, "The Dream Weaver." There is probably no creative act (unless it be weaving) for which we do not use weaving as a habitual metaphor.

If weaving is so involved with our ancient history, it is no less entangled with the building of our peculiar modern society. It was among the artisans, and especially among weavers, that the revolutionary religious ideas of the Albigensi took firmest root. Perhaps no single invention was more crucial in developing our special way of living than was the power loom. In this primeval skill, free craftsmen had to work as only slaves or manual laborers had worked before, not for fulfillment in their work but rather to get the money and free time to buy other enjoyments outside their work. Work became a burden, an imprisonment; the modern itch for fun was born. How much of good and of ill came there into our world! Throughout Europe, the early inventors of power weaving equipment were drowned, hanged, stoned, driven out—as if men knew what a Pandora's box was opening before them. But no use; modern society was not to be escaped.

One of the first plays involved with the revolutionary history of our modern democratic and communistic states is *The Weavers* by Gerhart Hauptmann, a play even more relativistic than is *A Midsummer Night's Dream*. It has no central character, no central group of characters, not even a central theme beyond a never-ending complaint: "It ain't fair!"

The most memorable representation of weavers in modern art, however, is rather to be found in the marvelous early drawings of Vincent van Gogh. In those rough, monumental scribbles I find something oddly bisexual: weaving is an art we always associate with the mother who nourishes, shelters, and comforts, yet it is most often practiced by men—and, in Vincent's drawings, men who are specially square-cut and rough-looking. Watching someone weave, I have always been impressed how satisfying the craft seems to its practitioners. Yet I have to be amused, too: it is as if the weaver had his own built-in sex act where he is both male and female; meantime, he rocks soothingly back and forward not only like the rhythm of sex but like the baby rocked by its mother or calmed by the rhythm of her heartbeat.

In Van Gogh's drawings, the weaver sits encased in his enormous loom like a man in the stocks, a child in his pen, the baby in the womb. Meantime, his own creation grows before him like an artificial belly or pregnancy. (It is a creation, too, embodying fundamental patterns, but usually centerless.) Like the fat man Auden mentions in *The*

Dyer's Hand, he has a built-in image of the mother he would join once more. (In the play, he rejoins her in the body of Titania. In the playlet he does not; he perishes.) The weaver, then, is symbolically self-sufficient; has taken over all roles. He has rid himself not only of the sex difference but of the size and generation difference—he is not only the contained baby, but also the containing and nourishing mother.

Vincent's weavers seem to me like the devotees of some goddess of fertility and motherhood—say Cybele, whose priests castrated themselves in consecration to her. They sit self-imprisoned in the loom as if in the stocks, totally absorbed in the fabric of their rites. The goddess of their devotion is bodied forth by the almost ever-present lamp hanging over the loom—in his letters, Vincent writes with near-ecstasy of finding one of those lamps. We may trace that lamp and its symbolic relatives all through Vincent's work, beginning with the cradle scenes. The lamp (in my mind, it resembles that "lanthorn" Starveling carries into the Duke's chamber as Moon) represents that light which announces to the baby that he will soon be fed and is, ever after, associated in his mind with all that is warm and comforting. It glows over the world of these trapped and shackled weavers just the way the moon glimmers above the world of changeling and Starveling, the enchanted world of *A Midsummer Night's Dream.*

X. Moonshine

In almost every overt way, the play gives victory to the male, hands the child to its father. The little changeling boy is awarded to Oberon —presumably to be trained and follow in his image. True, Theseus tempers Egeus's vengeful severity against his daughter, even helps her escape a full confrontation with the law by his "private schooling" of Demetrius. Yet he also makes it clear she cannot flout that law: had Demetrius not relented, she apparently would still have to choose between her father's will and chastity or death. Although neither the father's will nor Athenian law, then, are left as immutable or inescapable forces, both remain operant powers which must at least be successfully evaded. That evasion will probably require help from the Duke, a male ordering authority or father-surrogate.

Yet the male's victory, like so much else here, may well be illusory. Theseus seems very much in control; he is, in fact, completely dependent on unrecognized forces. Oberon is awarded the child; his triumph never pervades the mind as does the recollection of the imperious Titania, supreme in her bower.

From our vantage in time, it is easy to see that Theseus's and Egeus's days are numbered; Bottom who has lain beside darker powers, will soon oust both of them. It is astonishing for Shakespeare, so near this culture's first greatness, to render so clearly the drives which first produced that greatness, and now draw us toward decay. He could hardly have imagined that the machine and the bomb would make Theseus, if not obsolete, expendable. He could not imagine a people so luxurious and leisurely they could dispose of Theseus's strength, authority, aggressiveness, ability; that mediocrity *could* drive out superiority. He did see, only too clearly, the complex of emotions which, once this became possible, would make it inevitable. As a tree or animal contains, in the structures of its growth, the principles of its limits and death, cultures seem to hold, in the very form of their successes, the forces which eventually destroy them. To have attacked so successfully the centers of direct and conscious authority seems to have left us at the mercy of unconscious powers whose despotism may be much more far-reaching.

The play's most powerful image—Bottom in Titania's cradle—holds both the constructive and the decadent side of this complex. On the one hand, we usually think of creative work in strongly phallic terms, and without considerable phallic drive, the creative man can scarcely perform. On the other hand, it must also be noted that most of our truly creative men have had very strong mothers and have been deeply attached to them, even directly imitative of them. We have already noted that the experience of Titania's bower may be quintessential to the creative act; we have also noted what incredible energies we have tapped in the boy's desire to replace his father in that bower, or in the opposing desire to lose his own sexuality in becoming his mother. Yet those desires are only valuable so long as they are frustrated, unfulfilled—so long as the child embodies the unresolved struggle of his parents. Naturally, we all would see that conflict resolved; to resolve it through the evisceration of either power may be to eviscerate the child and perhaps, also, that civilization built partly upon the tensions of that struggle. Detente implies that both opposed powers *remain* powers; for all the dangers of antagonism, we would not lose the enormous energies it has given us.

If the father is successfully castrated or driven out, or if one's own sex is successfully obliterated, then all that tension—the source of energy—is dissipated. How quickly all that phallicism turns anal and passive, all that invention turns sluggish, static, aimless. We fight our way, with what vigor, to the throne, to Titania's bower. Once there, we just can't seem to think of anything to do.

How imperceptibly competition turns to betrayal. Given our special circumstances, the boy's attachment to his mother can be used to enlist him in the general weakening of the male—ultimately, himself. The baby's fear of abandonment has always given the mother immense powers over the imagination. This makes her less subject to our natural compulsion to betray whomever we love. But add to this the Industrial Revolution which makes the male seem dispensable, Romantic Love with all its castrative possibilities, individualistic philosophies with all their self-deception; it scarcely bodes well for the male. What can the too successful young man do?—he has helped undermine the forces that might have sustained and directed him in this surplus of power. Now there is no one left to betray but himself.

Or he can betray the active ideals he used to reach the seat of power. Why not settle down to be babied, soothed and pampered, lied to, fed and cajoled?

Be kind and courteous to this gentleman:
Hop in his walks and gambol in his eyes;
Feed him with apricocks and dewberries,
With purple grapes, green figs, and mulberries;
The honey-bags steal from the humblebees,
And for night-tapers crop their waxen thighs,
And light them at the firey glow-worm's eyes.
To have my love to bed and to arise; . . .
Tie up my love's tongue, bring him silently.

Or, better still, feed him on endless beer and potato chips, plant his ever-widening buttocks before an inextinguishable television set, all channels of which play various episodes from an endless soap opera called "Bottom's Dream." We are not ruled by those who have an idea of what the state should do, nor even of what they want from it. We are ruled by any who can contact and control the dream life of the masses. It is not bread and circuses; it is ice cream and revolutions, equal pay and concentration camps. If I speak of Hitler and Stalin, it is only to avoid mentioning anyone closer home.

Nowhere is the mother's dominion over the unconscious world of the play more evident than in the omnipresence of the Moon. No doubt Dr. Gui is right to see it as the symbol of the mother's breast, of that nourishment the child must have or die. Titania, her earthly avatar, echoes that breast in her very name; Hippolyta, so closely kin to her, must lack one teat, thus already suggesting the possibility of starvation. Who is it, after all, that carried the Moon's lanthorn and thornbush?—none but Starveling. The Moon, then, is indeed "governess of floods," the tides of liquid in our world. But the Moon is also goddess of virginity and of marriage, of barrenness and of birth, of grudging coldness and of warm affection. She shines on the Lovers as on the raging, hate-filled Fairies. She is patroness of Art, of Illusion, of Dreaming, of Lunacy—of all those forces that control the wide-awake, sunlit, reasonable, paternalistic city of Theseus.

Dr. Gui reminds us that if Theseus's first speech is true, then

239

throughout the whole time of the play there is no Moon shining at all. The Moon, then, the symbol of Illusion, may itself be an illusion. Why talk so much about it, if one were sure that it was really there? Why weave so cunning a web as this play, so circular, so delicately filigreed, so glimmering with dew, if one were really able to catch the thing itself?

No one of the worlds of this play can be truly understood or located until we know its relation to the Moon. And, after all, in so relativistic a play as this one, all worlds may very well revolve around the Moon.

Glorying in Failure:
Cervantes and Don Quixote

W hat could Cervantes have hoped for in writing *Don
Quixote?* Did he suppose he was creating a masterpiece, one that
would outlast not only the Spanish empire, but probably all Western
civilization? Hardly. Did he think he was inventing the comic epic of
a nation and age—and so dissolving the myths and beliefs not only
of that nation, but of himself, a dedicated, an almost bigoted Spanish
Christian? Certainly not. Did he suppose he could be mocking all
idealism, all attempts to establish an ideal realm here, and most
particularly mocking the preposterous spiritual claims of the greedy
Spanish empire in its attacks on the Turks and on Flanders? Not
bloody likely. Could he have had even an inkling that he would make
a laughing stock not only of the Church militant, but ultimately of the
whole spirit of Christianity? He would have been the first to burn any
such book. Yet I think, in spite of his own beliefs and aspirations, in
spite of his own desperate efforts to write nothing of the kind, that is
just the book he wrote.

241

What, then, did Cervantes himself think he was doing? As to his subject matter, he counsels himself in his introduction:

> you have no other object in view than that of overthrowing the authority and prestige which books of chivalry enjoy. . . .

Later, speaking of hopes for readers, he says:

> Let it be your aim that . . . the melancholy may be moved to laughter and the cheerful man made merrier still; let the simple not be bored, but may the clever admire your originality; let the grave ones not despise you, but let the prudent praise you.

Clearly, he had in mind a light and popular entertainment, a spoof on those chivalric books to which he had himself been addicted. He must have hoped it might become popular and help lighten his chronic debts—perhaps, by great luck it might gain the favor of Lope de Vega or some great noble and help rescue him from lifelong obscurity and literary failure. Like Shakespeare, then, he wrote an incredible masterpiece which he probably thought was a potboiler. Cervantes's pot, though, steadfastly refused to boil. As in everything he undertook, he failed. Such failure, of course, makes success look paltry.

Of Cervantes's life, we know even less than of Shakespeare's; all we do know is disheartening. We don't even know his birthdate. The son of a wandering physician who had no diploma, he was afflicted with deafness, and was at least once jailed for debt. He was christened on October 9, 1547. His early life is a blank to us. At twenty-one, he was a student in Madrid; at twenty-two, chamberlain to Cardinal Acquaviva in Rome. He may already have fought with the Spanish forces in Flanders; at any rate, by the age of twenty-three, he joined a Spanish company stationed in Italy.

During this period, Spanish soldiers were the finest in Europe (fighting was perhaps the only thing the Spanish empire did well); Cervantes must have been one of the best. The next year he served under the famous Don John of Austria in the great naval battle of

Lepanto, where together, the Spanish, Venetians, and the Papal States broke the Turkish forces in the Mediterranean. Here, Cervantes particularly distinguished himself. Though sick with malaria, he demanded to be carried on deck to take part in the fighting; he was wounded twice in the chest and his left hand was maimed for life. Cervantes never doubted that the battle of Lepanto was the high point of this life which it had maimed.

After a period in the hospital, Cervantes entered another regiment, served in various parts of the Mediterranean, and fought in the battles of La Goleta and Tunis. In 1575, aged twenty-eight, he embarked with his brother to return to Spain, carrying letters of commendation from the Duke of Sessa and from Don John of Austria himself. These letters, which led him to expect high preferment, proved his undoing. His galley was captured by pirates and, since he seemed a person of importance, he was held for ransom in Algiers. Again he distinguished himself in courage and initiative, leading attempts to escape and winning even his captors' admiration. Only after five years was he ransomed and returned to Madrid, thirty-four years old and nearly destitute.

His family had made terrible sacrifices to ransom him and was deeply in debt. His father's health and livelihood were failing. Worse, Cervantes's hopes of preferment failed—perhaps the name Lepanto had already lost some of its magic. No post came his way. At this juncture, Cervantes apparently made a decision possible only to a man deeply in love with loss: unable to make a living in politics and government, he became a writer.

This, too, failed. Within three years he must have written almost thirty plays. Not one was performed; only two have survived. At that moment the Spanish theater was dominated by Lope de Vega, a star of such magnitude that no one else could even enter the field against him without his approval—that, Cervantes never obtained.

In the following years, a pastoral romance, *La Galatea,* was published, but apparently received little notice and less money. Of the many verses Cervantes wrote throughout his life, one poem received some praise and a second won three silver spoons. Otherwise, both stories and poems went unpublished. Meantime, his domestic situation deteriorated, with his own active collusion. In the early 1580s, he had an illegitimate daughter, Isabel, apparently by a Portuguese actress. In 1584, aged thirty-eight, he married a peasant girl of nineteen. So, like the hero of that novel he had yet to write, he became the head of a household of impoverished gentlefolk, a household of women—a wife, an illegitimate daughter, two sisters, a niece, and a maidservant. Early in this marriage he could not even provide a house; his wife lived at home with her brothers.

Finally, after three or four years of marriage, he *did* manage to obtain a steady position from the crown; he became a roving commissary to the fleet, requisitioning supplies for the Invincible Armada which was to attack England and end, once and for all, her power at sea. This position lasted some fifteen years. If Cervantes could have foreseen the tribulations it would bring him, he might well have preferred to go on starving.

During this period, Cervantes made Seville his home base, though from time to time he moved, apparently because of debts. He spent most of his time traveling through the villages and countryside of Andalusia and La Mancha trying to collect stores and taxes from the peasants. They demonstrated against him; he was excommunicated for appropriating church supplies. Twice, perhaps thrice, he was jailed for faulty accounts. Meantime his own pay was usually far in arrears and his creditors, as always, pressing.

Out of this background, then, in 1605, at fifty-eight years of age, Cervantes produced the first modern novel, probably the greatest novel. As already suggested, he must have felt his other works were of greater artistic merit but hoped this would relieve his habitual poverty and lifelong neglect. He was, of course, disappointed.

The book did receive instant acclaim. Six editions appeared within the first year; Don Quixote and Sancho Panza were the talk of everyone from the court down to the poorest peasant. Yet Lope de Vega had sneered at the book before it ever appeared—as a result, the publisher didn't bother to properly copyright it. Of those first six editions, four were pirated. Cervantes seems to have realized almost no money from the book. Though it made him famous, it seems not to have helped his position with the court or the literati: in 1610, he was deeply disappointed to be omitted from a group of literary men chosen to accompany his patron, the Count of Lemnos, to Rome.

Cervantes was able to publish his later works: *Exemplary Novels* in 1613, *The Journey to Parnassus* the following year, and *Eight Comedies and Eight Interludes* the year after that. *Persiles and Sigismunda* was published in 1617, a year after Cervantes's death, though a part of it may have been written in his youth.

The ending of the first part of *Don Quixote* had left the reader in doubt whether or not Cervantes would fashion any further adventures for his hero. In 1614, however, a spurious sequel to *Don Quixote* appeared, written under the pseudonym of Alonso Fernández de Avellaneda. Cervantes, enraged, hurriedly finished his own second part and published it the following year, 1615, when he was himself sixty-nine. Only a year later (April 23, 1616), he died, seventy years old and as wretchedly poor and neglected as he had lived. In England ten days later, Shakespeare died, though differences in calendars make it appear they died the same day.

We do not know the exact place of Cervantes's burial in the grounds of the Trinitarian Nuns in Madrid. It is a fitting irony that since the time of his death and burial there, those grounds have been renamed: the Calle de Lope de Vega.

If this is the author and his idea of what he was doing, what have the critics thought he did? The most common thing to say about the book, especially since Lionel Trilling's splendid essay, "Manners, Morals and the Novel," is that it concerns Reality and Appearance.

And no doubt a great part of the book is riddled with this theme. This was, after all, the Renaissance's greatest obsession; it would be hard to find any great book of the period that didn't touch on it.

Reality and Appearance is surely a thematic center for most of those farcical adventures famous even among those who've never read the book. The episode of the windmills, for instance: as usual, Sancho sees what is really there—windmills—while the Don sees great giants whirling their arms about. He charges in to the attack and is, as usual, battered and hurled down. This is true of the many scenes where the Don mistakes an inn for a castle, the innkeeper for castellan, the whores for princesses; or of the wild bedroom scenes where everyone gets entangled—Maritornes the servant-prostitute, her carter boy-friend, the watchmen, the innkeeper, Don Quixote and Sancho Panza —all thrashing about furiously in the dark unable to find out who is who. We are constantly faced with the effort to identify persons and things: is this a barber's basin or Mambrino's helmet; a steed's capari-son or a mule's packsaddle; is this Ginés de Pasamonte, Ginesillo de Parapilla, or a gypsy puppeteer named Pedro?

In the earlier chapters, Don Quixote is usually just plain wrong. He looks at one thing and sees another. We have no doubt about what the object "really" is, or about whether he's wrong. These episodes progress, often, into problems of madness and hallucination. For instance, early in Part I, we have an encounter in the Sierra Morena between Don Quixote and the lovelorn Cardenio, a madman of belief and a madman of love, each liable to attack others when his fantasies present them to him as guilty, as those who have caused his grief.

As the book progresses, however, we become less and less able to reject the Don's reasoning; partly because his rationalizations become subtler and more convincing, partly because the book's view of reality becomes more complex. We begin to wonder if the Don isn't right; we are not at all so certain that *we* are. He, himself, begins to realize that others see things differently and that their view may be correct. Meantime, his madness, his very errors seem less reprehensible, in-

246

deed they are so persuasive that they begin to draw in almost everyone who meets him. We begin to doubt the value of being right, even of sanity:

> As for myself, I may say that, since becoming a knight-errant, I am brave, polite, liberal, well-bred, generous, courteous, bold, gentle, patient, and long-suffering when it comes to enduring hardships, imprisonment, and enchantments; and although it was only a short while ago that I was shut up in a cage as a madman, I still expect, through the valor of my arm, with Heaven favoring and fortune not opposing, to find myself within a few days king of some realm or other where I may be able to display the gratitude and liberality that is in my heart.*

We scarcely share those sanguine expectations, yet concur in the Don's self-appraisal; he has shown those qualities which are seldom possible to the sane man.

Besides, the Don's ideas often are so close to noble religious and philosophical positions that we can't comfortably reject them. He is in love with a lady whom he has only seen once or twice, if that, and whom he calls Dulcinea del Toboso. Yet the reader, like Sancho, knows she is actually a strapping peasant wench named Aldonza Lorenzo, who heaves sacks of grain around and stinks of sweat. Early in Part II, Sancho shows her (or another girl who appears much the same) to the Don. Confronted by the crudity of her "appearance"— which we take for her "reality"—he decides that we have merely turned things around. He decides Dulcinea is *really* the beautiful princess of his imagination, but that evil enchanters have transformed her into the sweaty, jeering slut we all see.

Who can prove he's wrong? Besides, is he really any sillier, say, than Dante in his commitment to Beatrice? Like Dante, he has picked an earthly female he has scarcely seen to serve as symbol of his heavenly passion. If Dante had ever become closely acquainted with the human, physical Bice Portinari, wouldn't he probably have found

*All quotations are from the Samuel Putnam translation.

her ill-tempered, neurotic, as hard to live with as most humans? And wouldn't he have said this was not the *real* Beatrice but some evil transformation of her? "She's not herself today," we say of those we love, being careful never to tally how many days she *is*. Some of us never are. "Is it the real me?" we ask—meaning that self we wish we could become.

Moreover, in his commitment to Dulcinea, Don Quixote is paralleling not only Dante and Beatrice, but their supposed models, the true Christian and the Virgin Mary. In taking his image of Dulcinea (or of anything else—an inn, a whore, a packsaddle) to be more real than its appearance, doesn't the Don echo religion's noblest illusion: that we are not *really* animals who may or may not be capable of possessing a soul and attaining to certain good qualities—that is an illusion. *Really,* we are souls debased through birth, degraded by captivity in our human bodies, by transformation into the sweaty animals we now appear to be. Is not the Don echoing the notion of all dualists that nothing seen here is *real,* but only a debased shadow of some nobler reality? Is he not like the Neo-Platonist, or the Church militant, in his effort to make this world conform to an ideal, the really real, trying to build the City of God on earth?

Such questions have extended philosophical and religious complications. Many critics have noticed here a struggle between an absolute Truth on one hand, and on the other relativism, individualism, perspectivism. This turns up, for instance, in the continual question of names which reflect a social reality or appearance, a moral reality or appearance. Zoraida, the Captive's Moorish bride, changes her name to Maria when she converts; Ginés de Pasamonte (who is possibly Ginesillo de Parapilla) changes his name to become Master Pedro, the gypsy puppeteer. The lovelorn Dorotea becomes first a nameless boy, then the Princess Micomicona. The Bachelor Carrasco as he gets drawn into the Don's madness becomes first the Knight of the Mirrors, then the Knight of the White Moon. The Duke and Duchess—like the curate or the innkeeper—have no personal names we know of. They are known by their social function, though this does not prevent them from having distinct traits of character. Don Quixote, by contrast, has no social function, but has a whole raft of names. We do not know his real name. First, he is Don Quixote, or Quijada, or Quesada, or Quejana but as he begins trying to change himself he becomes for a moment Rinaldo of Montalban, then the Knight of the Woeful Countenance, then the Knight of the Lions. When a neighbor expostulates that he is "a respectable gentleman by the name of Señor Quijana," he replies, "I know who I am and who I may be, if I choose. . . ." Yet when he is defeated and dejected, ready to die, he says, "I am no longer Don Quixote de la Mancha but Alonso Quijano, whose mode of life won for him the name of 'Good.' " In almost a thousand pages of text we had encountered neither that name nor that epithet; what *is* the truth about him?

Much related to the names are the disguises of every sort—a typical device of Renaissance drama and fiction, one always involved with problems of reality. We meet women disguised as men, men as women, thieves as gypsies, students as knights-errant, rich men as shepherds, and so on indefinitely.

One step beyond this we have the open fantasies—the dreams and visions, the symbology of moons and mirrors, the conscious dream of art. In art, of course, we have a deliberately created illusion, yet one that may become in some way more real and true than the natural world. Don Quixote, as we should expect, can't distinguish what reality is proper to a work of art: he goes to a puppet play and gets involved in the puppets' struggle. All the characters of the novel have their own worlds of fantasy and projection, their chosen fictional heroes, their pet illusions. Even the curate himself, holding an Inquisition on the Don's books, gets caught by a favorite romance, begins reciting its wild-eyed adventures, and gives it to the barber to read. The Don's own fantasies, too, have special appeal for many of the characters—on almost any excuse they will get themselves up in costume or disguise to act a part in his private drama. In time, we hardly believe this is all done merely to cure the Don—you can seldom cure my cold by catching it. Yet the other characters maintain a distinction between their fantasies and their practical everyday affairs, between belief and action. They gallop off into Never-Never Land just as readily as the Don, but they find better excuses; they never claim it is really there. The Don believes in what he is doing, so we know he is insane.

A closely related meaning lies in the author's pretense that this is not a novel at all, but rather a true history which he is translating. At points, the story is interrupted while the pretended translator pretends he cannot find a text that tells the *truth* about Don Quixote; once, he denounces his own book as apocryphal. In the book, Don Quixote presumes to criticize his own author; the pretended author, Cid Hamete, makes certain criticisms of his as yet nonexistent translator even though we know Cid Hamete is himself a fiction of that supposed future translator, the real author. Again, early in Part II, the Bachelor Carrasco and Don Quixote discuss whether that same volume, Part II, will ever be written; they decide it probably won't! The Don and Sancho are then questioned about one of Cervantes's slips in Part I—the theft of Sancho's ass. When they try to set the record straight about this previous fictitious event, most of the new explanation is itself a patent lie! Before long, the Don begins to meet various characters who have already read about him either in Part I or in the spurious Part II. Next he begins to encounter characters he has never seen before but who claim, either lyingly or innocently, to have known him. The Knight of the Mirrors (actually the disguised Bachelor Carrasco) claims to have defeated him in combat; Don Alvaro Tarfe, whom he meets at an inn, believes he had induced him to attend a tournament at Saragossa. Since it was the false Don Quixote from the spurious Part II he had known, the problem here is to identify the *real* fictitious madman. Ultimately, Don Alvaro takes an oath that he has not seen what he did see and that what happened to him could not have happened. All this becomes, at times, positively dizzying.

These problems of authorship also echo into some of the theological areas we have already broached—especially in the book's insistence that there *must* be a true text, that these great adventures could not possibly occur without some author telling us what truly happened, just as the Don insists that his noble actions must be recorded by some later scribe. This could only be true, of course, of a holy text or a holy action. If one of *us* should happen to perform a noble act, that might drop into instant obscurity; in our world infamy has a far better chance of survival. Don Quixote, on the contrary, deliberately takes actions just so that his chronicler may truly report them; he avoids certain actions (e.g., going to Saragossa) just because the actual false author of Part II reported them. Beyond this, he accounts for certain actions of his own or Sancho's on the grounds that this must have been what his future scribe wanted them to do at this point. Much of this seems a direct parody of teleological argument or of Biblical interpretation: "All this was done to fulfill the prophecy. . . ."

No doubt, as Trilling suggests, such philosophical problems naturally rise in a society where money brings social fluidity and breaks down hierarchies of nobility. You tend to get all sorts of social pretense and falsehood, the need to keep up appearances. This enters the novel directly in Sancho's social climbing, his desire to govern an island, make his daughter a countess, dress up his son to look like what he is not. It is seen even more directly in the Don's poverty, his ragged nobility—for all the greatness of his ideals, he must sit up at night worrying about how to darn his stockings. This creates a strong contrast with the luxurious ignobility of the actual nobles, Don Fernando and the Duke.

This problem does encompass, then, much of the book. Far from all of it. I have been talking as if this were a tightly knit, idea-structured novel. Nothing could be farther from the truth. The book is almost a hodgepodge, almost a grabbag of odd and discordant materials many of which relate neither to a satire on chivalric romances nor to problems of Reality. This is specially true of the "inserted novellas"—the completely unrelated stories crammed into Part I. These insertions have been criticized from the beginning; early in Part II, Cervantes pauses to answer some of those who had already complained about them. For myself I would have to say that they may constitute an aesthetic flaw in the novel, but they raise such interesting and far-reaching personal and human problems that I would be sorry to lose them. They are, in a sense, so vastly incongruous as to suggest a breadth of spirit. Perhaps they make a poorer novel; they make a richer and deeper human document. In any case, there are five such inserted stories which I will list and briefly summarize:

1. Grisóstomo and Marcela. A young student dies for love of a girl who becomes a shepherdess to escape all lovers.

2. Cardenio and Luscinda; Don Fernando and Dorotea. Cardenio runs amuck after losing Luscinda to Don Fernando, the villain. Meantime, Dorotea—abandoned by Don Fernando—roams about disguised as a boy. All happen to meet at an inn and the villain reforms.

3. "A Man Too Curious for His Own Good." (The manuscript of a tale which has been left at the inn and which the guests read for amusement.) Anselmo, married to Camila, tests her virtue with his best friend, Lotario; she falls. This becomes entangled with a love affair of the maid, Leonela. Tragedy falls on all.

4. The Captive and Lela Zoraida. Cervantes's own story prettied up and given a happy ending: a soldier comes back destitute from the wars but brings back a pretty Moorish girl and finds a rich brother. Meantime the brother's daughter, Doña Clara, is pursued by young Don Luis. Everyone is reunited at the same time as those in story 2.

5. Eugenio, Anselmo, and Leandra. More students wandering about as shepherds, lamenting for Leandra, stolen by Vicente de la Rosa.

Now, what in the world *are* all these love affairs doing in the middle of the Don's adventures? We've grown accustomed to Renaissance dramas full of subplots which reflect back on the main plot to enlighten it. But this is ridiculous. These stories have nothing to do with knightly romance and little to do with Reality. Worse yet, they completely reverse the novel's attitudes. The book has taken a very hard line against romantic and idealistic beliefs. To mock them, we have turned loose a man holding such beliefs in a very realistic landscape, a world of inns, whores, convicts, muledrivers. We may not specially like this realistic world, but the whole aim of the contrast is to mock the insanity of a man whose beliefs and idealisms have divorced him from the only world that exists.

Yet if the Don should once meet a shepherd along the highway, everything is instantly changed. Not only do we cross into Never-Never Land—we are expected to believe in it. The shepherds, unlike the whores or mule skinners, are completely idealized. They never do things *real* shepherds do—chase wolves, worry about pasture rights, buy sheep dip. Instead, they sit about wailing for their false true loves, carving names in trees, writing sonnets. Men go mad for love; men die for love. Girls dress up as men and go hunting for faithless lovers. Long-lost relatives bump into one another just in time to prevent tragedies. Villains see their folly and marry the right girl; the right girl marries the villain and calls it a happy ending. In short, we plunge headlong into all the claptrap of Renaissance pastoral romance—a tradition every bit as silly and idealized as chivalric romance ever thought of being.

These inserted romances *do* have some relation to the main story; the lovers show some similarities to Don Quixote. First, both are in search of a Golden Age of virtue, peace, justice, and comfort; second, both are forlorn in love. And these two pursuits are probably not so diverse as they might seem. Both may well be an expression of a more basic urge—a need to seek and lament for an unattainable. One scarcely pursues the Golden Age or the heavenly beloved in order to

253

obtain it, but rather to localize and focus a sense of grief, to express and so release an abiding sense of loss. Of all the lovers, only Don Quixote is wise enough to see that he needn't trouble any actual, living girl with his passion. He need only pick out a girl, any girl, assume she doesn't return his love, then go up into the wasteland to lament. As Sancho tells us, his master enjoys these lamentations immensely.

The lovers and Don Quixote share another quality—they are idle. The lovers have no work because they are young and well-to-do; the Don because he is old and obsolete. No doubt one of the aims of his quest must be to recover a useful military past, his own or history's; what he romanticizes as the days of knighthood are in fact the days when the nobility had a real military function in a hard-pressed society. Yet he sees himself as seeking a future of significance and justice—he is a type of all wild-eyed reformers riding out to set the world straight. Like most of them, he is little help to the world— Andrés only gets his beating doubled—and for his troubles usually gets his teeth scattered, his bones rattled. Yet, if you have done little work, for whatever reason, you are likely to believe you *can* improve the world; the less you have done, the easier it is to believe in your own virtue. This helps account for the gradual deepening of the Don's character as the book progresses; as he gains experience, he loses infallibility. Losing battles, he loses certitude; he gains humanity.

But idleness not only leaves one innocently self-righteous; it also leaves one time to brood, to keep vigils, and so darkens his own sense of loss, his need for lamentation. The Don, like the lovers, must be careful to pick a Lady who is not attainable—at least not for a suitably long time. Again, like most reformers, he must only set out on impossible quests or he might deprive himself of those losses he needs to mourn. The lovers, too, though they seem to have time and money to construct a life and landscape to their liking, build their world around a central loss, an unattainable loved one. Fittingly, it is the Don who warns the shepherds and lovers that Marcela must not be too closely pursued. She (like Beatrice) is the symbol of the divine, so must be allowed to leave us when she wills or when she wills to pass among us, beloved, tantalizing, and untouchable. The divine must be unattainable, so all coldness, all cruelty must be forgiven.

In any case, such lamentation is not much needed by Sancho, the peasants, the working people of the novel. Sancho greatly enjoys griping; the deeper accesses of grief are a luxury denied him. For him, hard work and trouble take the place of forlorn love. He doesn't need a fantasy of persecution; he's persecuted:

> all the rest of the night was spent by Don Quixote in thinking of his lady Dulcinea, in imitation of Marcela's lovers. As for Sancho, he made himself comfortable between Rocinante and the ass and at once dropped off to sleep, not like a lovelorn swain but, rather, like a man who has had a sound kicking that day.

For myself, I am less concerned with what light these lovers cast on the hero by their similarities to him, than I am in what light they throw on the author by their dissimilarities to the rest of the story. Let me propose a heretical reading. In the author's continual interruptions, in the inserted novellas, in the break between Parts I and II, I think we have a record of Cervantes's almost desperate effort to not write a masterpiece. I think we see here a man trying fiercely, if unconsciously, to stop saying things which he, and everyone in his culture, would have found unbearable. It is one of his glories that he failed—he could not write the trivial entertainment he wanted; in spite of himself he wrote the masterpiece he must have dreaded. His special good fortune was that no one at the time, himself included, needed consciously to know why they were laughing so hard at his book.

While we state the book's theme so broadly as Reality and Appearance, or as a satire on Neo-Platonic idealism, on reformers, even on idealism generally, little threat appears. It is easy enough for the reader, and for Cervantes, to detach himself and think he is laughing only at the folly of others. If we narrow this, however, to a satire on Christian idealism, Christian reform, the militant Christian Spain, something very different appears. Cervantes surely thought himself a Christian idealist; so did nearly all his readers. Yet I have already noted quite a number of ways that the book parodies the church, Mariolatry, basic Christian theology, even the life of Christ itself.

No doubt other strands of satiric meaning will have already suggested themselves. Some readers may object that we could find nearly as many parallels to the life of Christ and the Christian in any of the chivalric romances. That is precisely the point: in a culture where many things take their name or form from the state religion, those things may easily become parodies of their models. If my parents had named me Jesus, my career would unavoidably stand as a mockery of that greater existence. Yet it would be hard to attack my career without also attacking the model standing behind me. The stories of knights-errant were deliberate imitations of the life of Christ. Many, of course, imitated it so poorly that they already approached parody. We should not be surprised that an attack on the knights-errant might reflect some criticism back onto their models—Christ and the Christian church.

Our hero, Don Quixote, comes to birth (or to christening; his birth as hero) in the stableyard of an inn where there was no room. His armor is baptized in a horse trough; his service read from an account book. He sets out into the world to "right every manner of wrong," to help maidens and widows, succor the oppressed, drive out the tyrant, the money changer, the evil-hearted. One widow (Doña Rodríguez, the duenna) tells her woes to him because he is the one "capable of remedying those of all the world." He treats whores and adulterous women better than we would, yet he is notably chaste himself. To men he would bring not only justice, but a gift of healing —the Balsam of Fierabrás. Knowing the miseries of the world, he becomes the Knight of the Mournful Countenance, a man of sorrows and acquainted with grief.

He battles in the name of an ideal lady who is to him as is the soul to the body. "She fights and conquers in my person, and I live and breathe and have my life and being in her!" At times he goes up into the mountainous wastelands to meditate upon her, to fast and mortify his flesh. In battle, he turns his eyes to her presumed abode, Heaven, and prays to her for that power which she, godlike, dispenses. He forces strangers to swear to her divine beauty and grace or else be branded disbelieving traitors and heretics who can be battered into submission. Probably her most striking resemblance to the Virgin is that these strangers must swear to her divinity or beauty without ever seeing her or receiving any proof; they must accept her on faith or be destroyed as unbelievers. The Jews and Moors of Spain had already been forced to swear just such an oath to the Christian deity—then had been robbed and driven out anyway.

Though a number of characters come to follow him on one pretext or another, the hero has only one true disciple: Sancho Panza does rise up and follow him, forsaking both wife and children. To him, Don Quixote plays both God and teacher. Whenever Sancho dares disagree, especially about Dulcinea's desirability, he is at once branded a "disbelieving traitor . . . heretic . . . a bad Christian" and "excommunicate." While the Don never washes Sancho's feet, he does in moments of humility curry and feed their animals, and once while teaching shepherds about the Golden Age, invites his first disciple to sit next to him at table. Sancho, of course, refuses the honor—he'd rather sit among the lowly where he can belch as he pleases. Though the loyal Sancho never sells out or denies his master (he merely denies his sanity), his first thoughts on the Balsam of Fierabrás concern what it would bring on the market. Like other disciples, Sancho finds it hard to stay awake while his master keeps vigils.

This hero is defeated in every worldly sense, captured and brought to stand trial. Three times he is brought in to judgment—the first time, riding on an ass, the second time on display in a cage. Just as he himself is several times accused of founding a heretic sect, a false religion, so his library is forced to stand Inquisition and most of it consigned to the flames. Like most epic heroes, he does descend to the

257

underworld in the Cave of Montesinos, where, like the supreme Hero, he believes he stayed three days. Later, he is permitted to pass among the heavenly spheres on the wooden horse, Clavileño. After his defeat, he is led through Barcelona on a mule to be mocked by boys and scoffers, as was Christ through Jerusalem. On his back is a sign: THIS IS DON QUIXOTE DE LA MANCHA. If he is not exactly crucified, he is trampled by cattle and swine, degraded and mortified, and finally destroyed by one of his false disciples, the Bachelor Carrasco, who has not even the grace to go out and hang himself. Instead, it is the Don's armor that is left hanging on the trees beside the bodies of criminals. He is brought home beside Sancho's dappled ass which wears a robe figured with fiery flames and wearing a miter—like the Lord of Misrule. Yet in his final defeat and mortification, he reaches his highest glory; as Sancho says on returning to their village:

> Open your eyes, O beloved homeland, and behold your son, Sancho Panza, returning to you. If he does not come back very rich, he comes well flogged. Open your arms and receive also your other son, Don Quixote, who returns vanquished by the arm of another but a victor over himself; and this, so I have been told, is the greatest victory that could be desired.

It is, of course, important that the Don is not specifically a teacher and healer, but rather a warrior. His enemies are usually identical with the historical enemies of the church: not merely infidels, but the Eastern pagan powers, the Moors or Turks. This is natural enough since many of the chivalric romances dealt with the Crusades and other wars against the Eastern powers; yet this too brings its element of satire. This is nowhere more prominent than in the battle of the sheep in Chapter 18 of Part I. The Don, seeing two large flocks of sheep being driven in opposite directions, imagines them two great armies approaching to do battle, one led by the pagan Alifanfarón, lord of Trapobana, the other led by the Christian Pentapolín of the Rolled-up Sleeve, king of the Garamantas. Standing to one side, the Don describes the great champions of each force (rather like a parody of the *Iliad*'s catalogue of ships) then joins the battle himself on what he takes to be the Christian side. Of course it is telling enough that beneath all the clouds of dust, beneath the gorgeous chivalric appearance, beneath the supposed cause of the fight (Alifanfarón's desire to marry the Christian king's beautiful daughter), beneath the ideological trappings, lies a sordid reality—all the warriors on both sides are nothing but sheep, probably being driven to market and to slaughter, driven in any case only for their keepers' profit. Even more revealing are the specific wounds received by the Don: several broken ribs, a couple of lost grinders, and two badly mashed fingers—almost precisely the wounds Cervantes himself received in the battle of Lepanto.

Further, in the Don's relation to Sancho and his promise to make him governor of an island, we tend not only toward satire on Spain's wars in the Mediterranean and Flanders, but more specifically its explorations and conquests in the New World, its desire to find and govern islands. Most of the explorers and conquistadors were led by priests, just as Sancho is led by Don Quixote. And most of them were just as greedy and stupid in governance as we would (wrongly) expect Sancho to be, when he talks about his desire for riches, his plans for advancing his children, his willingness to sell his new Negro subjects into slavery.

Is not this one of the noblest speeches Don Quixote ever makes?

If my wounds are not resplendent in the eyes of the chance beholder, they are at least highly thought of by those who know where they were received. The soldier who lies dead in battle has a more impressive mien than the one who by flight attains his liberty. . . . I still would rather have taken part in that prodigious battle than be today free of my wounds without having been there. The scars that the soldier has to show on face and breast are stars that guide others to the Heaven of honor, inspiring them with a longing for well-merited praise.

Of course not. He never made it. Cervantes made it in the Introduction to Part II, replying to the sneers of the pseudonymous Avellaneda

259

that he is old and one-handed. It should not surprise us too much that his own voice sounds so very much like the Don's.

Most modern Cervantists have seen a close relation between author and hero. Walter Starkie, for instance, writes, "Cervantes lived the whole of his life in the spirit of the Knight-errant. . . ." Don Quixote, like his author, is old, poor, without a function in society, the head of a household of impoverished women. Like him, he feels the most exalted sentiments and idealisms but cannot practice them because of neglect and poverty. Like him, he rode out into the world to make it tidy and Christian; and incidentally to become rich and powerful. But this same comparison has a threatening side which most critics have not cared to examine. Could Cervantes mock knight-errantry without mocking his own career, his life, his dearest beliefs? Worse, could he mock himself without mocking the Spanish empire and the Christian church in whose service he passed most of his life?

Where could Cervantes have found Don Quixote and his adventures but in his own psyche and experiences? Where but as a devout Spanish Christian could one learn so well how one's books and texts can divorce him from reality? Where but as a soldier of the Spanish empire could one learn how little good one does for others or for himself by trying to impose his vision of virtue on others? Where but as a tax gatherer among the peasants of Andalusia and La Mancha could one learn how little the common people believe or listen to all the high ideals and low lies dealt them by their leaders, yet how basically loyal and sound they are for all that? Where but in a debtors' prison could one learn how little the nobles of a nation care about the aspirations, the abilities, the dedication of those they rule? Surely in all the buffetings Don Quixote takes, Cervantes sees his own: surely in all the high-flown nonsense Don Quixote speaks, he hears his own.

I do not imply that Cervantes was any more a conscious disbeliever than most people. As to whether he was more of an *unconscious* disbeliever it is hard to tell—few people have left us so encompassing a record of their psyche. Certainly the breadth of Cervantes's experiences and the extent of his disappointments must have left traces. Besides, whatever beliefs any man espouses, large areas of his mind are bound to be unconvinced, skeptical, inimical. The more ardent and unquestioned a man's conscious beliefs, then it is likely that his unconscious doubts will be all the stronger and more threatening— especially in a man cursed with a lively intellect. From time to time, those doubts may begin to emerge into the more conscious areas. During World War II, many of us were astonished that all our comrades overseas knew what the war was really about, that not one believed the "official" explanations. Now, they usually cannot even remember what they then thought. It is more comfortable forgetting —not to mention safer.

I see no evidence that Cervantes was ever openly or consciously skeptical either of his religion or his nation. Yet parts of his mind *must* have harbored strong doubts and reservations. I think the structure of Part I preserves a record of those thoughts' struggle to rise and express themselves and of Cervantes's counterstruggle to choke them back at any cost. I see no reason, however, to think he was ever conscious either of his own doubts or of his own drive to suppress them. It seems to me very unlikely that, nowadays, a man like Cervantes could write a book like *Don Quixote*—now, he would *have* to know what he was writing about. If Cervantes had *had* to know what he was saying, he wouldn't have.

Even then, I think all these doubts were far too painful for Cervantes at the green and immature age of fifty-eight. Again and again, he had to relieve the pressure by distracting himself with romances —reaffirming his idealisms, his sentimentalities—stuffing his book full of pastoral love stories. When even that failed, he quit writing for perhaps nearly ten years, until he could bear so painful a thought— that all he had believed, and most of what he had done, had been nonsense. Only at the advanced age of sixty-nine would he be able to accept the notion that a man's beliefs could be foolish, yet if he added decency and courage, those beliefs might be ennobling. Perhaps Christianity was absurd; that did not mean that the Christian might not be wonderful.

The reader will recall that Don Quixote's first sally lasts only five chapters, covering three days and three adventures. Each of these episodes has a heavy satirical element: first, Don Quixote is dubbed a knight in the stableyard; second, he tries to save the farmer's boy, Andrés, from what he takes for tyrannical injustice; third, he tries to force some Toledo merchants to swear to Dulcinea's overwhelming beauty without any sort of proof. After such a display of subversive satirical intentions, Cervantes has the Don bludgeoned into near insensibility and carried home for the Inquisition on his library.

Purified by the barber and curate, his madness complicated and rationalized with the idea of persecution by enchanters, the Don is permitted to ride out again. Besides, he now has Sancho for ballast. Too many critics have already written about this brilliant archetypical contrast of characters for me to comment much. I would only ask why Sancho is introduced *here* rather than at the beginning of the book; I suggest that a part of his purpose is to insure against such dangerously open satire, satire that rises so close to the conscious surface. He *does* have such an effect for several chapters. We tend to be less interested in events and their meaning than in the interplay between these two characters.

This new group of adventures at the beginning of the Don's second sally will also last just five chapters before forbidden subjects start raising their heads and a new interruption must be found. The first new adventure, the attack on the windmills, is vastly successful in itself and avoids troublesome implications. The ensuing "liberation" of a Basque lady and the sword fight with her Biscayan squire seem equally harmless. That episode, however, is briefly interrupted by the search for a true text which raises the religious suggestion already noted. Further, while the Don nurses his wounded ear, we have not only the mention of the Balsam of Fierabrás, but also the first extended discussion of Sancho's promised island. Thus Sancho may have helped fend off or diffuse religious parody, but he has raised a whole new specter—the scarcely less threatening one of antinational satire.

At this point, Cervantes completely breaks off his story for the first time. For the next four chapters we completely forget knightly adventures; Don Quixote joins a group of goatherds, lecturing them about the Golden Age, hearing of Grisóstomo's love for Marcela, attending Grisóstomo's funeral, hearing Marcela's self-justifications. This not only gives the Don a new model for later kinds of madness, it also relieves the satirical thrust of the earlier chapters by engaging us in a sentimentalized landscape, a romantic view of life.

Yet this palliative, too, quickly wears off. The fourth of these chapters takes a sudden chilling turn. Marcela leads us into problems every bit as painful as, if less dangerous than, those we have been avoiding. Throughout the book, the beautiful beloved is closely identified with the ideal. This is what Marcela says over the grave of the young man who died for love of her:

Heaven made me beautiful, you say, so beautiful that you are compelled to love me . . .; and in return for the love that you show me, you would have it that I am obliged to love you in return. I know, with that natural understanding that God has given me, that everything beautiful is lovable; but I cannot see that it follows that the object that is loved for its beauty must love the one that loves it. Let us suppose that the lover of the beautiful were ugly, and, being ugly, deserved to be shunned; it would then be highly absurd for him to say, "I love you because you are beautiful; you must love me because I am ugly."

. . . .

. . . . I did not choose this beauty that is mine; such as it is, Heaven gave it to me of its grace, without any choice or asking on my part. As the viper is not to be blamed for the deadly poison that it bears, since that is a gift of nature, so I do not deserve to be reprehended for my comeliness of form.

. . . .

. . . . My life is a free one, and I do not wish to be subject to another in any way. I neither love nor hate anyone; I do not repel this one and allure that one; I do not play fast and loose with any. The modest conversation of these village lasses and the care of my goats is sufficient to occupy me.

Her reasoning, of course, is flawless; but that, if anything, only compounds the sense of icy-cold aggressiveness.

Besides, the whole speech is deceptive and subtle. If Marcela wanted only to be ignored by young men, why is she standing in the spotlight over the grave? She might at least let Grisóstomo's friends look at his body—instead she has them all looking at her. By the very way she tells them to leave her alone, she attracts them all to follow her. Who would say that was not what she wished? At least in *this* situation, Don Quixote alone behaves like a sane man—he stops the others from following her.

Thus it seems to me that the romantic and sentimental episode has turned as painful as the realistic and satiric one. If our ideal is this cold and cruel, cares for us no more than this, if it desires only to tease and torment us and will even let us die of longing without so much as one kind word, if it is as irresponsibly sadistic as this, what hope have we? We may as well rush back to the realistic world; that is just what the novel does.

In the next eight chapters, we return to farcical episodes of the Don and Sancho. The first is a comic reflection of Grisóstomo's and Marcela's love—Rocinante's ill-fated pursuit of the Yanguesan mares. This is followed by a human sexual tangle involving Maritornes and her carter boyfriend at the inn, followed by Sancho's being tossed in a blanket the next morning. In this block of chapters we have also the attack upon the funeral party, the terror of the fulling hammers, and the capture of the barber's basin as Mambrino's helmet, all relatively harmless. In the middle of this section, however, we come upon a very subversive episode, the battle of the sheep, which I have already compared to the pagan-Christian wars and to the battle of Lepanto. Again, at the end of this section, we find the freeing of Ginés de

Pasamonte and the galley slaves, another extremely threatening episode.

The book's first pastoral interlude, we may note, also followed a violent encounter (that in which the Don stopped the Basque lady's coach and battled her squire); immediately afterward, Sancho expressed a fear of the Holy Brotherhood, and within a few pages we had begun the first pastoral novella, the story of Grisóstomo and Marcela. Now once again, after this lawless and violent scene, it is Sancho's fear of the Holy Brotherhood that drives the Don and Sancho into the Sierra Morena—and a very similar fear, I think, that drives Cervantes into the love story of Cardenio, Luscinda, Don Fernando, and Dorotea.

During the several chapters since the battle of the sheep, Don Quixote's actions have become more and more openly lawless. While attacking the funeral party, he broke the leg of the Bachelor Alonso López. Next, he forcibly stole the barber's basin. Now he has directly attacked the officers of the king (one of whom is incidentally, like Cervantes himself, a commissary) and, in so doing, the legal system behind them.

Not only has the Don moved openly as an outlaw or perhaps a revolutionary; Cervantes has done much to put the reader into sympathy with him. Much of what the Don says appeals strongly to unreasonable but very deep and powerful emotions. We all feel that any punishment is an outrage, that it is outrageous ever to be forced to do anything one doesn't want to do. This doesn't mean that these things may not be necessary or even good; they are merely outrageous. We all, then, must violently resent the mere existence of prisons—whether we consciously approve of them or not. How else could revolutionaries so easily enlist us by merely promising to abolish prisons—despite our constant experience that the first thing successful revolutionaries do is *fill* prisons? Our fantasy is too powerful for our historical sense—even if we have not, like Cervantes, been imprisoned. He, of course, had very strong commitments on both sides—

had been both a prisoner and a commissary. But the reader is bound to be almost equally divided.

Beyond, the Don's questioning of the convicts is cannily designed to give them our sympathy, and even more to turn us against the morality of the legal system. First we are amused and attracted by the "lover"—jailed for hugging a basket of linen. Next we agree with the Don and the guard that the "canary" deserves prison for "singing" under torture; unnoticed, we have accepted the convict's code, ignoring the legal morality which asks whether the man is guilty. The next prisoner, jailed for lack of five ducats, moves us farther in the same direction by pointing to general inequity and corruption in the legal system. Next, we are moved to real sympathy for the tears of the aged pimp-sorcerer. Finally, we encounter the arrogant, but strong and dignified Ginés de Pasamonte. Surrounded, as he is, by the comparatively faceless guards, he draws our deeper and more rebellious passions subtly but firmly into his orbit. Small wonder, then, that having freed him and his comrades, we must flee to mountains and to romance.

This episode, then, closes the third block of the Don's adventures, each ended when they become too suggestive or critical, the first by Inquisition, the second and third by pastoral romances. Cervantes must now have drawn up his fullest powers to fashion a climactic episode which might combine and resolve the conflicting styles and attitudes already introduced and so close the volume. This must have cost an enormous effort of will, but it is accomplished by that sustained scene which begins with Don Quixote capering in the Sierra, then returns to the inn where the Don can be enchanted and all the lovers joined. Here, Cervantes introduces not one type of interruption or interlude, but both types used previously. Having engaged Don Quixote with Cardenio and the lovers in the mountains, he sends Sancho to the inn where he meets the same curate and barber who'd held the Inquisition. Still wishing to cure the Don, they plot to enchant him through the pretended distress of the Princess Micomicona.

Next Cervantes brings to this inn the Don and Cardenio, then all the other lovers—Dorotea, Don Fernando and Luscinda, the Captive and Lela Zoraida, then Juan Pérez de Viedma (the Captive's brother), his daughter Doña Clara, and the young Don Luis. In this setting Cervantes can engage the Don in several more rowdy adventures against a realistic background—the battle of the wineskins, the entanglement with the puppet show, the temptations by the innkeeper's daughter. This provides a mockery of idealism without dangerous satirical leanings. At the same time, Cervantes can satisfy some of his own idealism or romantic leanings by having the love affairs come out happily (all at once!) and by including his own life story and giving it an absurdly happy ending. In the meantime, the plot to enchant Don Quixote and bring him safely home is successfully carried out.

The one inserted novella we have ignored is the story the travelers read at the inn, the abandoned manuscript, "A Man Too Curious for His Own Good." This story within the story, where Anselmo deliberately provokes his best friend to seduce his wife, seems entirely out of place. It, obviously, cannot involve any of the same characters and has scarcely any thematic relation to the other stories. It certainly does little to enlighten the career of Don Quixote; it *does,* I think, enlighten the dilemma of his author. Though it echoes the earlier unhappy ending of the story of Grisóstomo and Marcela, this is the only story in this section that ends unhappily. It stands, I think, as Cervantes's warning to himself, reflecting what disaster falls on the man who will not accept the possible. Anselmo is warned again and again that if his wife is faithful under the normal conditions of their life, he should not ask more. Further, this story warns Cervantes that we must not be too curious, too demanding. The other romantic love stories suggest that you may hope to obtain the actual girl you want here in this world; the story of the Don suggests that the more the lady is identified with the ideal, the less attainable is she. This story warns that we had better not be too curious about our ideals, too inquisitive about our beliefs, too demanding of our lady.

267

Having brought off his climactic scene and stylistically resolved (or perhaps escaped) his problem, Cervantes takes the enchanted Don Quixote in tow (in an ox cart) and hauls him rapidly home. Along the way, he has the curate pronounce him a heretic, a founder of a new sect. Then, capping the many scenes in which Don Quixote tried to free a captive lady, Cervantes lets him attack an image of the Virgin Mary. This, of course, deflects from Cervantes any guilt involved in the Don's earlier adventures. Having branded the Don insane and heretical and washing his own hands of any complicity in the Don's actions, Cervantes closes the book as swiftly as possible.

In Part II, such problems seldom rise. We have no inserted novellas, no such split in style and attitude. Instead of moving between poles of style and feeling, we tend to keep those extremes continually present in the richer, more various tone. This is true both in the presentation of Don Quixote and Sancho and in the book's grasp of the nature of Reality. At the same time, we come to be much closer to the Don himself. This alone cuts off some of the threatening aspects we found in Part I, since we lose the detachment needed for satire. Actually, we tend to be more involved in the action, to see its paradoxically good qualities. I think the final implications of Part II may be far more threatening and subversive than those of Part I. But deeper sympathy and identification with the Don make them less of a problem for two reasons: first, we tend to be dealing less with symptomatic social entities like the Church or Spain, and much more with deep-seated human energies and needs; second, and partly because of this, the troublesome meanings are less likely to rise to the conscious surface of the story.

The difference in tone can probably best be seen by comparing scenes on related subjects. For instance, the handling of the liberation of Ginés de Pasamonte and the galley slaves as contrasted to the later treatment of Roque Guinart and his band of noble robbers. Or we might take the Don's crucial fantasies about women. On his very first adventure, we watched him come to an inn where he mistook a whore for a princess. It is a simple blunder and we laugh rather simple-mindedly at his inappropriate actions and high-flown address. Later in Part I, Sancho lyingly tells the Don about his supposed visit to Dulcinea. Again we laugh at the Don's expectations that she will act like a highborn lady, while Sancho pokes holes in this bubble by describing her realistic and lowdown attributes. Here the fact of Sancho's lying adds some complication, may lead us to wonder whether Sancho is not deliberately baiting his master, enjoying his discomfiture. After all, Sancho did not really go to Toboso; he could have agreed with the Don's fantasy as easily as not. Yet if this is a complication, it does not much sophisticate the view of reality.

In Part II, however, is a comparable scene we have already mentioned; in it, Don Quixote and Sancho both go to Toboso to visit Dulcinea and Sancho leads his master before a vulgar peasant girl who is, he claims, Dulcinea. She must, in fact, look very much like Aldonza Lorenzo, on whom Dulcinea is based. Yet when Don Quixote looks at her, he sees not the princess of his fantasies or of Sancho's ecstatic description; he actually sees the ugly wench who is there. He and Sancho have completely switched roles: Sancho talks high-flown nonsense while the Don, for once, sees the simple physical fact. And he manages to do this even though Sancho, who alone can claim to have seen Dulcinea, has knowingly lied to him. Yet, even though he accepts the report of his senses, he does not accept them as real. He decides that she has been enchanted, so bringing into the book that tremendous complication of philosophical and religious implications already outlined. Even this is further complicated later when the Duchess convinces Sancho himself that *he* was enchanted—that what he had witnessed actually was the real and beautiful Dulcinea but that he and his master were both enchanted and unable to see her true being. And all of this is, in turn, further enriched by the later scenes of the enchanted Dulcinea and the enchanted Altisidora (a sort of false Dulcinea), both of whom must be restored through punishment of Sancho, which raises the possibility that his guilt may be the original lie about his master's enchanted beloved.

We may trace a similar progressive enrichment by comparing on the one hand the Don's encounter with Dorotea disguised as the Princess Micomicona in Part I, and on the other, his encounter with the Bachelor Carrasco disguised as the Knight of the Mirrors and the Knight of the White Moon in Part II. In the first episode, we follow the plot from beginning to end. We hear the barber and curate planning to entrap Don Quixote, we watch the curate disguising himself as the princess and the barber as her squire, then watch them switch roles, and finally see Dorotea drafted to play the princess. At all times we are in a position of superior knowledge to the Don; part of our laughter is at anyone who could be so foolish as not to see what is obvious to us.

In the later adventures this is not at all the case. We may have some suspicions who the Knight of the Mirrors is—some hints were dropped in advance. But this is only inkling—a guess, which at first reading, we would not at all trust. When the Knight of the Mirrors has been defeated and unmasked, we may not be quite so astonished as Don Quixote is, yet we have generally shared his ignorance and confusion. We have not felt free to say who is who and what is what; Reality is nearly as baffling to us as to the hero.

Later, when Carrasco returns as the Knight of the White Moon, the whole episode is handled with such speed that we are halfway through it before we even realize it is happening. Like the Don, we are bowled over and confused by this sudden and overwhelming attack. Again, there were a few hints beforehand—the Bachelor after his first defeat had sworn revenge. But we have scarcely time to even ask who this is or what is happening before Don Quixote is lying flat on the ground.

It is not only our ignorance and confusion that has brought us closer to the Don. From the beginning of Part II, he has displayed a new and increasing nobility; we have come to admire, more and more, his courtesy, his courage, his dedication and endurance. Almost alone of all the characters, he and Sancho have shown a concern for others. Throughout Part II, his voice has suggested a richer, more various spirit: a sense of humor, of self-criticism, a sense of reality. Not only does he realize that virtue or its reward may never appear upon this earth, he realizes that he himself may be wrong. Yet, for all that, he sees his actions as insignificant in themselves, yet as allegorical parts in a morally conceived universe. So, even when he is wrong, his blunders show a certain grandeur of spirit, a kindness of intent.

As many critics have noted, the Don and Sancho do tend to grow more like each other throughout Part II; this is particularly noticeable in the effects of the Don's teaching upon his squire. This appears first in minor and comic ways—e.g., the Don's corrections of Sancho's speech, which Sancho much resents, but which he then imitates in correcting his wife. Yet this same influence appears much more powerfully later on, especially in Sancho's governorship.

I have already mentioned the very effective contrast between the nobility and poverty of Don Quixote (and I may add, of Sancho) as opposed to the ignoble extravagance and ostentation of the Duke and Duchess. Even at his worst, the Don does not deserve to be the kept lunatic and freak of a bored rich man—and by the time he encounters the Duke he is nearly at his best. The Duke and the Don are most directly compared in the two episodes of distressed duennas. Perhaps Don Quixote has not been able to really help Doña Rodríguez and her pregnant daughter—he has at least shown a real concern and effort on their behalf; in the same matter the Duke has acted with a base and greedy callousness.

Again, while in the Duke's household, the Don and Sancho have shown real fortitude and constancy in their discussions with the Duchess and in the Don's temptations by Altisidora. We are of course amused at his thinking she *could* be enamored of him; we are still much impressed by the constancy which could so continually though politely refuse the favors she so frequently offers. Through all the indignities and pranks heaped on them by the Duke and Duchess— the beard washings, the cats and bells, the pinching and slapping— Don Quixote and Sancho maintain a real dignity and sensitivity.

Besides, as already noted, one of these pranks, the ride on the back of Clavileño, gives a symbolic expansion which associates master and squire with the greater literary and mythic heroes. Of course we cannot take this too literally; it is not handled as a conscious pattern in the novel. Nonetheless it exists as an ambience and gives to the Don's adventures in Part II an imaginative breadth and dignity missing from Part I. The Don himself saw his descent into the Cave of Montesinos as comparable to a descent into Hell; in all the trials and temptations of Part II, most especially in Sancho's penance of three thousand lashes, we have a definite purgation of the heroes, if not a Purgatory; in this ride on Clavileño we have an imaginary journey to the Heavens. Our heroes have not, of course, been actually taken through Heaven and Hell to be shown the extremes of existence. Yet they imagine they have, which suggests a certain breadth of spirit in itself. And for Sancho, at least, this has been as deeply humbling as one could ask from any real trip through the Heavens:

> Ever since I dropped down from Heaven, . . . ever since I looked at the earth from up there and saw how little it is, I am not as anxious to be a governor as I was once upon a time. What greatness is there in ruling over a grain of mustard, or imperial dignity and power in governing half a dozen human beings the size of hazelnuts?

Yet, finally, through another prank, Sancho does get to govern his island. And we are only partially surprised that he does it with such credit to himself and to the master who taught him. We believe his wonderful speeches reporting his governorship:

> I was naked when I entered upon my government and naked I find myself now, and so I neither lose nor gain. . . . I answered questions, solved problems, and decided cases at law, and all the time I was dying of hunger. . . .

272

The short of it is . . . ; it is no load for these ribs of mine. . . . And so, before the government threw me over, I decided to throw over the government; and yesterday morning I left the island as I found it, with the same streets, houses and roofs that it had when I came. I asked no one for a loan nor did I try to make any money out of my office; and although I had it in mind to make a few laws, I made none, since I was afraid they would not be kept and then it would be all the same whether I made them or not.

. . . . And so, . . . Sancho Panza . . . has come to learn that he would not give anything whatever to rule, not alone an island, but the entire world. . . . I kiss your Highnesses' feet; and . . . pass over to the service of my master Don Quixote; for with him, even though I eat my bread with fear and trembling, at least I get my fill, and in that case it's all the same to me whether it be of carrots or of partridges.

Would that more governors could say as much! Yet we know that Sancho could not have risen to this true, if comic, dignity and integrity without his master's teachings. And those do not lie merely in the precepts the Don gave him at the start of his governorship, but through his counsel and example in all their time together. The Don may be insane; he is not only noble, but ennobles others.

No wonder, then, that Don Quixote's destruction at Carrasco's vengeful hands is such a blow to us, that his voice in defeat is so unbearable:

At once the victor leaped down and placed his lance at Don Quixote's visor.

"You are vanquished, O knight! Nay, more, you are dead unless you make confession in accordance with the conditions governing our encounter."

Stunned and battered, Don Quixote did not so much as raise his visor but in a faint, wan voice, as if speaking from the grave, he said, "Dulcinea del Toboso is the most beautiful woman in the world and I the most unhappy knight upon the face of the earth. It is not right that my weakness should serve to defraud the truth. Drive home your lance, O knight, and take my life since you already have deprived me of my honor."

His voice *is* a voice from the grave—without the fantasy that controlled his life, without the belief that he could not only adore but in some way serve the distant and untouchable beloved, he is as good as dead. As one degradation after another is heaped upon him, as an ever deeper and more terrible despair opens inside him, we move from farce into the deepest tragedy. Not only has the Spanish Christian author, Cervantes, grown to a oneness with his hero; we, regardless of our background and belief, have done the same. Like every tragic hero, Don Quixote represents a part of us that cannot survive, that is essentially wrong. Yet we are not sure, either, that we can survive without that mad energy, that noble dedication—or if we can, that such a life would be worth living.

The last chapter begins:

> Inasmuch as nothing that is human is eternal but is ever declining from its beginning to its close, this being especially true of the lives of men, and since Don Quixote was not endowed by Heaven with the privilege of staying the downward course of things, his own end came when he was least expecting it.

He could not stay what he saw as the downward course of history, or more basically the downward course of his own life, that paradigm on which all fantasies must be based, the text of which all fictions must be truly translations. Yet if life *is* that relentless decline, then perhaps only madness, perhaps only a wrongheaded and senseless devotion can give an acceptable meaning, can give the zest and appetite we demand. Like most of us, Don Quixote could become rational and accept the real world only after his downfall and defeat; could become sane only by humiliation. But it is a real downfall; he has become merely human and must die. The forces that have made him endurable to live with have ended his endurance and his life; that brought him back to sanity, to his niece and housekeeper, to humanity and to us, have taken him away from us for good.

Analysis of Dehpts:
The *Inferno*

Critics commonly speak of the *Inferno* as a sort of psychoanalysis, a probing of the soul's sickness. Then, they change the subject rapidly as if they feared the notion false. Or as if they feared it true—to find any man's soul much like that sinkhole of corruptions could easily embarrass us all.

The subject of Dante's analysis, the hero of this journey through the abyss, must be Dante—or that Pilgrim in his poem who carries his name. Yet if this Pilgrim *is* sick, his symptoms certainly appear mild: he has seduced, killed, betrayed no one. He has merely lost his way, though he admits he was so sunken in sleep that he has lost all conscious recollection how this happened. Yet, when Virgil, representing Reason and the conscious mind, comes to guide him back, he once again wavers "like a man who unwills what he willed" and "turns back from honored deeds" questioning whether he should go on. This timorousness, Dante's lack of constant purpose, is hardly admirable, yet it seems almost trivial compared to the horrors, the great sinners we must soon witness.

275

Yet, is this trivial? Each of those sinners, after all, is actually an image of Dante's own soul at a deeper level; each is shown him precisely to explain his own failure, since it is a deeper and truer image of that very failure in the upper world. His inconstancy has exposed him, there, to three terrible beasts: a Leopard suggesting worldly appetites and passions, a Lion suggesting violent pride, and a She-Wolf suggesting unappeasable hunger, faithlessness, and fraud. These beasts, too, signify no merely external evil: they symbolize the three divisions of the Inferno, the three worst diseases of Dante's soul.

We should not confuse luridness with significance. Seduction, murder, and betrayal may be less serious than losing one's way. Into such momentary failures even the noblest might slip; losing one's way suggests something about one's whole life. Besides, mightn't a man get lost *to* seduce himself; *to* kill his spiritual self; *to* betray the principles he conceives in himself or his universe? A general, leading an army to battle, might well find many of his soldiers had a less-than-admirable tendency to get lost. Many of those soldiers, too, might be quite unable to recall how that happened. Few generals are so stupid as to think betrayal is less betrayal when compounded by fraud. Since Dante's general, his leader, is the principle of right action, both in the universe and in his own spirit, getting lost may be no small betrayal. Perhaps the full experience of Hell, all the soul's evil, is needed to place its full enormity in his grasp.

The *Inferno,* if I may jog the reader's memory, has nine circles, the last three containing many subdivisions. The first five circles contain the sins of the Leopard, of worldly appetites. Here, men lost the way through lack of opportunity or, much worse, were distracted by earthbound passions—lust, rage, hunger, or greed:

1. The Virtuous Heathen
2. The Carnal Lovers
3. The Gluttons
4. The Misers and Spendthrifts
5. The Angry and Sullen

The next two rings hold the sins of the Lion, of violent pride. Here,. the simpler crimes have been complicated by rationalization. We find not mere error but a willful pursuit of wrong. Not mere lust, greed, or rage, but an arrogant violence, which not only breaks God's law but subverts its substance.

6. The Heretics
7. The Violent against:
   (a) neighbors
   (b) self [suicides]
   (c) God and natural order [blasphemers, sodomites, usurers]

Finally, the last two rings hold the sins of the She-Wolf, of fraud and betrayal. Here, rationalization and falsehood are the way of life. The intellect, meant to be one's light toward the right path, has been used instead to obscure and disguise one's self and one's intentions. It has been made a weapon against the innocent or, much worse, those who trust or love one:

8. [Malebolge] Types of Fraud:
   (a) seducers and panders
   (b) flatterers
   (c) simonists
   (d) diviners and soothsayers
   (e) grafters
   (f) hypocrites
   (g) thieves
   (h) evil counselors
   (i) schismatics; sowers of discord
   (j) forgers; liars; impersonators
9. Betrayers of:
   (a) kin
   (b) country
   (c) hospitality
   (d) benefactors

The quality most common to all these images of evil is faithlessness. Sometimes this appears as a lack of deep commitment, at others a commitment to deliberately wrong objects and principles; sometimes as a violence done to Nature; sometimes to the self. At its deepest level, we see it as a rebelliousness, a compulsion to betray whoever should receive our gratitude, reverence, or loyalty.

The overall tendency of movement (despite exceptions along the way) is from turbulence to stasis, from the enormous swirling of the Trimmers and the lovers, inward and downward to the Traitors frozen in the ice of the Judaica. At the same time, we tend to move from images of social and public ills toward evil in its more private, childlike, and fantastic images. That is, we move from social symptoms to personal cause; from our restless perversions of love, politics, economy, belief, to the deep and unchanging sickness of the individual psyche. In the later circles we see more childishness and, at the same time, more rationalization. Reason, meant to be a maturing force, has been misused to freeze the adult in the grip of childish urges and compulsions, especially the urge to deny the world's nature and his own.

Despite exceptions, then, each deeper ring of the *Inferno* tends to reflect an earlier layer in the development of the psyche, though one still present in the rationalizing adult; partially causal to the layers above it and to the actions of the adult. As already noted, those adult actions tend to be represented directly in the Sins of the Leopard, the sins of worldly appetite. As we move down into the Sins of the Lion, we make a sudden leap backward in time. This second section tends to reflect, both in its direct concerns and in its symbolism, the problems of the adolescent, overwhelmed by his own sexuality and aggressiveness. Descending to the Sins of the She-Wolf, we will once again take a large leap backward into early childhood and babyhood. When we finally reach the Judaica and Satan, we have reached the realm of Original Sin, of that envy which led first Satan and then Adam to resent God's greatness and so rebel against Him.

Theologically, Satan's sin is seen as the basis of all later sins; so, personally, this deepest level of experience is seen as the basis of the later illness of the psyche. Just as Original Sin is seen as universal, so this traitorous rebelliousness is seen to be part of the psychic equipment of any child at birth.

From a point so early in the child's development, we can regress only one step further; that is, to birth itself:

> As he [Virgil] desired, I embraced his neck
> and he took advantage of time and place
> so that when the wings [of Satan] were opened wide
>
> he caught hold of the shaggy sides
> and climbed down from tuft to tuft
> between the matted hair and the frozen crusts.
>
> When we reached where the thigh turns
> on the swelling of the haunch,
> my leader, with strain and great difficulty,
>
> turned so his head was where his feet had been
> and grappled at the hair like a man who climbs up,
> so that I thought we were returning into Hell.
>
> "Keep a good hold! since it is by such stairs,"
> said the master, panting like one exhausted,
> "we must depart from so much evil."
>
> Then he passed out through a cleft in the rock,
> placed me sitting on its brink
> and directed his wary step toward me.
>
> I raised my eyes and expected to see
> Lucifer the way I had left him,
> but saw him with his legs stuck upward.
>
> And if that puzzled me,
> let that coarse crew consider, who do not see
> what point it was that I had passed.
>
> —*XXXIV, 70–84*

Just as the baby, under the tremendous pressure of the body, turns over inside the womb to be born, so does Dante, under the burden of all the evils he has witnessed, under the gravity of the whole world in that "dismal hole which all the other rocks bear down upon"—so does Dante turn over to issue "through a cleft in the rock" and so re-enter the world of light and life. Re-enacting the trauma of his human birth and its attendant ills, he is at the same time re-enacting the death and rebirth of Christ in himself, so being reborn into the new life, La Vita Nuova. The poem began on Good Friday of the year 1300, so this moment of birth and rebirth must occur on Easter Sunday.

Paradoxically, however, Dante can be reborn into a new life only by fully accepting the old life, yielding his prideful rejection of the life God gave him. One of the first things he sees in Hell are great droves of the dead waiting to cross Acheron; they blaspheme "God and their parents, the human race, the place, the time and the seed of their conception and of their birth." To leave the damned, he must accept the unpardonable gift of birth. Further, he can only accept his human self by accepting the existence of things outside himself, then by fully committing himself to something other than self. His past failure of commitment is seen as a refusal to accept the separation between himself and others—the facts of life and so life itself.

Like any other child entering the world, he must make a series of almost unbearably painful recognitions: first, that there *are* other existences, painfully separate from him, yet demanding his commitment; then, that many of these are larger and more powerful than he; next, that still other painful differences, especially of sex and ability, abound; finally, that the world is little concerned with his sense of loss and betrayal. He must surrender his prideful sense of being all-powerful, all-pervasive, all-important; must recognize that he is tiny, terribly limited, and all-important only to himself. He must see that he is not God, though his envy of God and others may make him into Satan. No doubt things are worse than he would like; he can have them better, or be better, only in accepting what is. Again and again, throughout the *Inferno*, desire (above all, desire to be other than one's self, above human limitations) is the crucial drive and torment of the damned.

This whole paradox is stated most directly much later in the *Commedia* when Dante has purged himself and moved on toward the realms of the blessed. The first person he meets in the *Paradiso* is Piccarda, sister of his friend Forese Donati. Significantly, her low place among the blessed is caused by a sin similar to Dante's own—an inconstancy or neglect in her vows. When Dante asks if she does not want to be in some higher plane, she replies:

> Brother, the power of love quiets our will
> and makes us want only what we have,
> and we thirst for nothing else.

> Should we long to be higher up,
> then our desires would be discordant
> with His will Who disposes us here

> for which, as you will see, these spheres have no place
> if we by necessity have existence here in love
> and if you think about Love's nature.

> Rather, it is the essence of this blessed state
> to hold ourselves in the divine will,
> so that our wills may be made one.

> So that our state, here, from threshold to threshold
> of this realm, delights the whole realm
> as it does the King who brings our will to His.

> And His will is our peace;
> it is that ocean to which all things move
> which it creates and nature makes.

> *—Paradiso III, 70–87*

Piccarda has achieved that serene rest, that freedom from desire, which all the damned—those who could not quiet their will, their desire to be higher—constantly reject and yet constantly mourn. Her words, then, may fittingly turn us back for a closer look at the damned —those whose frantic hatred of their lot led them to rebel against the Divine Will that they be born as nothing grander than human beings.

We begin with the Trimmers, the Neutrals in the vestibule of Hell —those whose failure of commitment to anything outside the self is so deep that they have lost the self. They were only for themselves and now, paradoxically, are "envious of every other lot." They "who never were alive" have also "no hope of death." Heaven will not have its radiance stained, and Hell rejects them lest the damned feel superior looking at them. They are a powerful warning to Dante of where his failure is leading him. Stung by hornets and wasps, this train of nonentities endlessly pursues a banner which can never rest and they can never catch. This is the first image of the psychic restlessness of the damned. Since each ring of Hell is smaller than that above it, this vestibule may well contain the greater part of Mankind—it holds, at any rate, "so long a train of people, I should not have believed death had undone so many."

Like all the *Inferno,* this is a vision not merely of punishment hereafter, but essentially of that life (Dante's own life) whose lack of serene purpose is its own punishment. That anyone would choose such a life seems incredible. Yet choose it they do. When Virgil first found Dante lost in the woods, lingering in pain, he had asked, confounded:

> But you, why go back to such trouble?
> Why not climb the delectable mountain
> Which is the beginning and the cause of all joy?
>
> —*I, 76–78*

This sounds, at first, like a bad joke: "Why have you got that knife in your back?—it's bad for your health!" Rather, it is like those concerned questions we ask our friends, "Why do you keep marrying girls you don't like? Why do you keep getting fired?" The facts have been so disguised that our concern *seems* callous; it seems a tasteless joke merely to point out that the victim has chosen his suffering.

On leaving the Trimmers, Dante's next vision—the hordes of dead waiting to cross Acheron—shows that they are eager for Hell, no one forces it upon them. In the words of an expert, Minos, Hell is actually a refuge *("ospizio"),* a refuge from birth, from life; the scene itself is a parody of the *Aeneid*'s vision of the souls waiting to cross Lethe and be born. The damned, cursing their parents, their conception, and their birth, are anxious to get unborn.

As for the Trimmers, it is not merely that they lived only for themselves and so in death must be "envious of every other lot." The true cause and effect are nearly reversed: because they were dissatisfied, envious of every other lot, they came to be only for themselves, committed only to self-aggrandizement. This is an image of Dante's mind; no less, of his society. Or ours. Equally tormented by envy of greatness, and much more able to afford driving it out, we too create a faceless mediocracy where one can endlessly pursue the swirling banner of self-fulfillment, self-service. Endlessly trumpeting the importance of the individual, of our own great significance, yet rightly fearful that our own performance may not justify any such estimate, we make a life of no standards, no sex, no authority, an equality where each can play at being more important than the rest, where one cannot commit himself even to his own work lest the damning facts of unequal ability become clear. Having refused all roles, definitions, faces, how could we be adjudged to either Heaven or Hell?

Nowhere is Dante's rejection so immediate and complete. Later, he may feel pity and sympathy for certain individuals; for others, scorn and rage. Yet even when he strikes or kicks at one of them, he only shows his need to fully reject a part of his nature not more easily spurned. For the Trimmers, those who could not commit themselves even to evil, could not even make an admirable mistake, his rejection is immediate. He is on his way already to salvation, even if by way of those who have committed themselves to actual evil. At least he will be alive, not completely despicable.

Dante next visits those who are not only less despicable, but truly admirable—the Unbaptized and the Virtuous Heathen in Limbo, the first circle of Hell. Here, he sees no punishment, no warping of the psyche or misdirection of vital energies, only a great sadness. The affliction of these is to "live in desire without hope." Dante could not imagine any man living happily or joyously without that Faith which gave him purpose, gave peace to his desires.

Yet, from those calm, virtuous figures who live in longing only because of the accidents of history, he descends to those who deliberately chose desire—the Carnal Lovers. After relative peace, we are plunged into the tempests of passion and lust that hurl the Lovers endlessly, aimlessly, through the black air. After scenes where Dante himself was comparatively at peace—his easy rejection of the Trimmers, his triumphant acceptance among the greatest pre-Christian poets— we move into an area of his feelings so troubled that he will faint when Francesca da Rimini tells of her love.

It is this deep emotional involvement that makes Francesca so compelling for us, as for him. Just as Milton, much troubled by hatred of authority, created a figure of his own rebelliousness, Satan; so Dante, much troubled by carnal passion, created here a figure of that force to haunt us. In Francesca's faithlessness we see the sick perfidy of our love, our deliberate choice of whatever we cannot have.

It might seem that much of this canto's hold upon us derives not from the brilliance of Dante's treatment but rather from historical accident—from the increasing power that Romantic Love has had in our culture since Dante's time. He *was* ahead of his time—had fallen victim to a violent passion which every suffering teen-ager soon claimed as his due. Yet, is that not the function of the great artist— to take the pulse of passions so deeply powerful that, even if not consciously recognized in his society or in himself, they will become commanding forces in the future? No doubt that is one of the reasons works of art are more accessible to later ages.

Francesca—like almost every figure in the poem—begins by telling of her birth, birthplace, and parentage, those very facts which all the damned curse and desecrate:

> The city where I was born lies
>   on the shore where the Po descends
>   to have peace with its pursuers [i.e., tributaries].

Allen Tate has noted how touchingly this image reflects her present unrest, merely by looking back to that childhood home where she knew peace. A few seconds earlier, she began self-pityingly, "If the King of the Universe were our friend, we would pray to him for your peace, . . ." Yet it is her choice to reject peace. The King does not reject her; she rejects Him.

However strongly we must, and *do* sympathize, something is clearly wrong. Not only that Francesca has broken her vows to Malatesta, her husband. Who can imagine her living happily with Paolo; do we *seriously* believe she would be more faithful to him? Too plainly most of us are equally unhappy with whomever we marry and quickly need a second love—one we can pretend we would *like* being committed to. Then, if we are dissatisfied, if we betray our first love, this appears the fault of the love's object, not the nature of our love. Meantime, we have set up a second love, betrayed in its very conception. Can we seriously doubt that if Paolo had not been there, someone else would; that if her husband died and Paolo became possible, he might lose allure? Eventually, we scarcely know whether the lover is

285

an excuse to hate the husband, or the husband an excuse to love the lover.

If this seems far from the text, what does that text show of nobility in Francesca's love? We see, chiefly, the Pilgrim's tremulous sympathy with her:

> As soon as the wind bent them to us
> I raised my voice, "O wearied souls,
> come speak with us, if no one forbids it."
>
> As doves summoned by desire,
> with uplifted, steady wings to their sweet nest
> bear through the air by their own will
>
> so those spirits came forth from that company
> where Dido is. . . .
> —V, 79–86

"Doves summoned by desire"—that is, in part, by Dante's voice and its quality of desire like their own. Yet, even here, we find the questionable phrase "by their own will"—not by Dante's; certainly not by their Maker's. And though we admire Francesca's heroic and tragic constancy of will

> When we read how that desiring smile
> was kissed by such a lover,
> this man, who shall never be divided from me,
>
> kissed my mouth, all trembling. . . .
> —V, 133–6

even that has its questionable side. We partake of the strength of her passion, just as we do that of Milton's Satan. Yet we must see its ultimate foolishness, since it is, above all, a commitment to what cannot exist, a love of the impossible. Our life begins in separation; in it there is nothing and no one from whom we shall not be divided —it is the first and worst recognition we must reach. Romantic Love, offering the illusion that it can unite us forever with some new person, can only damage us further. Meantime, some of those we cling to may be damaged by our blindness—her lover's welfare seems never to have entered Francesca's mind.

Beyond, she tells quite frankly how she and Paolo were drawn simply by physical attraction:

> Love, which swiftly takes fire in the noble heart
>> caught him, by that beautiful body
>> which was stolen from me, in a way that still torments me.
>
> Love, which pardons no loved one from loving,
>> so strongly took me with delight in him
>> that, as you see, it has not left me yet.
>
> Love led us to one death. . . .*

—V, 100–6

That, and reading the wrong book. There is surely no more delicate, more touching passage in Western literature than this:

> We read, one day, for pleasure
>> of Lancelot, how love compelled him;
>> we were alone, lacking all suspicion.
>
> Sometimes our eyes were drawn together
>> by that reading, and this discolored our faces,
>> but one single moment overcame us.
>
> When we read how that desiring smile
>> was kissed by such a lover,
>> this man, who shall never be divided from me,
>
> kissed my mouth, all trembling.
>> The book was a Galeotto, and he who wrote it;
>> in it, that day, we read no further.

*The Italian contains a vital pun here: *"Amor* condusse noi ad un *a morte."*

> While the one soul said this,
>   the other wept so that for pity
>   I fainted as if I were dying;
>
> and fell as a dead body falls.
>   —*V, 127–42*

She so subtly involves us in the scene, demands our sympathy, so passionately reaffirms her love, and in the marvelously vaginal image of the book, implies all the opening of passion and lust: "in it, that day, we read no further." Her one tiny phrase, "that day," tells exquisitely how, day after day, they went back to read their book again and how, each day again, their eyes wandered, their color changed, their lips . . .

Even here is a deepest irony. We sometimes hear Francesca praised for acting on her own heart's truth, for not "living a lie"! Yet she says nothing about the nature of her heart's needs or how Paolo can fulfill them. She mentions, in fact, no excellence or nobility of his whatever. Only that they read together about two other lovers—as the young now go to drive-ins for a fantasy of other idealized lovers while making "their own" love. Francesca and Paolo have betrayed themselves, acting the part of someone else. And, in choosing the roles of Lancelot and Guinevere, they have re-enacted Lancelot's betrayal of his king, his lord, his people.

Then, too, Francesca's false commitment is to an expressly forbidden love-object, to her husband's brother, not only adulterous but incestuous. Love of the impossible, too, has its seamy side. We have no reason to suspect Francesca constant to, or inseparable from, anything that *could* exist. She knows that somebody sold her: "The book was a Galeotto, and he who wrote it"; she fails to see that she played both whore *and* pander.

Not in spite of this, *because* of this, we adore her. No doubt it is pleasant to imagine that what we sympathize with must be good and noble. That is very much more flattering than what we would find in even the least experience of the world or knowledge of ourselves. Like any tragic character Francesca brings to evil a persuasive dedication, an energy which entangles our deep emotions. If Dante's poem is to be a comedy, he will have to shake off her glamour; that will take much of the rest of the poem.

It is easy enough to see how the next few cantos begin freeing Dante from his sentimental involvement with Francesca, casting their image back and coloring our feelings about her. Like Ciacco the Glutton, wallowing in his mucky sty, she has wallowed in her emotions, demanded more than her share of love. Like the Misers and Spendthrifts of the fourth ring, she has given away too much, has held back too much; she too moves in an endless, senseless circle. By the fifth ring, Dante has partially outgrown sympathy for her self-pity. Here he must cross the muddy River Styx, in whose slime the Sullen lie buried and the Angry, naked, battle one another. Out of that muck rises one "covered with mud," Filippo Argenti; just as Francesca spoke like "one who weeps and speaks," so now he says, "You see that I am one who weeps." Dante *has* learned to see that, yet to see deeper too:

> In weeping, and in wretchedness,
> remain, accursed spirit; for I know you
> in spite of all your filth.
> —*VIII, 37–9*

which wins him the approval of Virgil:

> Indignant soul!
> blessed be she that bore you.
> —*VIII, 44–5*

Dante *has* moved one step closer to blessedness in his birth, away from the damned who curse their birth. Better, he wins the sight of Argenti torn not only by other furious souls, but especially by his own teeth. This is the first overt image of that urge to devour which will

289

much concern us later; of evil as not merely a cursing of one's birth, but a devouring of one's own existence.

Dante's rejection of Filippo Argenti, the implied rejection of Francesca, Virgil's praise—all suggest that Dante has passed through the first section, the Sins of the Leopard, triumphantly. We should be ready, then, to pass on to the Sins of the Lion; Dante, however, may not himself be so ready.

At the barred gates of the City of Dis, Dante is threatened by the fallen angels who refuse to admit him, by the Furies and Medusa who threaten to turn him to stone. Once again, he turns weak and cowardly, wants to turn back. His reluctance is seen not only in this cowardice but also in those very rebellious forces which threaten him—they, too, represent parts of his own spirit. Against these forces, Virgil and Reason are little help—he is entering the realm of *perverted* Reason. Virgil can only send for divine aid; had no heavenly messenger responded, the travelers' case might have been desperate.

Apparently Dante's triumph over his own stasis, over carnal love, over Francesca's urge to betray, is not so real or complete; he has been given this first moment of triumph only to sustain him in plunging deeper into the true nature of these same problems. The directly sexual symbology of this section's flaming gates suggests only too plainly that Francesca and carnal love are not to be so easily dismissed. Dante has only begun to fathom that profound motive, and further understanding may show him many things less flattering to himself.

Besides, once he has passed this threshold, he must encounter the tombs of the great Heretics, among them Farinata degli Uberti and Cavalcante Cavalcanti. Like the Trimmers at the start of the first section, these great Heretics at the start of the second point out to Dante his great and humiliating failures. I think we can only grasp the uncanny resonance most readers feel in this scene if we see what deeply guarded guilts it embodies, guilts that pervade the whole emotional life.

As Dante and Virgil pass among the immense tombs, where burn the souls of the great Heretics or Atheists, suddenly, within one of those tombs, arises the towering figure of Farinata degli Uberti, visible from the waist up and filled with scorn for Hell. A great leader of the Ghibellines, an enemy of Dante's ancestors, he asks about his one concern, his own family. His pride provokes a like pride in Dante; they exchange insults, Dante apparently getting the better of it.

Suddenly they are interrupted by the querulous voice of Cavalcante Cavalcanti, apparently risen to his knees, only his head being visible. He asks about his son Guido, Dante's friend and fellow poet. Mistaking Dante to have implied that Guido is dead, he falls back, as if in a faint. Completely oblivious to this pathetic interruption, Farinata resumes, predicting that Dante will be exiled from Florence (as were, incidentally, both Guido and Farinata). Finally, he remarks that though he had once saved their city from destruction, the Florentines are now relentless to his family. Only after finishing their talk does Dante think to ask him to tell Cavalcanti that his son still lives.

Since this drama is set in April of 1300, the Pilgrim can truthfully answer that his friend Guido lives; only four months later he could not have. The canto itself points out that the only reason Cavalcanti doesn't know whether his son is alive is that Guido's death was so close at hand. Two months later, in June of that same year, Dante was elected one of six Priors, the highest officers of Florence. Attempting to calm the turbulent city, he acquiesced in exiling the leaders of both Black and White Guelphs. Among the Whites was his "first friend" Guido Cavalcanti, who, in exile, contracted malaria and came home only to die; by August, Dante's term of office was over and his "first friend" dead. "From this priorate," writes Leonardo Bruni, "sprang Dante's exile from Florence, and all the adverse fortunes of his life, as he himself writes . . . 'All my woes and all my misfortunes had their origin and commencement with my unlucky election to the priorate; . . .' "*

The appearance of Guido's father, then, and his question "Where is my son and why is he not with you. . . . Isn't he still alive? Doesn't the sweet light strike his eyes?" can only be a bitterest accusation, one Dante must still have felt even at the time of writing, fifteen years later.

After this accusation, Farinata's prediction of Dante's own exile comes very much like a pronunciation of judgment, a punishment. (Like Guido, Dante was banished and he, too, contracted a fatal malaria while in exile.) Beyond this, Farinata's charge that, after his own defense of Florence, his family has been exiled unjustly suggests that Dante's banishment may be just, that he has performed no such heroic service. No more than any other reader do I imagine Dante guilty as charged of barratry, of corrupt dealings in office—his banishment of his friend shows him above graft or partisan dealings. Nonetheless he appears to *feel* that he failed his city and his friend in some way; such feelings are seldom much based on fact. That very year, 1300, when he was at the height of his political fortunes as Prior of Florence, is the year he himself says he went astray in the dark wood. Small wonder that the torments of the historical Dante in the city of Florence should be reflected here in the City of Dis.

Moreover, the Pilgrim Dante *is* guilty of a shocking act in this scene itself. Many readers are impressed by Farinata's obliviousness to the powerful drama happening at his feet—none seems to notice Dante's callousness. Surely he owes Cavalcanti respect and reverence—to let him think his son dead is fiercely, if passively, cruel; his excuse is totally inadequate. His obliviousness must rise partly from a desire to ignore Cavalcanti's accusation, partly to retaliate against it. But this scene also relates to his oblivion at the poem's beginning when, sunk in sleep, he first went astray, and to the end of the poem when he sees

*Quoted in Toynbee, *Dante Alighieri* (London: Methuen, 1924), p. 100.

Satan frozen in the ice and must recognize his own desire to defeat and destroy the Father-God—partly by being half-alive, sunk in sleep, oblivious, frozen. Cavalcanti's accusing cry of grief, "Where is my son?," must echo, then, the grievous accusation of the Father or Father-God against the lost and unconscious Dante. Again, in this scene, Dante has committed the sin he is witnessing: he has dabbled in theories about the future and ignored his present duty—revering and responding to a paternal figure. Just as the Trimmers showed Dante his own lack of commitment, so the Heretics show him that underlying this is a denial, a passive participation in the injury of those he loves.

These episodes have also been concerned with other problems relating to love; we have already noted how the sexual symbology has suggested a deeper concern with carnal love. The section began with images derived from a childlike fear of sex and the vagina: Dante's fear of the great gates, the presence of the fallen angels (who rebelled against the Father-God), the Furies (avengers of crimes against the mother), and the Medusa, a standard emblem of the child's fear of the vagina.* Small wonder it takes a messenger from the Father-God to admit one through so fearful a portal. Yet this imagery continues even after we have passed the gates: there we encounter the flaming tombs, those hot containers from one of which suddenly rises, erect, the phallic and fatherly image of Farinata.

Moreover, Professor John Freccero has recently pointed out a number of literary and biographical references in these two scenes which not only underline their echoes of illicit lust and guilt, but help clarify the relation of this guilt to other failures in the affectional life. Very significantly, the appearance of Medusa and the threat that she may turn Dante to stone contain several deliberate poetic echoes of Dante's

---

*This is a somewhat comforting representation of the fear. The child, petrified by fear of the vagina, invents a pubis with *many* penises as a more manageable fear than the everyday fact of a pubis, a hairy area, with none.

earlier "Pietrose" rhymes, his love poems about that stony woman he had apparently courted, who, if he could not soften her heart, would turn *his* heart to stone. This, in turn, relates to Beatrice's accusations when Dante finally encounters her at the end of the *Purgatorio*— that he has been faithless to her, has been involved with some *"pargoletta"* and has had a mind turned to stone.

Professor Freccero points out that poems of illicit love are important in the following scene as well. There, Cavalcanti echoes the best-known poem, "Donna mi Prega," of his son Guido. This poem is an Averrhoistic definition of love, a secular and opportunistic view of sexual passion. Dante himself had apparently shared Guido's views as a young man and acted upon them even longer. Guido's poems were so intimately involved with illicit love in Dante's mind that when he created Francesca, his great exemplar of that passion, he could not help having her parody one of Guido's poems in her lines. Beyond this —and directly in line with the overall tendency of our argument—we should note that romantic love in Guido and the other poets of the *dolce stil nuovo* was, both in style and content, a direct development from the courtly love of the Troubadours—a love based immediately on the urge to deceive and betray one's overlord in seducing his wife. Thus romantic love is related to those rebellious and treacherous drives we shall encounter in the deep ice of Cocytus—the deep compulsion to betray the father, the master, the Father-God.

I have already noted that imagery in the deeper circles tends to be drawn from ever earlier periods of the child's development, simply because the deeper sins tend to be fixations of earlier drives. In this section we are concerned with childhood and early adolescence, when a child must come to terms with his growing passional nature, his violence and sexuality. For a boy, of course, the father will be a major influence as a power to emulate and oppose, a limiting force which forbids and permits, a teacher and civilizing force on the child's brute nature, an overwhelming presence to be constantly appeased.*

---

*Dante's father died when he was twelve; we know, too, from certain poems of

This whole section is charged with images of the growing child and his father. We have many visions of that half-human, half-bestial nature which the child fears in himself, in his father, in his mother: the centaurs, the Furies, the harpies, the Minotaur, even the Old Man of Crete in his split nature—gold, silver, brass, iron, and feet of clay. In the genital imagery of the whole section, we see the growing sexuality and aggressiveness which puts the child in danger from his father. We see figure after figure of familial guilt—Geri de Bello, Ulysses, Bertran de Born—and of adulterous passion and incest— Myrrha and Potiphar's wife. We see the child's rebelliousness in the unrepentant Capaneus; familial murder in Guy de Montfort, who killed his cousin, and Obizzo d'Este, killed by his son. We find every type of father-image, substitute and surrogate: beginning with Farinata, the enemy ancestor, and Cavalcanti, the friend's father; ending with the "dear and good, paternal image" of Brunetto Latini. We meet the great teachers, "the gentle father" Virgil in his long lecture on Hell's structure, Chiron who taught Achilles, Brunetto who taught Dante. We also encounter the other side of the father— Attila and the great tyrants, Zeus the adulterous father, Athamas who slew his son, Saturn who devoured his children.

In pointing out the unconscious genital and sexual derivation of this section's images, I would negate none of the more conscious interpretations. In noting the sexual source of Dante's terror and despair before the gates of Dis, I no less accept the theological and philosophical interpretations. The Furies *do* stand for remorse; Medusa *does* stand for the obduracy of the prideful heart. My point is that the images embodying these ideas draw on images and patterns established in that period when the child struggled with genital problems —which patterns are bound to shape his later thoughts and actions.

Forese Donati that Dante's father was not apparently very admirable. So, Dante may have tended to deal with images of that paternal force, more than with the qualities of his actual father.

Before Dante can continue through this section of his journey, he must pass one more obstacle, a curious and seemingly arbitrary one. First he must pass by the Minotaur, and then must cross a great "discharge of stones" which occurred when Christ was crucified and

> on all sides the deep loathsome valley
> trembled, so that I thought the universe
> felt love, by which some believe
>
> the world has often been converted to chaos; . . .
> —*XII, 40–3*

Critics have puzzled much that this idea from Empedocles should be introduced here; critics habitually think too much and feel too little. If any man can report of his early experience of love and orgasm, that it was not a landslide, his foundations were not shaken, and his world not thrown back to chaos, I submit that that man is deficient in affect.

Dante, then, has successfully passed the flaming gates, sustained from his encounter with Farinata no wound worse than his predicted exile, slipped past the monster (offspring and evidence of a bestial intercourse), and now crossed the wreckage left by an almost universal upheaval. He may turn, then, to the other side of the libidinal energies—violence.

Scrambling down this rockslide, Dante arrives among the military tyrants and murderers immersed in boiling blood—a more extravagant version of the Angry, immersed in mud. Both guards, the Minotaur and the centaurs, give this violence a somewhat sexual coloring. The Centaurs, however, are a tempering influence; they share the military background of their prisoners, but have also a reasonable and humane side. They show us the male, no less steeped in violence, yet able to control and channel that, and so to teach the child or the hero. As Chiron taught Achilles, so Nessus teaches Dante, at Virgil's own suggestion:

Let him be your first guide, now, and me, second.

—*XII, 114*

In the following canto, we see the immediate effect of this effort to contain or control these passions, to turn them inward. In the Wood of the Suicides, we see those who turned their violence back against themselves, either at once so as to perish, or gradually, to become a kind of vegetable. The unconscious side of the imagery shows the corresponding sexual inversion, the turning of the sexual energies back against the self in masturbation. This is seen not only as Dante breaks off the twig to let the tree bleed and so express itself; but also in Piero della Vigne's story of destroying himself to escape the calumny of that harlot (Envy) who never turns "her adulterous eyes" from his master's court; again in the description of souls of the suicides being sown as trees:

When the fierce soul leaves
    the body from which it has torn itself,
    Minos sends it to the seventh pit.

It falls into the woods; no place is chosen for it
    but wherever fortune casts it
    there it sprouts like a grain of wheat,

grows into a sapling and a wild tree;
    then the Harpies, feeding on its leaves,
    give pain, and an outlet for the pain.

Like the others, we shall go for our remains
    but not so that we may wear them again
    for it is not just that a man have that of which he robbed himself.

We shall drag them here and throughout
    this dismal wood our bodies shall be hung
    each on the thorn-bush of its tormented soul.

—*XIII, 94–108*

297

FOUR STUDIES IN THE CLASSICS

If sex appeared, earlier, as a form of Crucifixion, body upon body, onanism is here a self-crucifixion, the body eternally nailed on its own spirit. An extension of this meaning appears in that Florentine suicide who says, "I made a gibbet for myself of my own house."

The next circles—the Violent against God, Nature and Art—take us into the other subtle inversions and perversions which are a normal part of a child's development, of the tremendous, and partially successful, struggle to channel his passions. We witness the sterility of the burning sands where the Blasphemers, Sodomites, and Usurers dwell, recollect the Prostitute's stream at Bulicame, see the weirdly athletic sexual dance of the Sodomites, the suggestions of perversions and of spurious fecundity in the Usurers. Not only do the Usurers give money that fertility which should belong only to life; they wear the vaginal purse hung about their necks, which surely suggests some order of perversion—in view of that Usurer who "twisted his mouth and stuck out his tongue like an ox that licks its nose," possibly *cunnilingus,* or an urge to devour the feces.

We are even more concerned with the appealing figure of Brunetto Latini, the Florentine politician and author, whom Dante identifies not only as a "paternal image" but as his teacher.* This identification of the father-teacher with certain homosexual tendencies has already been prepared in the treatment of the Centaur, Chiron, who, for all his huge masculinity, partakes of certain feminine qualities, both in having been a nurse ("il qual nudri Achille") and in that curious action when, with the nock of an arrow, he parts his beard to uncover his great mouth.

We find a similar vaginal suggestion in the Old Man of Crete—the island where Zeus was hidden from his devouring father, Saturn. Every part of this huge allegorical figure, excepting its golden head, "is cleft with a fissure that drips tears . . ." Where we previously saw

*Dante could not have known well the historical Brunetto, except from his books.

298

the male organ issue from the female, we now see the female organ grafted upon the male.

This imagery is drawn from that part of the boy's experience when he is so terrified of his own sexual rage, and his father's punishing violence, that he must temper his view of the male both in himself and in his father by giving it certain of the female qualities (including—fortunately—gentleness, nourishment, flexibility); and will tend, at the same time, to disguise his Oedipal urges by direct inversion—by seeming to lose all interest in the female and transferring all affectional and libidinal interests to the father or to other males as a substitute. This is, of course, both normal and valuable in tempering the male's wilder impulses, so long as it does not turn to overt and permanent homosexuality or terrify the child with fear that it might.

Immediately after the image of Saturn, the evil Father-God who devours his children, we meet Brunetto, who, as a *good* father and teacher, shows Dante how to avoid being devoured by his countrymen, by those of his fatherland:

> Your lot reserves such honour for you
> that one party and the other will be hungering
> for you; but the grass shall be far from the goat.
>
> Let the beasts of Fiesole make fodder
> of themselves and not touch the plant—
> if one still springs up on their dungheap—
>
> in which there lives once more the holy seed
> of those Romans who remained there when
> it became the nest of such wickedness.
>
> —*XV, 70–8*

Yet there is a curious irony in Brunetto's statement, for his specific crime is homosexuality, a goatish devouring of others' seed—something of a cannibalistic nature survives in much homosexual imagery.

Thus, if homosexuality provides a kind of bulwark against the swollen seas of sexuality and passion (as is suggested by Brunetto's imagery of the Flemish dikes), it opens a deeper and even more destructive area of cannibalistic drives. This problem will more concern us, later. For the moment, it is enough to see Dante's admiration for Brunetto:

> I did not dare go down from the path
> to be level with him; but I kept my head
> bent down, like a man who walks with reverence.
> —*XV, 43–6*

Even Dante's description of his past journey suggests a rejection of the female:

> Up above there, in the radiant life
> I lost myself in a valley
> before my years had been fulfilled.
>
> Only yesterday morning I turned my back on it;
> he [Virgil] appeared to me when I was returning to it
> and by this road, leads me home.
> —*XV, 49–54*

and a strong attraction to the male:

> Then he [Brunetto] turned, and seemed like one of those
> who run in the field at Verona
> for the green cloth, and he appeared
>
> like one who wins, not like one who loses.
> —*XV, 121 ff*

Again, speaking to Jacopo Rusticucci, another homosexual, in the next canto:

> If I had been sheltered from the fire,
> I would have thrown myself down among them,
> and I believe my teacher would have permitted it.

But as I would have been burned and baked,
    fear overcame my good will
    which made me voracious to embrace them.

Then I began: "Not disdain, but sorrow
    has your condition fixed within me
    so deep that it will not leave me quickly

as soon as my Lord spoke to me
    words through which I came to think
    that such men as you were coming.

I am from your city, and always I
    with affection have recounted and listened to
    your deeds and your honored names.

I leave the gall and go for the sweet apples
    promised me by my truthful guide,
    but first I must go down to the center."

"So may your soul long direct
    your members," . . . he replied . . .*
                  —XVI, 46–65

Small wonder, then, that Dante, ready to descend into the last circles, looses the cord from around his waist and throws it down into the pit as a signal for Geryon. As in each of these highly sexual or suggestive passages, Dante specially asks for the reader's attention:

Ah! how cautious men should be
with those who see not only acts

*I know nothing of Renaissance slang, but this sounds like a rather affectionate homosexual joke, which would be in keeping with the earlier joke about Bishop Andrei de Nozzi's "mal protesi nervi"—his high-strung nerves, or penis. There seems to be much sexual implication, too, in the image of the "family" of sodomites squinting at Dante and Virgil "as men . . . look at one another under a new moon"—or "as an old tailor does at his needle's eye"—how conscious, I have no idea.

but with their judgment look into thoughts!
—XVI, 118–20

Interpreters have been much puzzled. Dante is leaving a realm of sexual perversion; he may well cast off that cord with which he had "meant once to catch the Leopard with the painted skin." He is casting off his sexuality, not only to escape the sterile fires of perversions, but more especially so he may descend into a pre-sexual area. He is returning to the child's earliest impressions, even those of birth. So the casting off of Dante's belt must suggest not only a casting off of sex and the penis, but also the earlier casting off of the navel cord. No doubt the two bodily appendages are closely related in the child's thought and thus may be embodied in a single image.

Seated on the back of Geryon and circling slowly down through the murky air, Dante comes to the Eighth Circle, the *Malebolge* (Evil Ditches, Pouches or Pockets). Here are "new anguish, new torments and new torturers"; he has entered the realm of the She-Wolf, of Fraud and Betrayal. As noted, the imagery of this section tends to come from earlier periods in childhood and babyhood, finally reaching the moment of birth (already quoted) in the last canto. We will be less interested in the figure of the father and more in a mother or parent of undefined sexuality. At the same time, largely coincident with the *Malebolge's* image of Fraud, we will find many images of the child's attempts to change, disguise, transform, or pervert the truth about his body and his psyche; then, coincident with the last circle's images of Betrayal, many images of hunger, of nourishment, of devouring and being devoured.

Yet when we first enter the *Malebolge,* there is no immediate change. The first *bolgia* holds the Seducers and Panders, whipped on by horned devils to walk their ceaseless round; the second, the Flatterers dipped in excrement. Both clearly carry on patterns already established. So does the third *bolgia,* where Simonists (dealers in church offices) are stuffed head-down into the rock.

During this episode, however, something odd occurs. Dante asks to go down into the *bolgia* to question one of the sinners (who turns out to be Pope Nicholas III—a wicked if religious *Papa,* guilty of seizing the beautiful Lady, Mother Church, and fornicating with that "whore that sitteth upon the waters"). Virgil not only agrees, he picks Dante up on his haunch and carries him both ways, like a child. This happens three different times in the *Malebolge* and, moreover, we twice see Dante crawling like a baby and, once, Virgil teaching him how to do it. For Virgil to carry Dante is specially surprising since Dante has weight while Virgil has none. Every reader, no doubt, will think of good theological explanations. Yet the real point is that this did not happen at other times in the poem when it would have fit as well narratively or theologically; it does happen just as we approach the problems of the very young child.

This becomes clear, however, only in the following canto; there, in the fourth *bolgia* we see the "wondrously distorted" bodies of Diviners and Soothsayers. Throughout the *Malebolge* we are dealing with Fraud, with those who "resent God's judgment" and so try to change His creation through intellectual and emotional falsifications, pretenses, disguises. Here, we see that such falsifications have their beginning and their later models in certain efforts of the child to deny "God's judgment," the nature of reality, particularly of sex as he finds it in others and in his own body.

This horror of sex in others, particularly the parents, has already been represented—most recently in the emphasis on prostitution among the Panders and the Simonists, and probably also in Virgil's long story about Manto, the "cruel virgin" soothsayer who founded his city. On the one hand we have a maternal virgin, on the other a maternal whore; both are efforts to deny the simple facts of everyday sex—to suggest that the mother either had nothing to do with sex (Manto abjures all human intercourse, *"consorzio umano"*) or that if she *did,* it was only to get the father's money, certainly not because she was pleased by the sex act or by that particular male. Thus, the

303

child enacts a self-comforting fraud upon his own psyche which may profoundly affect his view of whomever he loves in later life.

The child's efforts to escape sexual definition in his own body are reflected in Tiresias, who twice changed his sex, in the pronounced anality of this and the surrounding cantos, in the emphasis on failures to fulfill one's assigned role in life.

The old parables always showed that if the gods *really* wanted to wreck you, they gave you what you wished for. Many of the things Dante only fantasied we are rich enough to have. By now we can afford the anality of our wasteland, can all afford to evade any assigned role; most of us can afford to look and act like the opposite sex; a few have even managed to get it changed—behold, Christine Jorgensen! What hath man wrought?! Even if none of us has managed yet to change it *twice,* even if we haven't re-created the complete *Inferno,* right now—don't give up, we have a crash program under way.

The Diviners had tried to foresee the future. As a result, their heads are on backward:

> . . . the face was turned toward the back,
> and they had to go backwards
> since they were denied to see ahead.
> —XX, 13–15

The effect of this transformation is to replace the sexual organs with the anus and buttocks, as we are twice reminded:

> how could I keep my face dry
>
> when close at hand I saw our human image
> so distorted that the tears from the eyes
> washed the buttocks at the crack?
> —*XX, 22–4*

She [Manto] who covers her breasts,
which you do not see, with her loose tresses
and has her hairy skin on the other side, . . .
—*XX, 52–4*

Such distortions are the result of the child's desperate effort to place his future, especially his sexual future, in his own will, not at the mercy of God's will or of his own birth.

Among the barrators (grafters) in the boiling pitch of the fifth *bolgia* we continue the excrementary interest already evinced. This is seen, too, in the behavior of the Malebranche, the guardian devils, both in the childishly obscene parody of military form, their salutes and anal trumpetings, and in their torture of the captured Ciampolo like a gang of sadistic boys who have caught some small animal or smaller boy.

In the sixth *bolgia,* we find another attempt to escape reality—not by transforming the body, but disguising the spirit. Here are the Hypocrites, a "gilded" and "painted people" circling even slower than the Diviners, weighed down by the exhaustion of maintaining a false appearance: cloaks that are dazzlingly beautiful outside, but all of lead inside. This loss of self through disguise is carried on in the image of the Evil Counselors clothed in great tongues of flame—of "thievish fire." The basic theft here is of the self—the removal of the self through lies and falsification. But only among the actual thieves of the seventh *bolgia* do we see the full interrelation of these ideas of falsification, loss of self, bodily transformation, and sexual degradation.

There is probably no scene so fantastic or so horrifying in all the poem. In their hideous pit full of snakes, the thieves are running, their hands tied behind with serpents whose heads and tails pass through the loins and are knotted in front. A horrible series of transformations begins at once. First, Vanni Fucci, bitten by a serpent, takes fire, drops into ashes and is then re-created—only to speak an utter blasphemy and be attacked by several other serpents and the centaur, Cacus. Another thief, Agnello, is then attacked by a serpent, Cianfa; both merge into one serpentine body. Next, a tiny lizard springs upon Buoso, bites into his navel, and the two exchange bodies, Buoso becoming a serpent, the lizard becoming a human, Francesco.

Perhaps the best possible gloss for this scene has been provided by Jean Genêt in *The Thief's Journal*. All those things that Dante knows symbolically, Genêt knows literally and in detail. First, the transformations, beginning in the wilful drive to insult and invert the moral nature of the universe, to pervert the natural physical order of the body. Then, the close interrelation of blasphemy, theft, and sexual corruption, of different ways to invert the normal order. Next, the conception of a man's property as an extension of his personality; its theft as an attempt to pre-empt or destroy some part of his power or ability. Above all, the gang of thieves as a sort of family group founded on mutual victimization, on acts of corruption and thievery meant to pass on one's own degradation. Perhaps some brief reading in de Sade might be helpful, but I suggest that any reader who thinks this still too far from his own experience might take a second look at his own society—one larger and more proper, yet again formed after a conception of the family group, and founded not on buggery but glamour as a sex substitute, not theft but open and recognized deception as its currency of membership.

The thieves' blasphemies, transformations, degradations, satisfy a real desire—to pervert and degrade the nature of what is. Recalling all the shoddy deceit we seem to demand in advertising, news, politics, the many ways we have of being cheated, diminished, degraded (and so accepted and cared for as members of the group), the reader may decide this episode is not so strange as he might wish.

I have already suggested that the next *bolgia,* the eighth, where Evil Counselors burn in tongues of flame, reveals how lying and bad counsel are a kind of theft, too—above all, theft of the self. Throughout the *Malebolge* we deal in perversions of identity; here it is implied that identity is the embodiment of parental voice. As others have noted, all the sinners in this *bolgia* are men of great ability and authority—those who are able, both by gifts and position, to take a parental role, to teach and give counsel. Betraying such a position is no slight offense. Small wonder that Dante, the poet, must

> . . . rein in
> my talent more than usually,
>
> lest it run where virtue does not guide;
> so that if a good star or something better
> has given me blessings, I may not grudge myself that.
> —*XXVI, 21–4*

And that the Pilgrim, who nearly slips and falls into this *bolgia*, must, when he stands before the huge, fiery, forked-tongue of Achilles and Diomedes, refrain his own tongue and pass through the mediation of Virgil.

Moving on to the Schismatics, or Sowers of Discord, we see the body not so much transformed as mangled and dismembered. This re-creates not only the child's fear of being dismembered, but suggests that in attempting to change himself the child may be maiming himself, producing schisms in the self.

In Bertran de Born, who holds his severed head aloft like a lantern, we see the divorce of the mind, the eyes, and tongue from the body —that same process of rationalization we have noted before. This is in part the punishment for separating others (in de Born's case, separating father from son); it is also something sought by the child in his effort to deny the reality of the body. We have a vicious circle of schisms which produce schisms. Most significantly, we are only a few verses away from the last circle, the circle of birth and betrayal, into which Dante will be lowered by Antaeus, who was killed by separation from his mother. I suggest that all these schisms in the mind, between mind and body, between the self and others, between others,

307

FOUR STUDIES IN THE CLASSICS

are re-creations and re-enactments of the original shock of separation.

In the last *bolgia,* the impersonaters, the counterfeiters, the alchemists, lie about on the ground afflicted with every disgusting disease. Dante has advanced to a recognition of transformation, falsification, rejection of reality, as a disgusting blight.

If it seems that I have moved through the *Malebolge* very rapidly, that is because I have skipped over what are perhaps its two most important events, both of which oppose the overall tendency of the section. First, Dante's change of heart after witnessing the Hypocrites of the sixth *bolgia;* second, the great speech of Ulysses in the eighth *bolgia.*

As Virgil and Dante leave the Hypocrites' *bolgia* they discover that one of the Malebranche had tried to trick them—the bridge ahead is out. One of the hypocritical Friars smirks:

> I once heard them tell in Bologna
> of the Devil's many vices, among which I heard
> that he is a liar, and the father of lies.
> —*XXIII, 142–4*

which angers Virgil; he, however, manages to lead an exhausting climb to the next *bolgia,* meantime exhorting Dante.

> The breath was so wrung out of my lungs
> when I was up that I could go no farther,
> but sat down as soon as I got there.
>
> "Now you must shake off sloth,"
> said the master, "for sitting on featherbeds
> no one comes into fame—nor under comforters—
>
> and whoever consumes his life without that [fame]
> leaves as much trace of himself on earth
> as smoke in air or foam on the water.
>
> Get up, then! conquer your panting
> with your soul that wins every battle
> if it does not sink with its body's weight.

A longer ladder must be climbed;
  it is not enough to have left these souls.
  If you understand, act now so that it will profit you."

I got up, then, showing myself furnished
  with better breath and nerve than I felt,
  and said, "Go on, for I am strong and fearless."
  —*XXIV, 43–60*

This reform from timidity and cowardice is extremely significant. Dante is learning to handle his cowardice; Virgil is teaching him to crawl so that he *can* return to his right journey. Like the good father, he now exhorts his pupil to really *try*. Yet, why are those efforts successful when, in the past, Dante responded so poorly? First, simply because of Virgil's affectionate yet stern, humane yet truthful ministrations. Second, Dante has just left the Hypocrites after discovering that the devil, the father of lies, has attempted to impede his progress. He must realize there has been something lying and hypocritical in his past cowardice, that his progress has been impeded by a Satanic and lying part of himself. Surrounded here by false and lying transformations, Dante has managed to work a real transformation in himself.

The other episode I have skipped over is the great story of Ulysses's last voyage. This is a truly remarkable episode which in its final meaning seems to me to oppose every idea, every belief put forward by the rest of the poem. This is not a flaw; it is one of the poem's greatest glories. We are dealing, after all, with the human spirit where ideas do not become false in the presence of their opposite, but truer. Every twopenny poetaster from Dante's time till ours has been able to create an airtight system of ideas and beliefs to conclusively demonstrate what life means, what the soul needs. It takes a true poet to see that a man needs walls on his house, but he also needs a window or three. Just such a window is Ulysses.

So far, we have been concerned with the soul's need for limits and

309

directions, man's need to divert and channel his energies, to master his drive to rebel and subtly betray. This is a truth specially valuable now it is so unfashionable. Yet merely because Freedom has become the slogan of every mediocre fantast, every tyrant and would-be tyrant, Freedom is no less valuable for that. Ulysses, the great adventurer, stands for that freedom, for the soul's need to follow its own bent, for the fact that a man of great drive and ability can fulfill himself and his work only by going his own gait, can find his way only by getting lost. Many analysts nowadays assert the same truth in saying that the completely identified man, the man who is always *mature*, is likely a bore. A comparatively happy bore—one rescued from the depths and from the heights—nonetheless a bore. And our world would be poorer if *everyone* became so. We cannot afford a world of regression, yet often the creative man can operate only by regression.

This does not deny the dangers of such freedom. It makes no man happy; makes most men less interesting, less creative. Ulysses is clearly *not* most men. If in his abandonment of father, wife, and son, he reminds us of the irresponsibility that drives most of us to damage these we love, yet he reminds us, too, of our other adventurers—those whose passionate curiosity, whose love of the impossible, whose rejection of what *is,* drove them to great explorations, great creations. And, incidentally, whose private lives often fill us with compassion if not downright horror. If Ulysses is little better than a pirate, then we must admit we love pirates and piracy and had better put that love to some use, else we waste one of the great powers in the only world we have.

We often embody this conflict in the opposition between Athens and Sparta; it is equally easy to see it in the present world division between ourselves and the more channeled communist states. Here, it is easy to grow disgusted with a free people's unproductive self-service, their neurotic and self-destructive violence, their demand for subtler tyrannies, their myriad ways to undercut ability. No doubt the Eastern peoples, having got rid of freedoms they couldn't use, are in the mass happier and more productive; we must also see the deep frustration and waste of ability and aspiration there. If this were not a *real* problem, if the truth lay on one side or the other, not in the necessary tension of the two, it would be a great deal easier to make a sensible world—or a meaningful poem.

At any rate, the figure of Ulysses goes far to redress a balance which would otherwise be lost. For all Dante's diligence to show what's wrong with Ulysses, the final impression is of almost awe-stricken reverence. And in all Dante's later journey surely one of the great driving influences upon him is the recollection of this tragic and powerful wanderer. How could it be otherwise to a man and poet whose life was spent in wandering, for whom life very nearly came to equal exile?

Of course, it is easier for us to admire Ulysses than it was for Dante. We know only too well that there *is* no Divine Will to guide our wanderings, that if our journey is ever to have great value, it will probably have to roam outside the direction of our conscious will. (If there is one thing I aim to do here, it is to show that much of the value of Dante's poem lies in creation at a level he was not aware of, and which may reach a reader at a level far below his conscious awareness, far below the rational mind with all its ingenuities, its numbers, patterns, its easy meanings.) One of Dante's greatest triumphs lies in overcoming his conscious beliefs to sympathize with the tragic passion of such a figure—a passion and a sympathy far deeper and more meaningful than anything he had felt for the triviality of Francesca.

So Dante, now, is ready for the last, the ninth circle.

> To describe the bottom of the whole universe
> is no undertaking . . .

for a tongue that cries *mama* and *papa.*
                                    —XXXII, 7–9

No task for any child. Nor for any man who can't return to his earliest passions and emotions, to the center of his world. Dante passes into the frozen well of Cocytus ringed by the giants who rebelled against Zeus. They tower above him there with terrifying force, as adults and parents surround the child, picking him up, putting him down, talking some kind of stupid, long-forgotten gibberish. As Rossi has remarked of this somewhat comical scene, "Virgil has much the air of a father who accompanies his bright boy on a visit to a menagerie and makes him notice the beasts one by one and quiets his fears and restrains his idle curiosity."

As noted before, it is significant that Antaeus, whom Hercules picked up, now picks up Dante to lower him into the frozen cistern of Cocytus. Antaeus was killed by that separation from his mother, Earth; Dante will re-enact here his birth and smallest babyhood.

By an odd and very human ambiguity, the giants stand both for those adults the child rebels against, and also for his rebelliousness against them. Feeling in their presence stupid, hate-filled, rebellious and treacherous, it is natural to project these feelings onto the persons they are directed against—then viciousness seems justified. By their mere presence, they remind him that his word is not law, his mere wanting will not produce what he wants, he is not a god. And that very weakness fills him with a rage so vast that it seems to him a sort of elemental force which must be kept chained at the center of the world or it would destroy Olympus and his gods. Yet, at the center of his world they stay—so he will always have a desire to undercut greatness in himself and others—to cut it down to his size and betray it. There is no loss worse than that of powers we never had. Having felt most free and powerful at a time he was completely contained and helpless is the sort of thing to make a man uncompromising—to make him seek either absolute power or complete helplessness. It's clear which of those is easier to get.

Not only are the adults large and powerful; far worse, they feed the child. Nothing kills you like getting born; nothing starves you like being fed. Speaking of his lifelong exile, Dante remarked on "how bitter is the bread of others." It is a bitterness a child may never forgive—his parents' generosity only shows him his own need. Even if he finds no revenge beyond refusing to eat (rejecting the life they offer), he will find more ingenious revenges against any who try to help him in later life. Most of us are dangerous only to those we love.

Thus, a godlike generosity in others tends to turn most of us into something Satanic. By a related ambiguity, the giants here ring Satan around like disciples or like the priests in a baptismal font, yet priests of irreligion. We even hear a parody of Venantius Fortunatus's hymn "Vexilla Regis prodeunt Inferni." Earlier, among the Simonists, Dante spoke of such a baptismal font, keeping birth imagery ambient even there by mentioning that he once broke one of these marble fonts to save a child wedged in and drowning. There, too, we saw the Simonists stuffed into holes in the rock, just as now the traitors are stuffed into the ice, into the mouths of Satan, or as Satan himself is wedged into the rock of the world's center. On the one side we see his upper parts protruding like Farinata, or the frozen sinners; on the other side we see his legs exposed and sticking up like Pope Nicholas or like the traitors in his own mouth.

The child's violently mixed feelings about food help account for the many images of hunger and devouring in this section. We recall that the She-Wolf

> . . . has a nature so vicious and perverse
> that she never satisfies her greedy cravings
> but after eating is hungrier than before.
>
> —*I, 97–9*

313

We find image after image of this craving: Ugolino gnawing his knuckles, tempted to eat his starved sons,* finally gnawing on the head and neck of Archbishop Ruggieri; Tydeus gnawing the skull of Menalippus, Satan endlessly devouring Judas, Cassius, and Brutus. This reflects not only the child's humiliating hunger, but also his resulting rage to devour. It reflects his fantasy that if he was within his mother, he must have been devoured to get there; his self-comforting fantasy that she does not want to feed him but to devour him. (This fantasy may have its element of truth, literal or symbolic: that has little to do with its power in the child's mind.)

The terrible cold here, too, must reflect the newborn infant's discomfort. So, too, must the continual weeping. Here, everyone weeps —Ugolino, his sons, the brothers Alberti, Satan—or they try to. One of the worst torments of the last sinners is that they cannot weep:

> There, weeping itself keeps them from weeping
> and the grief which finds a blockage in the eyes
> turns inward to increase the pain:
>
> for their first tears form a clot
> and, like a crystal visor,
> fill the whole cavity beneath the eyebrows.
> —*XXXIII, 94–8*

This impacted grief and rage, given no expression, turns to bitterest rancor. The dead are spiteful and hateful, cursing and mocking each other's misfortunes, telling each other's names to blacken each other in the world. All demand pity; none show any. Ugolino says that when Dante hears how he, with his sons, was starved

*The historical Ugolino was imprisoned with two grandsons and two sons who were full-grown men. Dante, who must have known this, changes them to four infant sons. This makes the episode more pathetic, but also more horrifying in its suggestion that Ugolino has devoured his dead children—a suggestion so strong that some critics have mistakenly asserted it to be the case.

> . . . if you do not weep, what do you ever weep for?
> —*XXXIII, 42*

Yet oddly enough, he admits that when he first realized their plight himself

> I did not weep, I so turned to stone inside;
>   they wept; . . .
>
> I shed no tears, nor did I answer
>   all that day nor the night after, . . .

Our final impression is of a man gone utterly to stone. He tells us a terribly grievous story—but only to harm his enemy. He clutches every morsel of suffering to him, for it gives him an excuse to hate. He is as tied to Ruggieri as to a lover.

This, perhaps, more than anything else, gives us perspective back from this last set speech of the *Inferno* to its first, the story of Francesca. As critics have noted, each begins his tale in words derived from the *Aeneid:*

> And she to me: "There is no greater grief
>   than to recall a happy time
>   when in misery; and that your teacher knows.
>
> But if you have such desire to learn
>   the first root of our love,
>   I will do as one who weeps and speaks.
> —*V, 121–6*
>
> . . . You want me to renew
>   desperate grief which wrings my heart
>   only at the thought, before I speak.
>
> But if my words will be a seed
>   bearing fruit of shame to this traitor I gnaw
>   then you will see me speak and weep together.

Meantime, the companion stands aside, silent. Like Francesca, Ugolino wallows in self-pity, and so in hatred. He *has* been wronged. (So was she. Who has not been?) Even here he says nothing of his own wrongs which put him in the tower and finally in the last circle of Hell. We see only his deep fixation in hatred which makes him a true follower of the She-Wolf (in his dream he sees himself as a wolf with whelps pursued by hounds; in Hell, we see him as a hound, gnawing a bone). He and Ruggieri are locked together much like the brothers degli Alberti in the preceding canto:

> . . . I saw two so squeezed together
> that they had the hair of the head mixed.
>
> "Tell me, you who press your breasts so tight,"
> I said, "Who are you?" And they bent their necks
> and when they had raised their faces toward me,
>
> their eyes, which before had only been moist inside,
> gushed out at the lids and the cold
> froze the tears between and locked them again.
>
> No clamp ever fastened timber to timber
> so strongly: then they, like two billy-goats,
> butted each other, such rage overcame them.
>
> *—XXXII, 40–51*

Locked together by the frozen tears of their mutual rage and hatred. That earlier passage, too, reminds us that the Caina holds the brother Paolo and Francesca betrayed, as well as that Mordred whose betrayal and murder of his father, King Arthur, the lovers shared through the figures of Lancelot and Guinevere. The little familial groups, each based on hatred and betrayal, the victim and victimizer equally dependent on each other: if Ugolino and Ruggieri are locked in hate as close as lovers, are not Francesca and Paolo locked in love nearly as close as hatred? In them we first saw sketched that compulsion to betray the beloved, the benefactor, the lord, which we here see fully delineated in Ugolino, in Judas, and in Satan. Here we see the ice beneath the lovers' heat, the clutch beneath the embrace, the teeth beneath the kiss.

Crossing the ice, seeing thousands of faces "made doggish by the cold," Dante kicks one of them violently, admitting he's not sure it was an accident. When that sinner will not confess his name, Dante falls upon him, yanking out the hair. Later, he tricks Fra Alberigo, who begs:

> "Lift the hard veils from my face
> so I can pour out the grief impregnating my heart
> a little, before the tears freeze up again."
> —*XXXIII, 112–4*

Dante gives him a false promise, hears his story, then does not open his eyes. Many readers have found this cruelty puzzling and distasteful. It carries out one of the poem's most important themes.

One of the most marvelous things about the *Inferno* is its incredibly complex structure of balances and reciprocities: crime balanced against punishment, scene against scene, figure against figure. One of the most meaningful aspects of this structure lies in the way Dante, again and again, displays the very sin he is witnessing. With Francesca, he was sentimental and faint; with Filippo Argenti, angry; with Farinata, proud. Here among the cold-blooded traitors, he is cold-blooded and treacherous; he himself feels so cold that his face becomes callous.

Just after his scene with Fra Alberigo, a sinner asks him, "Why do you mirror yourself in us so long?" Why indeed!—so that he may truly see and know his own evil, so that cowardice may no longer "turn him back from honored deeds as false sight makes an animal [to] shy." To witness that evil only as he may see it in others is comfortable and innocuous; if Dante is to find a new life he must first experience, in himself, the evil of this life. Only by descending to the deepest passions can he reach powers strong enough to release him from their grip;

317

only by descending to betrayal can he find the forces that have controlled him and turned him back against himself and his God, so that he may now turn them back against themselves.

Before he can return to that first purpose, then, he has one vision left:

> "Behold Dis! . . . and behold the place
> where you must arm yourself with courage."

Not only must he arm himself for the sight, he must arm himself *with* it.

Coming before Satan, Dante is as frozen and powerless as the vision he sees; is neither living nor dead. Yet this experience must bring him warmth and power, a new and livelier birth. This abyss of blindness must give him new sight, must clear the crusts from his eyes. This pit of numbness, total stasis, must show him that his own insurrection has taken the form of being frozen, unresponsive, half-alive. If we feel the "honey of generation [has] betrayed" us, there are ways enough to return the betrayal. If we dare not lose the life we hate, we can still deaden it. If we feel devoured, we can always justify our feeling by devouring ourselves. If we dare not attack the powers of our life, we can still wound them by attacking what they love—ourselves . . . can defeat their hopes in us.

It should be clear, then, why Dante's movement in the world above had come to a halt, a false stasis, why he had turned from honored deeds. He should now be—at least in part—ready to resume his path. It is a path hard enough to demand considerable courage and endurance. The historical Dante—never fully divorced from the fictional Dante—had lost his mother even before his father; his mature life was one long exile from homeland, wife, and children. So he may speak for that sense of banishment our human birth gives us all. If at times Dante seems almost wilfully to have prolonged that exile, that does not diminish its bitterness. He is, at any rate, fortified to go on with a life not of containment and stasis, but of movement and change, of continual exile, yet of purpose and direction. He has completed his nine cycles of evil and may now turn over at the dead center of his world to issue forth into a new life.

He may not yet be ready for that realm described by Picearda, that realm of fetal contentment, "that sea to which all things move which it creates and which nature makes." He is ready to set foot on the inconstant surface of the earth, to begin his Purgation:

> We climbed up, he first and I second,
> so far that I saw the beautiful things
> which the heavens bear, through a round opening,
>
> and from there we came forth to see again the stars.
> —*XXXIV, 136–9*

Gods of *The Iliad:* Memoirs
of a Brainpicker

"I have come here today to convert you all to polytheism."
I really said that. Golstrom had warned me it might not work. I
should have seen it was the worst possible attack for *my* class. I
suppose I was desperate to impress them, to be admired and honored.
Besides, there *she* sat—who had brought the whole thing up.

She wasn't really dumb. She really was lovely. Worse, she bore the
name of a famous psychoanalyst. Who could help pinning false hopes
on her? If I could just answer her brilliantly enough; if she would say
only one bright thing, or even just agree with me once—then the
others might stop hating me. Overborne by her glamour, the boys
would follow her; the girls, though they must hate her, would still
have to follow the boys.

I had lost the girls in the first week, on the *Bible.* My few poor
snippets of encyclopedia Higher Criticism had shaken their faith.
They thought me a militant cynic enlisting them for godlessness.

Actually, I had merely failed to realize how deep was their ignorance —and how badly needed.

The boys saw me the same way—but then, that's how they saw themselves. As tough-minded challengers of authority, they liked my apparent questioning of established religion. Also, they liked the girls' discomfort. For days, we were almost buddy-buddy.

Then I gave the first test. The raging girls read hard, hoping to disprove me; they got high grades. The boys supposed that after all their nodding and grinning, they surely needn't read the books, too. They failed. An air of betrayal ran high in the room.

On *The Iliad* things had picked up a little—after all, I knew something about it. I could crib from my own teachers—Gerald Else and Robert Lowell. I could read the poem aloud—after hours of secret practice. I could give them notebooks full of background: Leda and the swan; Leda's two eggs, Castor and Polydeuces in one, Helen and Clytaimnestra in the other; Paris's judgment of the goddesses; his theft of Helen from Menelaus; the gathering of the Greeks for revenge, the ten years' siege of Troy.

Beyond, I thought I could help them through that cool, formal surface to those turbulent underlying passions still so close to their lives. Surely they should recognize Achilles, the impetuous rush of his language:

> Son of Atreus, I believe that now straggling backwards
> we must make our way home if we can even escape death,
> if fighting now must crush the Achaians and the plague likewise.
> No, come, let us ask some holy man, some prophet,
> even an interpreter of dreams, since a dream also
> comes from Zeus, who can tell why Phoibos Apollo is so angry,
> if for the sake of some vow, some hecatomb he blames us,
> if given the fragrant smoke of lambs, of he goats, somehow
> he can be made willing to beat the bane aside from us.

The Greek is still less grammatical, jerkier, yet even in translation (we, of course, used Lattimore's) this is a childish and petulant mind spewing out idea on idea, jamming one thought into another in a disorderly rush of energy and passion.

He is so unlike a movie hero, so far from anything young people have been told of heroes, yet so true to what they have seen, they must find it hard to believe the poem means what it says. The heroes *are* just as piratical, grasping, petulant as they seem. Achilles is using the plague and Calchas's prophecy only to start a quarrel. He is eager to attack Agamemnon just because he hates authority, arrogantly refuses that anyone should rule over him:

> King who feed on your people, since you rule nonentities; . . .
> So I must be called of no account and a coward
> if I must carry out every order you may happen to give me.

Once the quarrel is joined, rancor and envy simply pour from Achilles:

> You wine sack, with a dog's eyes, with a deer's heart. Never
> once have you taken courage in your heart to arm with your people
> for battle, or go into ambuscade with the best of the Achaians.
> No, for in such things you see death. Far better to your mind
> is it, all along the widespread host of the Achaians
> to take away the gifts of any man who speaks up against you.

Though Agamemnon has tried to be reasonable throughout this scene, Achilles's arrogance finally moves him to retaliate. No king could afford to permit such open defiance.

True, it is unjust that Agamemnon takes Achilles's prize, Briseis, to replace his own. Still, Achilles himself possesses her only by rape in a raid where he destroyed her city, her husband, her three brothers, and probably the rest of her family as well. Now, as she is led away, she seems to weep for Achilles. Later, we learn better; when the heroes have patched up their quarrel, she is led back, still weeping. Openly she laments for Patroclus; actually, she weeps for her own fate. She wants to stay with Achilles only because his greater ferocity might promise some stability for his slaves.

Once she is gone, this terrible fighter, the terror of both camps, runs sniveling to his goddess-mother:

> Since, my mother, you bore me to be a man of short life
> therefore Zeus of the loud thunder on Olympus should grant me
> honor at least. But now he has given me not even a little.

He is like a spoiled brat wailing how he's been mistreated so she will pat him:

> She came and sat beside him as he wept and stroked him
> with her hand and called him by name and spoke to him: "Why
>   then,
> child, do you lament? What sorrow has come to your heart now?
> Tell me, do not hide it in your mind, and then we shall both know."
> Sighing heavily Achilleus of the swift feet answered her:
> "You know; since you know why must I tell you all this? . . ."

But Achilles is not merely whining; he asks for the death and maiming of his own comrades, men blameless of his injuries. As the gods so often do, Zeus will give him just what he asks, though with circumstances which, for the moment, he does not see. In answer to his prayer, his dearest friend will die.

What a splendid irony that Achilles should have such awful power, yet be driven by the self-centered passions of a spoiled three-year-old. Could it have been different with Hitler? Stalin? General MacArthur? With the Wall Street tycoons? With men?

Helen, too, that paradigm of fatal beauty—how different from a movie heroine. Still, how very like the glamorous women who played such roles—say Jean Harlow or Marylin Monroe. Everyone seeks her;

only the hero can obtain her (Menelaus, Joe DiMaggio); not even he can stand her. The old men of Troy whisper of her beauty in dry, delicate voices like cicadas; even they pray that she will go away.

Her beauty has made her too feminine, too passive; in the great robe she weaves, she celebrates only the deeds of others to obtain her. She is almost as much a slave as Briseis; she will simply be handed to the victor. Having no history in commitment, she cannot now choose. When she was with Menelaus she ran away with Paris. Now she curses that act and wishes herself again with Menelaus. Yet when Aphrodite appears to her she is quick to refuse that possibility, too. The desire of others has made her hate both them and herself. She cannot call herself names enough. Not seeing her brothers in the Greek camp, she assumes they are too ashamed of her to show their faces.

Even her own goddess treats her with brutal dominance. After Paris has been fairly beaten by Menelaus, Aphrodite spirits him away to his bedchamber, then goes for Helen to make love to him. When she refuses, the goddess answers with curt ferocity:

> Wretched girl, do not tease me lest in anger I forsake you
> and grow to hate you as much as now I terribly love you,
> lest I encompass you in hard hate, caught between both sides
> Danaans and Trojans alike, and you wretchedly perish.

And Helen goes. When she tells Paris she wishes Menelaus had killed him, he does not even mind. He merely says he wants to lie with her. Within fifteen lines of her curse, she has turned to get into his bed.

So far, so good. Notebooks were open, pens flew briskly over the pages, my students were almost smiling. Perhaps these small victories led me to try for a large one. It still seemed academic. Obviously I couldn't draw examples from *their* lives; I took one from mine.

Once I had almost known a Helen of Troy. She came through high school, then our little college, about five years ahead of me; I would never have dared speak to her. Her name, Rosamond, held everything fatal, evil, unspeakably lovely. When our high school orchestra played Schubert's "Rosamunde Overture" we all became subject to sly looks and attacks of snickering. Had I touched her, my arm would have shriveled to the shoulder. I still retain the image of her flanks, encased in an incandescent blue Bemberg silk, passing up the main street of town one Saturday night, away from me where I stood in a gang of tongue-tied, scandalized boys, sweating with lust and despair.

(I never told them that she looked very like—shall I call her "Miss Freud"?—sitting there in their own class.)

She went, we thought, with the whole football team. Who, in their leather helmets and armoring, were our local heroes—hulking brutes from the mills and minefields of Pennsylvania, hired gladiators who kept solvent our tiny hyper-Christian college. What orgies we fantasied of her with them I would not dare now report. The day she stood before us all in the college stadium to be crowned May Queen —a stupefying vision—the loudspeaker announced that she had been elected by the football team. The whole crowd (God forgive us all!) roared with laughter.

I had always imagined her hard as nails. Yet recently, visiting in my home town, I had stumbled on two books (privately printed) of her poems. When I met old friends of hers, I asked. She had been a model student, sang with the choir, wrote poetry, painted. Actually, she had been too soft, too sweet—so very feminine that perhaps she felt safe only with those burly thugs.

She, who could have had almost any husband, any life, had fallen into something nearly tragic. Her first marriage, to a steel-plant executive, fell apart. Her poems, like mine, were about the loss of children. Apparently on the bounce, she had married a musician. That might seem closer to the life in the arts she wanted, but had turned into a nightmarish parody. She lived on the road, playing drums in her husband's dance band—one-night stands, night after night, in unknown towns throughout the South.

(Years later, I actually met her; most of this was utter nonsense. She was one of the strongest, finest persons I ever knew. She was very happy. But that is another story. Or even two.)

Why should the loveliest women be dogged by this air of doom? End up tied to brutes or fools? The most ethereal girl I ever met (whom I annoyed with weariless puppy love all my school years) married our town bully. Surely they, my students, had seen similar things?—I paused to see how they felt. They didn't feel. They sat silent, nervously ruffling their notebooks. Someone almost snickered. Perhaps the notion that I had ever desired any girl was obscene if true, probably impossible. In any case, even if I *had* once been alive, they did not care to know of it.

I ended the class; with lowered heads, they cluttered out. Yet, in all the general embarrassment, there in front of my desk stood Miss Freud. Asking me what all that had to do with *The Iliad.* I had scarcely begun to stammer when she broke in, "And besides, what are all those gods doing in there? I just don't get it. They aren't even real gods at all—they're weak and stupid and always muddling into the story where they aren't even needed in the first place. It would end up just the same without any gods at all. What in the world are they *for?*"

So that was how I came to be converting them that day. To show, in a sly and spectacular way, what the gods were all about. So she would *have* to admire me. At first, her question staggered me. It had never occurred to me that there was anyone who did not know what the Greek gods were about. I had never wondered whether *I* knew. In a panic, I had run to Golstrom. This is what he'd suggested. With warnings I didn't quite hear.

I began by sketching some of the disadvantages of monotheism. To Miss Freud, a "real" god was all-good, all-powerful, all-knowing. Yet those qualities are so far from the qualities of our world that such a god must be very distant, nearly inconceivable. Even the most contentious theologians admit Him to be paradoxical, indescribable. Nothing in this world can either prove or disprove His existence or His qualities. How can we be sure of His relation to our daily lives? We have a Thanksgiving Day, assuming Him responsible for the things we like. We have no Gripepitching Day—who in the world is doing all the rest of this?

Think of the friendlier world the Greek saw: he had someone to praise and blame, to propitiate and enlist. Suppose he lost a battle—that merely meant that next time he should try to have better luck and stronger gods on his side. It did not prove a man either wicked or unworthy. Just as among men there is no necessary relation between virtue, knowledge, and power, there was none for the gods. The Greek's gods were concerned not with virtue, but with narrow and selfish drives, just as *we* are. At least the Greek lost to forces a man could understand.

For us, totalities of loss are possible. Not only must we endure misfortunes; we must ask whether they imply God's judgment against us. Worse, this may lead us to judge God. We have committed ourselves to believe things which mere human logic denies; yet, that faith which must overcome such contradictions is constantly threatened by events. Our world is full of darknesses, inexplicabilities, crises of belief.

Several blocks up the hill, a truck's brakes give way; it crashes down, killing our little girl. Was she wicked and deserved to die? Were we wicked and deserved to lose her? Is God wicked to permit this? Has some anti-God usurped a part of His power? Does God merely sit back unconcerned with our little troubles, having once set the universe in motion?

The polytheist has no such worries. He merely sees a god, a great force named Slippage, who hates little girls and insurance companies and who loves to turn loose semi-trailers which crash through housewalls and crush the loved ones of any who fail to appease or counter his malign whim. Of course, the polytheist is wrong—no such god exists—but he's not far wrong. Skeptical and cautious as I am, Slippage remains pretty powerful in my world. He kills my little girl just about as often as the Greek's.

Having come this far, I supposed no one could fail to realize that I was spoofing. I had hoped that, at first, they might suppose I could be serious. By now they must have regained their footing; it was time to jog them off balance again.

I apologized. It was absurd to try to convert them—I had just realized that they already *were* polytheists. Always had been.

We all see many gods in our world—Allah, Brahma, Jehovah; we follow one, yet we usually grant to the others a sort of second-class divinity. Again, do all Christians follow the same God? All Mohammedans? Did Savonarola really follow the God of Sir Thomas More? We ourselves do not follow the same God tomorrow as today: our mind, our spirit matures and decays; our apprehension of Godhead changes. Even now, we may hear the voice of diverse gods. In any decision, we feel the call of disparate forces: sex, love, money, fashion, power; our preacher warns us that we are following strange gods.

Polytheism corresponds, then, not only to the diversity of our world, but also of our minds. The Homeric pantheon is very much an image of that family of interrelated yet conflicting forces which makes up the human spirit.

Just because of this diversity of ours, even our church has tended to become polytheistic. God *is* One; He can be *asserted* One. He can only be described in terms of linked opposites: love and wrath; mercy and damnation; foreknowledge and free will. If he is to be presented, He can only become humanly experiencable in terms of differing aspects: the church first split Him in three, then added Satan, then the Virgin, next (corresponding in many ways to the Greek gods) the whole corpus of the saints and the blessed. Thus the monotheistic church itself has created a pantheon larger than the Greek ever imagined.

328

This is not to criticize the church. Jehovah Who made and must know us must also realize that we are too limited to ever grasp Him single and entire—we must utilize all hints. To understand Him, however faultily, we must use terms we can understand—terms of multiplicity, diversity, conflict. But if this makes Jehovah seem almost polytheistic (I had preplanned this qualification fearing to offend my students), at the same time Zeus was something of a monotheist. The Greek had a term—$\mu o \iota \rho a$, which we usually translate as "Destiny" or "Fate"—which means much of what we mean by "God" or "Jehovah."

Offend them? "Outrage" would be closer. Three of them got up and walked out. There was open talking, expressions of disgust, slamming of the room door. And Miss Freud walked up to my desk once more, followed by a Phys. Ed. girl, both white as chalk, biting their lips, then turning to walk out without saying a word.

I hoped I was mistaken about all this; I was not. Within three hours I was summoned to the Dean's office.

And in the interval I had begun to sympathize with them. I had not answered Miss Freud's question; I had tried for a virtuoso display. The real question was, what do the gods do in *The Iliad?* We know that no one took them very seriously outside the book. And just as Miss Freud had complained, they do not help the narrative of the Trojan War or Achilles's wrath. If anything, they impede that.

Achilles's withdrawal, Patroclus's death, Achilles's return to kill and despoil Hector, yet finally to yield his body—we understand all this on its own grounds. We scarcely need the side issues which involve the gods—Thetis's entreaties to Zeus, Hera's opposition, Zeus's wranglings with Hera, Athena, or Poseidon. When the gods do interfere in the main action, they seldom perform anything we would not understand on natural grounds. The gods' acts offer an arcane explanation for simple events: Apollo may stun Patroclus, Hector kills him. Often the gods appear only as a dream or as a man's own thoughts would; a bystander would see nothing. When the gods *do* appear as something external, we usually understand this by a simple symbolic transformation. If Athena comes to the hero disguised as Polydamas, we see that wisdom came to him in that form. If Apollo snatches a wounded man from the battle, that is close to what we call a miraculous escape. Even that marvelous episode where Aphrodite whisks Paris away from Menelaus and into Helen's bed is readily grasped as a summation of Paris's life and character. The gods may have defined the outcome of the battle; nonetheless, like concerned parents, they usually sit back and let the humans fight their own fights.

Why have the gods? Above all, why underline their unheroic, amoral qualities? Though they punish our moral failures, they themselves act only from self-interest or whim. They are cowardly, self-indulgent, sneaky. Why should Zeus, ruler of the universe, spend his time squabbling with his wife, his rebellious daughter, his envious brother? Why, above all, should we interrupt the battle story at its height with a scene of Zeus and Hera making love?

I was ready to admit I had not answered these questions—though, of course, no one would have accused me of *that*. They'd have called me an atheist, or a sadist, or Communist, or pervert. Still, if I admitted some real failures, the Dean might honor my protests against false charges.

"But," said the Dean, "I don't see why you feel that anyone is accusing you. Really, we're only here to help you." He peered over his joined fingertips like the 4th Vice-President of the 5th National Bank.

"Look, I know my class is upset. They simply don't understand that what I've been trying to . . ." I choked with confusion.

"Then wouldn't it be best . . . simply to give us a copy of your lesson plans? Then we could help defend you . . . supposing some of your students *were* to complain . . . at any later time. You know, it happens in the best of families." That creep had come around his desk and actually laid his hand on my shoulder like the kindly old judge in a soap opera. "What do you imagine they might accuse you of?"

"I will submit nothing of the sort. I have never made a lesson plan in my life."

He could not turn away quickly enough to hide the smile sliding across his face. Triumph? Did he imagine this proved me incompetent?

"Well, now. Well. That *is* too bad. Very." The smile slithered into a grin. Not triumph; relief. He was off the hook. He didn't have to take a stand anywhere. He could support me; he could join the students and attack me. Best of all, he could sit back and watch us hassle each other until he saw his own advantage.

"All right. I am willing to draw up a résumé of my teaching since the semester started. But only if I know who is accusing me and of what. After all, any person has the right . . ."

"But nobody said you were being accused of anything. After all, we have many reasons to be interested in your work. For one thing, we have to consider . . . you *are* up for promotion this year, aren't you? And it's always our responsibility to maintain the level of teaching . . ."

That floored me. The *one* thing nobody had *ever* been promoted for was good teaching!

"If you will not state the charge against me, I will take this matter to the President and to the AAUP. This is a clear attempt to intimidate me, to control what I teach . . ." I felt stupid even mouthing such a gutless threat—the AAUP! Shaking your fist at the thunder!

"But," he went on happily as I stomped to the door, "you are simply making it impossible for me to help you out, if . . ."

I raged down the hall. That bland smile! And my tenure lost before it ever came up. Lesson plans! Besides, right now I needed one—I was due to go teach that class. I'd spent so much time stewing about this, I hadn't prepared anything.

I wanted terribly to counterattack. But what could I say? I didn't even really know (not officially) they'd attacked me. But even if I'd known every word, it was none of my business. (Even if it *did* cost my job.) My business was teaching *The Iliad* and I was about to bungle that.

I started off toward the class. And there, in front of me, stepping out of the elevator like some *deus ex machina,* was Golstrom, my private brain trust.

"Try this," he said: "The hero always is guided and controlled by a code of honor. Obtaining honor, he dies happy; losing it, he dies wretched. Everything he does is always and only for honor. So, he's not like anything in our culture—except for certain teen-aged mobs —juvenile delinquents and such-like. Motorcycle gangs."

"Motorcycle gangs!"

"What have you got to lose? If they're out for your blood anyway . . . Here." He handed me a copy of Robert Frank's great photograph of a cyclist—he must have just come from his own class. "Might as well have some fun, kid—go teach 'em up!" Well, maybe it had worked for him—besides, there wasn't time to argue.

I walked into my class, pinned up the photograph, and asked them to compare the Homeric heroes to Hell's Angels.

I was more shocked than the students were. They had never seen the Frank photo and could barely remember the Angels. All they *could* remember, seemed to make the comparison unthinkable: raids on small California villages, bloody rumbles, girls in hospitals for unspecified reasons. Yet once you *did* think about it, those things *were* the comparison. After all, how did Achilles come to own Briseis? Hadn't the Greeks raided Mynes, an apparently innocent town, and carried off the women? Was the Trojan War so different from a rumble?—longer, crueler, better organized, but essentially different? What started the rumbles they'd heard of? A rival gang member insulted an Angel's colors and so challenged his honor; one rumble was actually about a girl.

And that young rider of Frank's: alert, strong, intelligent. More and more, he looked like—not Achilles or Odysseus—maybe Patroclus. More and more, that bike looked like a warrior's horse or chariot; the leathers, that armor the heroes fought over. Not that an Angel would strip his fallen enemy; he'd take his colors as a token.

And the eyes, for all their intelligence: how downright arrogant! Whoever gave him orders would have his hands full. How easily they could tangle over a woman, over precedence, over honor. What if he lost and sought revenge; wouldn't all that intelligence, ability, aggressiveness be capable of any excess?

One of the boys had his hand up. "What's that got to do with religion?"

I didn't understand the question.

"I mean, like, you come in here yesterday with all that . . . stuff about . . . I mean, like, all that about . . . like, what's this got to do with whether there's a god or not?"

Well, now. Well. That clarified *some* things. Maybe the girls hadn't gone to the Dean at all; thank God *she* hadn't. Then what were the girls up to? It was clear what *he* was up to—overstepping and challenging his leader. Still, before I dealt with him, I had to show I could deal with his question.

What *does* the hero's arrogance have to do with God or gods? Only everything; around that contrast is evolved the whole structure of the poem.

Meeting something stronger than himself, the hero will always overstep and be struck down. Faced by a similar obstacle, a god will threaten, complain, bellow, but in the end he will be persuaded, give in, take a substitute. The gods don't much care for honor; they are so frankly dishonorable, they *might* just live forever. No such choice is offered the hero—dishonor could lengthen his life; nothing will save it. That, of course, is why he needs honor. Just as Achilles told his mother in the passage already quoted, or as Glaucus later tells Sarpedon:

333

> Man, supposing you and I, escaping this battle,
> would be able to live on forever, ageless, immortal,
> so neither would I myself go on fighting in the foremost
> nor would I urge you into the fighting where men win glory.
> But now, seeing that the spirits of death stand close about us
> in their thousands, no man can turn aside nor escape them,
> let us go on and win glory for ourselves, or yield it to others.

Knowledge of his approaching death makes the hero seek honor; pursuing honor hastens his death.

Being immortal, the gods are essentially limitless. So they can bear minor limits, can face the fact that another may be stronger. The humans are essentially limited—tragically, heartbreakingly. Not all will die so soon as Achilles; all will die. So they resent any force stronger than themselves; they will not face facts. If this rejection of reality costs their lives, it wins honor, the admiration of their fellows. Not only do they win such immortality as lies in being remembered by men, they achieve things both terrible and splendid which are impossible to those who accept the limits and behave reasonably.

The highest compliment Homer pays any man is "godlike." Yet, oddly enough, just in this overstepping to become godlike, the hero does something no god would ever do.

The gods never think of what they *should* want or do; only of what they do want and whether they can get it. Their concern is with the facts of power—am I strong enough or can Zeus stop me? Thus they become identified with the great elemental forces of Nature and with the child's view of his parents as embodiments of those forces. That is why they are so stuffy, domestic, downright middle-class. This accounts for those scenes of Zeus's family troubles, his quarrels with wife and daughter, his troubles with his brother, Poseidon, his stepson, Hephaestus, and finally, that scene of Zeus and Hera copulating.

"All wars," said Melville, "are boyish and are fought by boys." The hero bodies forth the adolescent in rebellion, his refusal of life's limits. The gods stand for that world he rejects and flees, yet which still limits and controls him. To the adolescent, that family of gods *is* immortal; they are the unchanging, undying forces of his psyche. They are the inculcators and agents of limit in his thought; they are his conscience.

How strange that the gods should be the only sustained image in *The Iliad* of normal domestic existence—the average, ignoble struggles and pleasures of family life, from which the heroes are cut off. All are separated from parents and children—Achilles grieves for his father, Peleus, and his son, Neoptolemus. In place of wives, the heroes have only such temporary bedmates as they can capture. (Hector alone sees his wife and child; this makes him more touching and vulnerable, but also less heroic, less adolescent.) In place of the normal quiet pleasures of sex and affection, the heroes have the lonely excitements of rape and conquest. If that seems a poor exchange, notice that they order their women about with a grandeur which Zeus, master of the universe, would never dare. He needs his wife's affection.

During World War II, the most savage man I knew—or saw; I wouldn't have dared speak to him—was a red-haired Marine sergeant with moustaches waxed up into long, sharp points. We knew he would kill you for looking at them. He was in a detachment that had fought in the Pacific for two years, had just been home for thirty days' leave and was now bound out again for the invasion of Okinawa.

Many years later I *did* speak to him—I had been talking to him for two days before I recognized him. He taught Government at Syracuse University, where I went to read a lecture. He now looked so much like myself that the night before, sitting at the opera, we had decided I should introduce him and he would read my paper. The next day (we lost our nerve; *I* read the lecture), we sat at the lake reminiscing; I began to suspect who he had been. Our hair had faded to nearly the same null brown; years of the G.I. Bill had given him the thick, horn-rimmed glasses I had always worn. We both wore curly brown moustaches. I had put on thirty pounds; his muscles had relaxed.

As we sat there, his five children raced up and down the lakeshore —swarmed up and down his sides. He was firm and admirable; his

335

daughter wore a straw beach hat on whose crown was painted a curly brown moustache and a pair of huge horn-rimmed glasses.

"Jesus Christ!" I gasped, "how the hell did you ever *do* it? Those invasions! How did you ever manage to make it up those beaches?"

"That was the easy part," he said. "The hard part of the war was that thirty days' leave. Going home to watch my mother devour my father. I was glad to go back out and kill people. I used to go out on Saturday when we didn't even have to."

Each time the gods manage to rig up a temporary peace among themselves, the result is renewed bloodshed for the humans on the battlefield.

All wars are boyish. My student, hot for heroism, for the honor of his fellows, had challenged me. (Only later did I notice that I had first aggressed against his beliefs, hoping to win the students' honor. And hers.) I did not strike him down; I did the next worst thing—I lectured at him for three weeks straight. I had come to class unprepared to say anything. Now, driven by Golstrom's insight, my rage at the Dean, my student's insolence, the need to be admired by my class, especially by *her*, I had bungled into problems that would cost me weeks of furious reading and concentration. At each step, I was sure I came closer to the center of the poem's meaning.

The poem starts where Chryses, priest of Apollo, begs Agamemnon for the return of his daughter. Dishonoring Chryses, Agamemnon prefigures the arrogance and downfall of the central figure, his chief competitor in pride, Achilles. Agamemnon oversteps first, but also is humbled and learns to yield first. His fault does not cost his life. Yet the plague which follows will cost his subjects dearly—almost as dearly as Achilles's anger. This may suggest that Achilles's rage, too, is a sort of illness, a plague upon his people. Even more, this first scene foreshadows that greater scene at the end of the poem when another aged father, Priam, will beg for the despoiled body of *his* child, Hector, begging Achilles to yield and accept the ransom.

The following scene is that council where Achilles and Agamemnon first openly collide. Throughout, Apollo's augur, Calchas, stands as an example of moderation, self-recognition; however high the god he serves, he respects the facts of power. Guaranteed safety, he points out Agamemnon's offense: the plague is already one defeat for the Achaians; worse is threatened.

To this, Agamemnon yields. For the first time, we see how a sound defeat can lead a man to common sense, can beat down his pride. Throughout the scene, Agamemnon is far more reasonable than before—and far more reasonable than Achilles. Yet Achilles's arrogance moves him to a lesser wrong: deprived of Chryses's daughter, he takes Achilles's prize, Briseis. Soon enough, this will bring him deeper losses and a deeper humility.

After this council, Achilles withdraws to work out his revenge. Meantime, the Greeks have returned Chryseis, praying her father to be propitiated; he in turn prays to Apollo, who yields and sends the Greeks a favoring wind. Achilles, in sharp contrast, "still sat in anger beside his swift ships" and "continued to waste his heart out/sitting there, though he longed always for the clamour and fighting." Apollo who lives forever can be propitiated; Achilles, "shortlived beyond all other mortals," cannot.

The last scene of Book I, the council of the gods where Hera quarrels with Zeus, is a brilliant contrast to the earlier council of warriors. Again, the lesser figures rise against the father-ruler; we hear all manner of unseemly scolding. But among the gods, Hephaestus, the crippled blacksmith god, rises to warn his mother Hera that "It is too hard to fight against the Olympian" and cites how sharply Zeus once punished his rebellion. So, a kind of peace is restored; Zeus and Hera, the father and mother divinities, go off to bed together. Peace between them is restored by a son who has been punished, crippled, even symbolically castrated into submission. Further, by the craft of his hands, he provides homes and beds for all the gods. The myth suggests that this violent repression not only makes him a peacemaker, but creative as well; he has no choice but sublimation.

337

On the one side lie the heroes, arrogant, unruly, noble, and destructive; on the other, the gods, domestic, persuadable, ignoble, and creatively useful. The heroes sleep with each other or with such women as they can enslave; Zeus sleeps with his uppity, quarrelsome, but supremely desirable wife.

Book Two opens on the first morning of that four-day battle which encompasses most of the poem. We begin with two examples of false persuasion, of delusion: first, Zeus persuades Agamemnon (through a dream) that the time is ripe for the Achaeans to enter battle; second, to try his men's mettle, Agamemnon pretends to persuade them to flee back home. He is far too successful: his weakness provokes rebellion and nearly brings on a general rout. The chief rebel is Thersites, a direct comic parallel to Achilles. Encouraged by Agamemnon's indecision and Achilles's successful revolt, he mimics many of Achilles's accusations—Agamemnon is greedy for gold and women, the warriors should not share their plunder with him, the Achaeans should withdraw and go home. Thersites, however, is quickly battered into submission by Odysseus, just as Hephaestus (also lame and bandy-legged) was beaten down by Zeus.

Many modern readers, like Simone Weil, feel a sympathy for Thersites—we would like to disapprove of war and hierarchy, and Thersites may seem to oppose both. If our morals have no stronger ally, we are in trouble. Like the others, Thersites came to Troy to kill, steal, and rape. Seeing an apparent weakness, he has now turned to attack his own leader instead. His are the morals of a jackal.

But Homer is not concerned with such moral questions anyway; neither is he concerned whether the war is good or evil, or how Thersites's acts may affect the war's outcome or his comrades' welfare. It is tempting to talk about such matters just because they are unknowns and so can always be twisted to our own advantage. Homer is concerned that a weak and ugly man (who, so, can expect little sympathy or support) should stand up and provoke the powerful, should think he can get away with the things Achilles got away with.

338

He has made himself a parody; what seems tragic, admirable, and monstrous in Achilles is ludicrous in him.

Thersites should probably give thanks that he is neither strong nor determined. He can be bludgeoned back into place with nothing worse than bruises and humiliations; Hector and Achilles will die for *their* overstepping.

"Sorry though the men were they laughed over him happily." Just as, earlier, "among the blessed immortals uncontrollable laughter went up when they saw Hephaestus bustling about the palace." Thersites, and the men around him, have given just this much play to their own rebelliousness. Seeing the least determination in Odysseus and Agamemnon, they turn and marshal themselves into battle order. That this battle order embodies their deeper desires is shown by the length and strength of that great catalogue of ships immediately following. By a mere recital of heroes' names, a whole civilization marches into the reader's mind. The driving motives of the individual soldier are stated only too clearly by Odysseus:

> I cannot find fault with the Achaians for their impatience
> beside the curved ships; yet always it is disgraceful
> to wait long and at the end go home empty-handed.

and by Nestor:

> . . . . let no man be urgent to take the way homeward
> until after he has lain in bed with the wife of a Trojan
> to avenge Helen's longing to escape and her lamentations.

This should not be taken for any final moral judgment on the Trojan War by the poet. From one point of view this war is a just vindication of Menelaus's injuries. From another, it is merely a pirates' raid; the theft and rape the Greeks have suffered are mere pretexts for the theft, rape, and murder they want to commit. Here again, Homer is true to experience. To have destroyed Hitler, ended the gassing of Jews, freed millions, cannot but seem worthwhile. To have taken control of half Europe and Asia, to have killed millions, needlessly destroyed Hiroshima and Dresden, to have betrayed and sold whole populations (like the Poles, for whose freedom the war was supposedly begun)—these things must seem different. If the poet's vocation is truly "justice of vision," then he must present the event in all its multiplicity of motives and results.

How splendid that the battle should begin with a general oath not to fight again—with the diversion (or provocation) of Paris's and Menelaus's single combat. This, of course, fools no one—the very oath is phrased in the assumption that it will be broken:

> let those, whichever side they may be, who do wrong to the oaths
>   sworn
> first, let their brains be spilled on the ground as this wine is spilled
>   now,
> theirs and their sons, and let their wives be the spoil of others.

Had Pandarus not fulfilled the assumption, someone else would.

Whenever nations swear great oaths of peace, we tremble, knowing these oaths (especially when couched in such bloodthirsty terms) are only part of the preparations for war. Things have gone so far that it only remains to find a suitable incident.

The hero of the first day is Diomedes. In Achilles's absence, he rises to such eminence that the Trojans think him Achilles's equal. For the reader, though, Diomedes stands in sharp contrast to Achilles. Above all, he never oversteps. Like Achilles, he has been injured by Agamemnon. While rousing the troops, Agamemnon had wrongfully scolded him:

> Ah me, son of Tydeus, that daring breaker of horses,
> why are you skulking, and spying out the outworks of battle?
> Such was never Tydeus' way, to lurk in the background,
> but to fight the enemy far ahead of his own companions . . .
> . . . yet he was father
> to a son worse than himself at fighting, better in conclave.

Diomedes neither answers nor permits Sthenelus, his charioteer, to answer this rebuke. Instead, he turns his anger against the enemy to show just how courageous he is. Indeed, just as Hephaestus's inventiveness may partially be caused by Zeus's ferocity, so Diomedes's greatness on this day may be directly caused by Agamemnon's unjust scolding. When, later, that same commander loses his own courage and suggests that the Greeks turn back, Diomedes may then properly rebuke him in turn:

> Son of Atreus: I will be first to fight with your folly,
> . . . I was the first of the Danaans whose valour you slighted
> and said I was unwarlike and without courage. . . .
> But if in truth your own heart is so set upon going,
> go. . . . and yet the rest of the flowing-haired Achaians will stay
>   here
> until we have sacked the city of Troy; let even these also
> run away with their ships to the beloved land of their fathers,
> still we two, Sthenelos and I, will fight till we witness
> the end of Ilion; . . .

Throughout the day's battle, Diomedes is warned and guided by Athena at each point. Taking her initial advice that he must not battle any of the gods excepting Aphrodite, he pushes this to the limit, never beyond. When Sthenelus advises him to back off from Pandarus and Aeneas, he can confidently refuse; when Aphrodite enters to rescue her son Aeneas, he dares attack and wound her. When Apollo tries to shield Aeneas, Diomedes moves against him three times, but on the fourth, Apollo's warning reminds him of the goddess's charge and he "gave backward, only a little."

Again, later, Diomedes gives way before Hector, who is supported by Ares. When Athena reappears with a reproach much like Agamemnon's, Diomedes reminds her that he is only following her instructions. Pleased, Athena now permits and helps him to attack even Ares. He moves on, then, to the ethical high point of the battle—that

341

scene where he and Glaucus (who also refuses to fight immortals) just at the height of the fighting recognize each other as "guest friends," shake hands, exchange armor, and swear friendship. In the midst of such carnage and savagery—one recalls the Scots and Germans dancing between the lines of World War I—it is a moment of touching humanity and decency. It is the kind of triumph available to the man who observes the limits. It points onward to that terrible scene at the end of the poem where Achilles, finally learning something of humility, will take the hand of his enemy, Priam.

Diomedes comes through this first day's battle alive and with considerable glory. As Dione assures her wounded daughter, Aphrodite, that glory does not come cheaply:

> . . . poor fool, the heart of Tydeus' son knows nothing
> of how that man who fights the immortals lives for no long time,
> his children do not gather to his knees to welcome their father
> when he returns home after the fighting and the bitter warfare.

For Diomedes, as for Achilles, the price of honor will be an early grave. Yet his careful behavior has saved him for the day.

Thus, through the courage of Diomedes, and later that of Ajax, the Achaeans are very successful in the first day's fighting, driving the Trojans almost back into their city. They would seem, then, almost as strong without Achilles as with him. As always, we find unreasonable pride in the victors, a sensible humility in the losers. The Trojans, losing, are able to see a part of their own fault; they offer to give back the articles Paris stole from Menelaus when he took Helen. Sadly, they are not so fully moved that they would forcibly take Helen from Paris and give her back. Not even defeat, apparently, can make men really just.

Success, however, is certain to wake an overweening pride. The Greeks, offered these goods with others of Paris's own possessions, flatly refuse. Diomedes himself (the model of rectitude) breaks the silence in which the Achaeans sit, perhaps attracted by the offer:

342

Now let none accept the possessions of Alexandros,
nor take back Helen: one who is very simple can see it,
that by this time the terms of death hang over the Trojans.

In short, why try for a reasonable settlement?—we're winning! It is a decision they will quickly regret.

On the second day's fighting, as we should expect, the tide of battle turns. Father Zeus calls the gods out of the fighting and goes, himself, to Mt. Gargargus to watch the Trojans drive back the Achaeans. Clearly, Hector is the hero of this day's fighting. Though we are given few details, by the end of the day the Trojans have driven the Achaeans back across their ditch and fortifications. Only the onset of night prevents them from crossing the ditch to fire the ships.

This reversal in battle, of course, produces a complete reversal in attitudes. The night before, the Trojans offered wealth to the Achaeans merely to go home; now they are so eager for revenge that they fear the Achaeans *might* leave. Hector advises his men to build huge watchfires so that the Greeks may not sneak away unseen. His triumphs lead him to see himself as a god:

. . . Oh, if I only
could be as this in all my days immortal and ageless
and be held in honour as Athene and Apollo are honoured
as surely as this oncoming day brings evil to the Argives.

For the Achaeans, however, and especially for Agamemnon, this day of defeat produces a new humility and recognition of reality. Like the Trojans the night before, Agamemnon can now see that he has committed a wrong—he answers Nestor's charge:

Aged sir, this was no lie when you spoke of my madness.
I was mad, I myself will not deny it. Worth many
fighters is that man whom Zeus in his heart loves, as now
he has honoured this man and beaten down the Achaian people.
But since I was mad, in the persuasion of my heart's evil,
I am willing to make all good, and give back gifts in abundance.

343

As if to pay for their pride of the night before, the Greeks must now humble themselves before Achilles.

Unfortunately, the events that bring Agamemnon to his senses deprive Achilles of his. Hector's victories are making him mad with pride; until he has suffered an essential loss, any embassage to him will be useless.

The Achaeans who come to him—Odysseus, Phoenix, and Ajax —are those most dear to him. Beyond, two of them speak in a strongly paternal role. Odysseus, the first, is not only one of the wisest of the Greeks, he speaks as representative of Achilles's king and overlord. His speech is both diplomatic and direct, describing the danger to the Greeks, reciting the list of rich gifts Agamemnon offers, warning how Achilles would come to regret allowing the Greeks to be slaughtered. He goes on to quote directly Achilles's own father's advice to contain his anger and avoid "the bad complication of quarrel."

For all his diplomacy, Odysseus receives an answer full of self-pity, sarcasm, and mockery. Achilles rejects Agamemnon's gifts:

> . . . not
> worth the value of my life are all the possessions they fable
> were won for Ilion, that strong-founded citadel, in the old days
> when there was peace, . . .

This may be true; nonetheless, Achilles does not fight for plunder, but for honor:

> For my mother Thetis, the goddess of the silver feet tells me
> I carry two sorts of destiny toward the day of my death. Either,
> if I stay here and fight beside the city of the Trojans
> my return home is gone, but my glory shall be everlasting;
> but if I return home to the beloved land of my fathers,
> the excellence of my glory is gone, but there will be a long life
> left for me, and my end in death will not come to me quickly.

This, too, is an equivocation. Achilles knows already that he will neither fight nor go home; he has found a third way to greater glory.

The second speaker, Phoenix, Achilles's teacher, guardian, almost his foster-father, calls Achilles "dear child" and is answered "Phoenix my father." His speech is all the more touching because his situation is even more Oedipal than Achilles's own. As a young man, he took his father's mistress. When his father cursed him, he set out to kill his father. His kinsmen locked him up to prevent this, but he finally escaped the country. Achilles's father, Peleus, took him in and made him a sort of foster-son, making him well-off once more. In his father's curse, however, he had been sterilized, magically castrated, and can never have a son of his own. He became a teacher and, in turn, raised Peleus's son, Achilles.

His long story of his care for Achilles is full of touching detail. He then tells a parable of Meleager, who stood aside from his people's war until too late and so lost honor. Finally, he begs Achilles to give in, to rescue him and the Achaeans before it is too late:

> Then, Achilles, beat down your great anger. It is not
> yours to have a pitiless heart. The very immortals
> can be moved; their virtue and honour and strength are greater than
>   ours are,
> and yet with sacrifices and offerings for endearment,
> with libations and with savour men turn back even the immortals
> in supplication, when any man does wrong and transgresses.

That is precisely the point: immortals can be appeased and assuaged; mortals cannot. Achilles speaks kindly to Phoenix, keeps him overnight, postpones decision. Yet we know both that he has decided and what he has decided.

Then something curious happens: for the first time, Achilles is humbled. Ajax, seeing they have been curtly dismissed, is hurt—not as an ambassador, as a friend. He tells Odysseus that since Achilles "does not remember that friends' affection wherein we honoured him by the ships," they should leave. In spite of himself, he gradually turns toward Achilles, saying that his rage is unreasonable, especially in the face of friends' affection.

Something in this huge man moves Achilles as not even Phoenix could. Perhaps it is that his role *is* less paternal. Perhaps he is more like Achilles himself—huge, dogged, not clever, not very sensitive. Certainly, what he says strikes deepest—that Achilles's fault (more fearfully than either could now guess) is a sin against friendship and affection. In any case, only for a moment, Achilles bends his pride:

> Son of Telamon, seed of Zeus, Aias, lord of the people:
> all that you have said seems spoken after my own mind.
> Yet still the heart in me swells up in anger when I remember
> the disgrace that he wrought upon me before the Argives. . . .

Achilles knows he is wrong; all the same, he will keep to his course.

When the ambassadors have returned to announce this to Agamemnon, it is fitting that Diomedes (who had risen to almost Achilles's greatness, yet always stopped short of madness) should see the reality of the situation:

> I wish you had not supplicated the blameless son of Peleus
> with innumerable gifts offered. He is a proud man without this,
> and now you have driven him far deeper into his pride. . . .

Victory has made Achilles half mad already; the Greeks have given him more victory. Only loss will teach him.

During the third day's fighting, the Achaeans rally, drive the Trojans back from the ships, across the plain, then nearly storm the city walls, only to be driven back again to their ships. In the course of the fighting, the fortunes of all the major figures are once again reversed. Agamemnon, who had humbled himself the night before, rises to new glories in the fighting. He leads in driving the Trojans back to the

Scaean gates and reaches a position of triumph entirely comparable to Hector's the day before.

Hector, meanwhile, who had been so prideful the previous evening, is paying for that. At first, taking what defeats he must, he abides by the gods' advice and holds back from the battle until Agamemnon is wounded. When he re-enters the fighting, he drives the Achaeans back to their ships. In this struggle not only is Agamemnon wounded, but Diomedes, Odysseus, Machaon, and Eurypylus as well.

Through momentary defeat Hector keeps a level head; momentary victory restores him at once to the foolish pridefulness of the previous night. For the first time, he refuses Polydamas's counsel—counsel that they not fight by the ships. (This is their first conflict inside the poem; clearly, they have clashed often before.) Since Polydamas's advice is based on bird signs, this amounts to rejection of the gods' warning—which had previously served Hector so well. The price of this rejection quickly becomes clear. At the beginning of Book XIII, Hector rejects Polydamas's advice, calls him cowardly, and threatens him; by the end of the same book, the Trojans have suffered such dire casualties that Hector will again listen to Polydamas and to reason. He learns what Achilles must learn later: "you cannot choose to have all the gifts given to you together"; for all his power in battle, another may be wiser.

So long as the Trojans fight around the ships, however, Achilles seems to be winning his greatest victories so far. In many ways, Achilles is now essentially of the enemy camp; already his fate is tied to that of Hector. He had prayed for his comrades to be injured; now, one after another, they *are*. It does not occur to him that these victories involve the worst loss he could suffer, his dearest comrade. He does not suspect that he is giving Hector a still greater victory which will cost both their lives.

It is early in the fighting of this third day that Hera decides to seduce Zeus. The effect of this on the overall battle is practically nil

—as my student pointed out. It allows Poseidon to enter the battle for a short while, driving the Trojans back from the immediate area of the ships. Yet Zeus soon wakes; this brief respite for the Achaeans has no ultimate importance.

These scenes are of greatest importance, however, both in establishing the parental quality of Zeus and Hera, and in creating a central contrast between the response of Poseidon and that of the heroes in the surrounding books. Faced with Zeus's greater strength, Poseidon at first bluntly refuses to leave the battle. Unlike those Greeks who plead so movingly but unavailingly with Achilles, Iris, Zeus's messenger, keeps a tactful detachment, almost as if she merely wanted information:

> Am I to carry, o dark-haired, earth-encircler,
> this word, which is strong and steep, back to Zeus from you?
> Or will you change a little? The hearts of the great can be changed.
> You know the Furies, how they forever side with the elder.

She not only makes clear the force ranged against Poseidon; she makes one of the most crucial statements in the poem: "the hearts of the great can be changed." Poseidon must admit both the significance and the tact of her speech:

> Now this, Divine Iris, was a word quite properly spoken.
> It is a fine thing when a messenger is conscious of justice.
> But this thing comes as a bitter sorrow to my heart. . . .
> Still, this time I will give way, . . .

Muttering threats and imprecations, he backs off and saves himself a good deal of useless pain.

In sharp contrast to this, of course, is that futile embassage to Achilles we have just discussed. Great as Achilles is, his refusal of his friends, his refusal to change course even after admitting the justice of the messengers' words, his refusal of his own recognition that he is wrong, suggests a terrible weakness. In yielding, Poseidon shows

348

how much greater (and not only in power or longevity) is an immortal heart.

We might also contrast that speech of Sarpedon to Glaucus earlier quoted. But the best contrast to Poseidon's yielding is probably in the transformation and death of Patroclus in the very next book. We have heard from Menelaus, Briseis, Zeus himself, that Patroclus is strong, gentle, and "kindly toward all." We have not quite believed the warning we have had of his temper—he first came to live with Achilles because he had killed someone in rage over a dice game when he was only a child. We have ourselves witnessed his gentleness in his pity for the Greeks, in his tendance of the wounded Eurypylus. We have heard him pray that Agamemnon might recover his sanity, that he himself might never be so incensed as Achilles:

> . . . you, Achilleus, who can do anything
> with you? May no such anger take me as this that you cherish!
> Cursed courage. . . .

Even as he arms Patroclus in his own armor, Achilles warns him not to go on out to fight with the Trojans after he has driven them back from the ships—that might diminish Achilles's honor. Even more, he must not try to storm the city wall. Achilles specifically warns that the Trojans are beloved of Apollo and that some one of the gods might crush Patroclus.

But even as we witness Patroclus's transformation, the battle itself is changing its tenor—an unspeakable hideousness is gathering over the struggle. Over the body of Sarpedon (as later over that of Patroclus), the warriors swarm so that

> . . . . No longer
> could a man, even a knowing one, have made out the godlike
> Sarpedon, since he was piled from head to ends of feet under
> a mass of weapons, the blood and the dust, while others about him
> kept forever swarming over his dead body, as flies
> through a sheepfold thunder about the pails overspilling

milk, in a season of spring when the milk splashes in the buckets.
So they swarmed over the dead man. . . .

In their zeal to strip and spoil their fallen enemies, the warriors seem
more and more like corpse-pickers, carrion beasts. In the midst of this
filth and carnage, we see Patroclus come to be filled with "a huge blind
fury./ Besotted." This strong and gentle man mocks arrogantly over
Cebriones, whom he has just struck down with a rock:

> See now, what a light man this is, how agile an acrobat.
> If only he were somewhere on the sea, where the fish swarm,
> he could fill the hunger of many men, by diving for oysters;
> he could go overboard from a boat even in rough weather
> the way he somersaults so light to the ground from his chariot
> now. So, to be sure, in Troy also they have their acrobats.

Not only does Patroclus cross the plain against Achilles's orders;
three times he tries to climb the city wall "like something greater than
human" or like a lion whose "own courage destroys him." In the
midst of the terrible fighting at the wall, Apollo merely strikes Patroclus with the flat of his hand "so that his eyes spun." Hector need only
finish him off.

Just as Patroclus, in killing Sarpedon, sealed his own fate, so Hector
in killing Patroclus. When Hector is dead, only Achilles will be left
to complete the cycle. Hector's vaunt over Patroclus's body is replete
with irony:

> Wretch! Achilleus, great as he was, could do nothing to help you.
> When he stayed behind, and you went, he must have said much to
>   you:
> "Patroklos, lord of horses, see that you do not come back to me
> and the hollow ships, until you have torn in blood the tunic
> of manslaughtering Hektor about his chest." In some such
> manner he spoke to you, and persuaded the fool's heart in you.

In the self-centered arrogance of victory, in his fool's heart, Hector cannot imagine that Achilles's instructions did not even mention Hector's name. As he puts on first the helmet, then the armor of Achilles, stripping them from Patroclus, we see him growing ever more prideful, see his death predicted on every side.

After the hardest, ugliest fighting of the poem, the Achaeans do save Patroclus's body, yet they are again driven back to their ships as the third day's fighting ends. By the end of the third day, then, Achilles's wish has been granted; his comrades have been wounded and in the death of Patroclus he has paid the price of that wish.

Like Kriemhild of the *Nibelungenlied,* he has caused the death of the only person he loved; he, too, will exact a terrible vengeance upon the world for the wrong he has himself committed. Unlike her, he will rise to recognize at least part of his wrong. Perhaps he has not caused Patroclus's death so directly as Kriemhild caused Siegfried's. He had no such direct motive: Kriemhild was beaten by Siegfried for misbehavior. Achilles has no grudge of any sort against Patroclus. Yet there might be a subtler motive: with Patroclus dead, his rage will be such that he may take a terrible revenge and so win the glory he wants. If that were his motive, Achilles could not even claim Kriemhild's excuse of passionate anger—instead we see the cold and selfish manipulation of his friend's death to glorify himself.

It is true that Achilles warned Patroclus against the acts that cost his life. Could he have made those acts more attractive simply through the warning? Possibly. In any case, he can hardly have expected Patroclus to risk his life only for Achilles's glory, not for his own. Besides, as he himself sees too late, if he had truly valued Patroclus, he should not have sent him into battle alone, but should have been there to help and protect him.

Like Kriemhild, he knows of his beloved's death before he has been told of it. Antilochus, the messenger, finds him

sitting in front of the steep-horned ships, thinking
over in his heart of things which had now been accomplished.
Disturbed, Achilleus spoke to the spirit in his own great heart:
'Ah me, how is it that once again the flowing-haired Achaians
are driven out of the plain on their ships in fear and confusion?
May the gods not accomplish vile sorrows upon the heart in me
in the way my mother once made it clear to me, when she told me
how while I yet lived the bravest of all the Myrmidons
must leave the light of the sun beneath the hands of the Trojans.
Surely, then, the strong son of Menoitios has perished.

There is no escaping that. Achilles knew his own life-term was short;
Patroclus's was shorter. Loving him as he did, he could scarcely forget
the goddess's prediction—not unless he had much to gain by forgetting. He had been warned, just as Oedipus was warned that he would
kill his father and marry his mother. That might have suggested to
Oedipus that he should not kill old men or sleep with old women; it
might have told Achilles not to let Patroclus fight alone. Both preferred not to understand until they had gained what they wanted.

When his mother hears Achilles's wail of grief and loss, she cannot
help asking

. . . . Why, then,
child, do you lament? What sorrow has come to your heart now?
. . . . These things are brought to accomplishment
through Zeus: in the way that you lifted your hands and prayed for.
. . .

When she tells him that he can revenge himself upon Hector only at
cost of his own life, he answers:

I must die soon, then; since I was not to stand by my companion
when he was killed.

He accepts his death as a just punishment for the guilt he feels:

Now, since I am not going back to the beloved land of my fathers,
since I was no light of safety to Patroclus, nor to my other
companions, who in their numbers went down before glorious
    Hektor,
but sit here beside my ships, a useless weight on the good land,
I, who am such as no other of the bronze-armoured Achaians
in battle, though there are others also better in council—
why, I wish that strife would vanish away . . .
that gall of anger that swarms like smoke inside of a man's heart
and becomes a thing sweeter to him by far than the dripping of
    honey. . . .
Now I shall go, to overtake that killer of a dear life,
Hektor; then I will accept my own death, . . .

Achilles's guilt, however, is deeper, crueler, more cold-blooded than this admits. He has not merely let his friend go out alone, then taken revenge, and, so doing, won incidental glory. He has sacrificed his friend so that he *could* avenge him and win honor.

Had Patroclus's death come as a mere accident of battle, had no part of Achilles's will been involved in his death, it would make little sense to take revenge; Achilles has already admitted his own guilt for that. Naturally, any warrior tries to avenge the death of a close comrade or relative; that is not vengeance on the scale of Achilles's. Such vengeance as his makes sense only if Patroclus were sacrificed for it. This may not seem just; *The Iliad* is not concerned with justice, but with what men do.

The sacrifice of Patroclus has been implicit in Achilles's prayer to Zeus from the beginning. It is not that the gods warp our prayers into something terrible; it is that they understand our prayer. Achilles did not exclude anyone from his prayer, none of those friends he says he loves best, not Ajax, not Phoenix, not Patroclus. And when he let Patroclus return alone to battle, he sent no postscript after his first prayer—surely a damning omission. Obviously, that prayer was being fulfilled—the Greeks were, indeed, "pinned back against the ships and the water,/ Dying." Already most of their greatest fighters are wounded. He shows no sense of pity for these, the "dearest of all the Achaeans." Indeed, he mocks savagely at Patroclus's pity for them:

> . . . . Why then
> are you crying like some poor little girl, Patroklos,
> who runs after her mother and begs to be picked up and carried, . . .
> You are like such a one, Patroklos, dropping these soft tears.
> . . . . Or is it
> the Argives you are mourning over, and how they are dying
> against the hollow ships by reason of their own arrogance?

Where Patroclus, merciful, stopped to dress Eurypylus's wounds, Achilles would see all the men of both armies dead, if that could increase his honor:

> Father Zeus, Athene and Apollo, if only
> not one of all the Trojans could escape destruction, not one
> of the Argives, but you and I could emerge from the slaughter
> so that we two alone could break Troy's hallowed coronal.

a sentiment worthy of Tamberlane.

Earlier, when Odysseus had offered him the return of Briseis with Agamemnon's oath that he had not lain with her, Achilles replied, "Let him lie beside her/ And be happy." This is to ask for greater injuries to increase the sweetness of his rage—"sweeter than the dripping of honey." If he wishes Briseis violated, would he not wish Patroclus dead for the same purpose—the rage that would lead him to glory?

Patroclus, of course, is far dearer than Briseis; that makes him a better sacrifice. Besides, to obtain honor he is willing to sacrifice the one person still dearer to him than Patroclus—himself. As he told Odysseus, he could still have a long life by simply weighing anchor and sailing home. But he could do that only at the price of obscurity. Indeed, "not worth the value of [his] life are all the possessions they fable were won for Ilion. . . ." Glory *is*—worth his concubine, his comrades, his dearest friend, his own life. Which is, perhaps, to say that men will sink to the deepest dishonor to win the honor of men. Throughout *The Iliad,* Zeus is called the "Father of Delusions." The basic delusion is that one could be like the gods, detached, superior, manipulating events to one's own advantage. It is shortly after Achilles withdraws that Zeus, too, withdraws from Olympus to Ida, where he observes that same battle, then calls the other gods also from the fighting. Like Zeus, Achilles sits apart "rejoicing in the pride of his strength." Again, it is just at the point that Achilles re-enters the battle that Zeus sends the other gods back into the fighting. Zeus stands for that delusion that we may be what we are not, the madness that drives us to overcome death, that our honor may live after us and make us somehow immortal. Achilles sees a part of his guilt; he never fully realizes what he has done to his friend. His need for honor demands that he remain deluded.

I could not believe that my students were accepting this. Surely I was saying things far more threatening than my earlier talk about the gods? My class sat docile and smiling, waiting for more things to put in their notebooks. Had my weeks of lecturing bludgeoned them into numbness? I stopped for questions, complaints.

That same boy, my own rebel, had his hand up. "This is off the subject, but . . . they say you are getting kicked out. Is that right?"

Not that I hadn't expected it, but how could he have heard before I did? What did he know that I didn't? And what did he mean—was he sorry for me? Or gloating over me?

Summoning the coldest tone I could command, I stated that this was off the subject. Actually, I suppose I had been lecturing so fiercely all that time partly to keep from thinking about my job. Now I wanted to escape not only that worry, but also my deeper puzzle about what he or any of the students intended. Had I ever known what was in their thoughts? Or feelings? There were only a few chapters still to go —I hurled myself back into them with a tripled fury.

Of all those men he kills, one at least has earned Achilles's wrath; that is Hector. Not only for killing Patroclus; he has stripped Achilles's armor from that body and put it on himself. So, he becomes a second pseudo-Achilles. This armor Achilles gave his friend for protection brought him death instead—just as Achilles's friendship proved so fatal. The armor will prove equally fatal to the second man who assumes it. And the armor of the gods will prove equally fatal to Achilles.

On this very night when Achilles is learning something of humility —that others are wiser than he—Hector is once again being maddened by victory. Wearing the armor he has stripped from Patroclus, he again opposes Polydamas, insisting that the Trojans remain camped on the plains to face the Achaeans and Achilles the next day. Meantime, Achilles is being armed by the gods to slaughter Trojans; Hephaestus is making him that armor and that dazzling shield which represents the full circle of man's life on earth.

The first day of battle was given to Diomedes; the second to Hector; the third to Patroclus. The fourth day will be given entirely to Achilles in his revenge and to the death and defilement of Hector. We have seen two false Achilleses, now we see the real one. Twice before, Hector has risen to the center stage, now he stands before Achilles. In the course of the day, they approach twice before their third and final meeting at the Scaean gates; Hector is chased thrice around the city before he stands and is killed.

We have noted that the fates of Hector and Achilles have become ever more closely bound together. Since Hector wears Achilles's armor, it is strongly suggested that in killing him, Achilles destroys himself. In any case, the death of each is now predicted on every side. Strangely enough, as they approach each other, Achilles, apparently the mover of the action, becomes less and less interesting. We see him in an incredible rampage of blood and carnage, slaughtering Trojans as if they were helpless children. Driving their army into the river, he kills so many that even the river itself rises up against him—the very forces of nature seem aghast. Yet, for all his violence, he seems nearly passive; he is in the grip of such passion that he seems almost mechanical. No decisions are left him.

I was reminded of my Marine friend who said that when they made those Pacific invasions, those of his buddies who didn't feel like killing anyone simply got lost for a while—there was no stigma attached to this. But if you had enough desire to kill people, the minute your foot touched the beach your mind shut off and your training took over. Such is Achilles.

Hector, on the other hand, has decisions, divided thoughts, fears, hopes. He makes the wrong choices, of course, but that, if anything, only makes him more human, more interesting.

Admittedly, we have always had a greater sympathy with Hector than with any of the Greek warriors. Even without the vastly touching scenes between himself and Andromache or his baby son, Astyanax, there is a great and wrenching pathos in his situation. From the start he has known he was fighting a useless battle for a wrongful cause. Common sense would say that even if he did not care about his own life, he might rescue his wife and son. Like Achilles, he sacrifices those he most loves to his need for honor, his fear of what the Trojans will say of him. Somehow we are more willing to partake of this passive guilt than of the starker guilts of Achilles. But if Hector has our open sympathy, Achilles holds our deeper empathy. Hector may be what we like to think ourselves; Achilles is what we terribly are.

Not only does Hector make the mistake of keeping the Trojans on the plain; when this brings disaster, he is unwilling to face his error, to accept the fact that his wilfulness has cost many lives:

Ah me! If I go now inside the wall and the gateway,
Poulydamas will be first to put a reproach upon me,
since he tried to make me lead the Trojans inside the city
on that accursed night when brilliant Achilleus rose up
and I would not obey him, but that would have been far better.

357

Now, since by my own recklessness I have ruined my people,
I feel shame before the Trojans and the Trojan women with trailing
robes, that someone who is less of a man than I will say of me:
"Hektor believed in his own strength and ruined his people."
Thus will they speak; and as for me, it would be much better
at that time, to go against Achilleus, and slay him, and come back,
or else be killed by him in glory in front of the city.

For one moment of half-madness, he thinks he might somehow yet
talk Achilles into sparing him. But he knows better:

.... There is no
way any more from a tree or a rock to talk to him gently
whispering like a young man and a young girl, in the way
a young man and a young maiden whisper together.

His choice is between death and disgrace, death and admission he was
wrong. He chooses death.

Thus, having wronged his people by his prideful decision, he
wrongs them further by getting killed. Now they are more nearly
defenseless. But Hector's choice is essentially the hero's choice at all
times—just as Achilles would rather die than face his mortality and
his guilt, so the hero always would rather die than face the facts of
his own limits, his own weakness and fallibility.

It seems almost miraculous that Hector's unwillingness to face his
error, then his flight around the city, does not destroy our sympathy
for him. It seems only to deepen our dread of his approaching death
and our horror that this humiliation, too, should befall him. The
whole point of this scene, I think, is to intensify our rather easy
sympathy with Hector. We dread his death and are shocked when his
body is dishonored—when those Greeks who once fled him gather
around his corpse to stab him and mock:

See now, Hektor is much softer to handle than he was
when he set the ships ablaze with the burning firebrand.

358

Alone of the heroes, we witness the grief of Hector's family, the aged Priam and Hecuba, his desperate wife Andromache who tells in two unbearably poignant passages of the brutal future she and Astyanax must face. We are revolted when Achilles despoils Hector's body, drags it behind his chariot, when in his futile rage he hauls it around and around Patroclus's bier.

Once Hector is dead, however, we have no choice but to return to identify with the survivor, with the bloody Achilles; we cannot identify with a corpse. Yet sympathy for Hector will remain and we will wish for ourselves—in our role as Achilles—to give over Hector's body for decent burial. The whole point of these scenes, then, is to make us long passionately that Achilles should finally yield, and to feel profoundly relieved and gratified when he does so.

The death of Hector is unquestionably the climax of the poem's action. Yet a deeper and more tragic scene remains; the meeting of Priam and Achilles. Before we plunge into that last scene the reader is given a brief comic respite in the funeral games for Patroclus. This scene also helps make credible Achilles's change of heart in the final scene.

The games, the next-to-last book, are an almost too artful commentary on the poem's theme, too artful a preparation for the last book. Achilles, once his rage is spent in that great bloody rampage, becomes astonishingly respectful, considerate, reasonable. Since he conducts the games, he is momentarily in the position of ruler; his judgments are both just and thoughtful. Even before the games begin, he counsels Agamemnon that "There can be enough, even in mourning." He has learned that at high prices, but we believe he *has* learned it. Meantime, the warriors also act with surprising moderation. Throughout the scene, we have a sense of comic relief and inversion of the main theme.

In the first contest, the horse race, Antilochus, in youthful recklessness, nearly collides with Menelaus. We are strongly reminded of Achilles's similar collision with Agamemnon. When Antilochus's prize, like Achilles's, is taken from him, we nearly have another

359

FOUR STUDIES IN THE CLASSICS

quarrel. But this is avoided partly through Achilles's generous arbitration (he has already healed a growing dispute between Ajax and Idomeneus) and partly because of Antilochus's respect for Menelaus's age and authority:

> Enough now. For I, my lord Menelaos, am younger
> by far than you, and you are the greater and go before me.
> You know how greedy transgressions flower in a young man, seeing
> that his mind is the more active but his judgment is lightweight.
> Therefore
> I would have your heart be patient with me. I myself will give you
> the mare I won. . . .

Again, this is almost too direct a comment on that youthful arrogance Achilles is unlearning. It certainly produces the desired effect: Menelaus, apparently eager to excel even in reasonability, relents and gives the mare back to Antilochus, after all.

This sets the tone for the rest of the scene. When Telemonian Ajax and Odysseus wrestle, and are apparently becoming incensed, the prize is split to avoid injury to either, as is done again in the spear fighting between Ajax and Diomedes. When Agamemnon enters the spear-throwing contest, Achilles is almost too quick to halt the contest and award the prize to the man he once so thoroughly abominated.

Jokes, bantering, quarrels wisely avoided—these characterize the games. Perhaps as much as anything, we recall the smaller Ajax falling in the cow dung during the footrace, then sputtering:

> Ah, now! That goddess made me slip on my feet, who has always
> stood over Odysseus like a mother, and taken good care of him.

Antilochus is able to cap this with a joke about the superiority of his elder, Odysseus:

> Friends, you all know well what I tell you, that still the immortals
> continue to favour the elder men. For see now, Ajax

360

is elder than I, if only by a little, but this man
is out of another age than ours and one of the ancients.
But his, they say, is a green old age. It would be a hard thing
for any Achaian to match his speed. Except for Achilleus.

Which afterthought wins him an additional prize from Achilles.

We are ready, then, for the final book, that unbearable scene where the aged and grief-stricken Priam comes to beg for Hector's body, kissing the hand of the man who has killed his sons, that scene where Achilles would take his enemy's hand and sit to weep with him for the griefs they have suffered, the wrongs they have done.

Everything has prepared us for this scene. In the first scene, Chryses prayed to Agamemnon to accept the ransom and give up his child. Immediately after that, Thetis came to her child Achilles, then carried his prayer to Zeus; now she comes from Zeus to Achilles telling him he must yield. This time, she too is grieving. He grieves for Patroclus; she grieves for him. Each of those scenes where, one after another, the heroes were humbled has led on to the humbling of this greater hero.

Achilles, who has been like a god in power and violence, must now become like a god in yielding, in recognizing the limits. Not only does he become more godlike in being humbled, he becomes more a man, less a machine, less a child. Even in the midst of that battle where the river rose against him, he prayed like a self-pitying child:

Father Zeus, no god could endure to save me from the river
who am so pitiful. And what then shall become of me?

Always, he has been self-centered, self-concerned. Now he will begin to see something outside himself. In Priam, his enemy's father and his enemy, he will see his own aged father, Peleus, for whom he longs. In the dead Hector, he sees his coming death. Just as Glaucus and Diomedes rose earlier to shake hands across their enmity, now Achilles and Priam sit to weep together. The scene between them has not only the unbearable poignance of Andromache's scenes, but far beyond them a deeper and more terrible tragedy.

Humility, yielding, comes far harder to Achilles than to anyone else. To many, of course, it never comes; they are merely killed. But those who can survive defeat (like Agamemnon or the earlier Hector) may come to humility, may lose their madness. Achilles is deprived of this simply because no one *can* defeat him. That is partly why he is so concerned with his father, Peleus, with his foster-father, Phoenix, with his enemy's father, Priam. For the other heroes, defeat takes the place of a father—beats down their pride, teaches them to yield. Achilles must learn to be humble without a father, without defeat.

This makes Achilles specially cogent to us. The father in most of our families, the government in most modern states, is so weakened or so distant that we too are essentially fatherless. Yet we must not —at least the great powers must not—seek the real defeats which could sufficiently humble us. We too must make do with the loss inherent in getting our own way, for that is essentially what we have.

All the poem's underlining of Achilles's violence, arrogance, viciousness, self-centeredness, has made his humbling all the more difficult—so, all the more meaningful and touching when it comes. Not that it saves his life, or Hector's life, or any of the Trojans already dead or still to be slaughtered, or any of the Greek heroes' lives. Yet if even so bloody a man as Achilles can rise to the sort of beauty and dignity he has in this final scene, there is a kind of redemption. A man may die, and may thoroughly deserve to die; he need not be despised.

The last day I lectured on this was almost sheer joy to me. I had answered the question I couldn't answer. By picking everyone's brain, I had come up with a view, partly my own, of the greatest poem men will write. And on that last day I had wrapped it all up in a tidy little package with a tidy little ribbon, then neatly flipped it into their tidy little laps.

It's true that none of the boys heard this. They were absent—that very day they had occupied the President's office. Apparently one of the very first riots about the war in Southeast Asia. Someone claimed they had made a fire of the papers on his desk and roasted weiners over it—for all I know, at the very moment of my lecture. And to my horror, I later heard that several of them carried signs demanding my reinstatement. Soon there were daily editorials in the college paper telling what a popular and stimulating teacher I was—how, even while having to teach irrelevant subjects, I had been able to help liberate my students from the falsities of authoritarian religion and materialistic American values.

Not that I wasn't flattered; it is hard to dislike praise whether it applies or not. Yet it was pretty clear they weren't talking about *me;* and dragging my case into this made me wonder if they were really talking about Vietnam, either. I could not go and talk to them for fear we might seem to be in collusion; I could not repudiate their support without seeming to condone American values or even the Vietnam war. Like it or not, I had dwindled into an issue. I had imagined myself a hero, a veritable Achilles of critical insight; they made me their Patroclus, an occasion for virtue in others. I became a "cause" which others fought over seeking their own honor and power. And, just as you'd expect, my new and unsought allies finished me off quicker than any coalition of enemies could ever have done.

I never got my hearing, since the President resigned within a week. It was almost certain that he would be replaced by that very Dean I was complaining against—since he was well liked by the students, it was hoped he could calm the beseiged campus. Even if they had rehired me, I wouldn't have been willing to teach under him. High time to find a new job.

Fortunately for me that day, I didn't know any of that—I only knew the boys were absent. But most of the girls (and even one or two stray boys) were present and heard my best lecture. Those few, I thought, were the real students, my true disciples. "Wherever two or three are gathered. . . ." Those few surely heard me, took it all in. No one walked out. Notebooks were open. Pens flew merrily over the pages. As the hour ended, I must have stood there in a glow of satisfaction and paternal benevolence.

And suddenly—beyond my wildest dreams—there she stood. In front of my desk for the third time—the magical number. My very own Helen Rosamund Freud, for whose sake I had lectured all those weeks. In front of my own desk in that, my finest hour.

"I was wondering," she said, "if you could tell me what the book is about, really. Like I understand those things you've been saying. But I mean could you just tell me in a sentence or two what's the point? I don't want any special favors. But, you know, what does it mean?"

74 75 76 77 10 9 8 7 6 5 4 3 2 1